Contemporary US Cinema

Inside Film

Forthcoming Titles

CONTEMPORARY
US CINEMA

Michael Allen

An imprint of **Pearson Education**

Harlow, England · London · New York · Reading, Massachusetts · San Francisco
Toronto · Don Mills, Ontario · Sydney · Tokyo · Singapore · Hong Kong · Seoul
Taipei · Cape Town · Madrid · Mexico City · Amsterdam · Munich · Paris · Milan

For Janet

Pearson Education Limited
Edinburgh Gate
Harlow
Essex CM20 2JE

and Associated Companies throughout the world

Visit us on the World Wide Web at:
www.pearsoneduc.com

First published 2003

© Pearson Education Limited 2003

The right of Dr Michael Allen to be identified as author of this work has been asserted
by him in accordance with the Copyright, Designs and Patents Act 1988.

ISBN 0582 43776 8

British Library Cataloguing-in-Publication Data
A catalogue record for this book is available from the British Library

Library of Congress Cataloging-in-Publication Data
Allen, Michael, 1957–
    Contemporary US cinema / Michael Allen.
        p. cm. — (Inside film)
    Includes bibliographical references and index.
    ISBN 0-582-43776-8 (alk. paper)
        1. Motion pictures—United States.   I. Title: Contemporary United States cinema.
    II. Title.   III. Series.
    PN1993.5.U6 A827 2002
    791.43′0973—dc21   2002025269

10   9   8   7   6   5   4   3   2   1
05   04   03

Typeset in 10/13pt Giovanni by 35
Printed and bound in China
EPC/01

CONTENTS

ACKNOWLEDGEMENTS

My grateful thanks go to Alexander Ballinger of the McLean Press, who has been the source of countless valuable thoughts and responses throughout the writing of this book. His patience and forbearing towards my many errors of judgement have improved the work immeasurably. He was the best editor I could have wished for. I would also like to thank him for his tenacity in clearing the rights to the stills.

My thanks also go to Tim Parker of Pearson Education for taking over the manuscript in its final stages, and guiding it through to completion, and to Anne Henwood, whose painstaking copy-editing repaired many an oversight, and led to some productive rewriting.

Finally, my love and thanks go out to my wife Janet, whose support, both emotional and intellectual, helped to get me through.

LIST OF PHOTOGRAPHS

Genre, Sequels and Remakes

12. Keanu Reeves and Hugo Weaving do battle with the aid of digital wire removal and time-slice cinematography in *The Matrix* (Andy and Larry Wachowski, 1999) THE MATRIX © 1999 WV Films LLC. All rights reserved **p.196**

Fixing it in Digital

13. Effects specialist Peter Jopling composits an image at Mill Film **p.207**

We would also like to express our thanks to Gérard Depardieu, Leonardo DiCaprio, Anthony Hopkins, Andie MacDowell, Keanu Reeves, Julia Roberts, John Travolta, Bruce Willis, Kate Winslet and Catherine Zeta Jones for approving the use of stills from Green Card, The Mask of Zorro, The Matrix, Pulp Fiction, sex lies and videotape and Titanic which include their images.

All pictures provided by the British Film Institute, The Ronald Grant Archive, Ellie James, Mary Ellen Mark and Good Machine International Inc.

CHAPTER ONE

The Background

In this first chapter I want to lay out the context which framed and created American film-making from 1970 through to 2001. The last 30 years of American film-making have seen a number of seismic changes in the industry and in the kind of films it produces. At the industrial level, new business models emerged which have given the major American film studios new owners and a different sense of their place within an economic marketplace. This new position, in turn, has resulted in changes in the management hierarchy and structure of the film companies, changing the way they make films.

Another phenomenon of the past 30 years has been the rise of independent American film-making to the point where it now offers a serious alternative to mainstream film-making. Again, the purpose of this chapter is to chart where that strand of independent film-making originated and developed, to show that its modern manifestation is not a bolt from the blue, but rather a continuation and expansion of earlier initiatives.

Recent decades have seen the rise of the 'multi-hyphenate': the film-maker who adopts multiple roles on a film production: as actor, director, and/or producer. American cinema had seen such figures before, but they occurred as exception rather than the norm. The contemporary period of American film-making has seen their exponential rise.

Most famously, even infamously, the costs of making films in Hollywood, in terms of both film production budgets and star (actor and director) salaries, have risen to alarming levels. While not a new phenomenon – spectacular films with exorbitant budgets have been an aspect of American film industry since at least the days of D.W. Griffith's *The Birth of a Nation* (1915) and *Intolerance* (1916) – big-budget films have become far more common in the last decade or two, to the point where they might almost be said to dominate public perceptions of the American film industry. The consequences of this phenomenon for the economics of modern American film-making, whereby big-budget films have to make increasingly huge sums at the box office to justify their investment, are being played out as this book is written, and will form a central focus throughout its pages.

The American film industry has periodically been required to redefine itself, technologically. Although the studio period lasted several decades, technical innovation was an integral part of production strategy. Changes in format, shape of screen, and quality of sound were introduced as and when the film industry needed to reinvigorate its market position. Though such changes might have been extremely expensive, they were seen as necessary investments to maintain the specificity and attraction of cinema as an entertainment form.

The last three decades have witnessed the latest phase of that technical innovation, with the emergence and development of a number of new media: computer-based, digital, non celluloid-based. These new media have entered into a set of increasingly complex interactions with more 'traditional' film-making, as both new sources of funding and as new distribution channels for films, to the point where they are substantially transforming the very nature of the industry. These developments and interactions are themselves changing rapidly as time goes by. It is the somewhat daunting aim of the final chapter of this book to try to chart the progress of these changes and to offer some thoughts on what might happen in the next few years.

Mostly, in this chapter, we will be looking at the post-Second World War period, although where relevant, our investigation will go back further, sometimes to the very beginning of cinema at the end of the century before last. The hope in doing this is not to risk redundancy or irrelevance but, rather, to show that the various elements that go to make up contemporary American film-making in all its aspects have a long history and complex genealogy. Nothing ever appears ready-formed; everything that appears does so because of innumerable prior events and decisions. And so it is with the American film industry as we now know it. This first chapter is designed to sketch out that history, to outline the framework in which the industry has developed to this current point in its story.

THE HOLLYWOOD STUDIO SYSTEM

The American mainstream film-making process between the 1920s and the 1950s has been given many labels – classical; studio system; production line; mature oligopoly. The 'studio system', as it has come to be known, can be defined as many things: a physical place, an industrial method, a developer of

audio-visual technologies, an aesthetic sensibility, and a structured employment situation.

The major film companies were sited in a particular geographical location –
Hollywood, in California – in extensive studio complexes which consisted of
sound stages, editing rooms, backlots containing huge scenery from past
productions, offices, and so forth, within which the films they made were
chosen, created, and sent out for release:

> [The MGM] plant – fifty-three acres, valued at a trifling $2,000,000 – is in
> Culver City, California . . . It contains twenty-two sound stages, a park that can
> be photographed as anything from a football field to the gardens of Versailles,
> $2,000,000 worth of antique furniture, a greenhouse consecrated to the raising
> of ferns, [and] twenty-two projection rooms . . . MGM's weekly payroll is
> roughly $250,000 . . . Actors' salaries are only a small part of MGM's outlay.
> The biggest and most expensive writing staff in Hollywood costs $40,000 a
> week. Directors cost $25,000. Executives cost slightly less. Budget for equipment
> is $100,000 a week. Average cost of Metro-Goldwyn-Mayer pictures runs
> slightly under $500,000. This is at least $150,000 more per picture than other
> companies spend. Thus, Metro-Goldwyn-Mayer provides $20,000,000 worth
> of entertainment a year at cost of production, to see which something like a
> billion people of all races will pay something more than $100,000,000 at the
> box office.
>
> (Fortune magazine, vol.6, December 1932, pp.51–2;
> quoted in Balio, 1985; pp.311–2)

The overheads required to keep such an operation going were therefore
sizeable, and could only be afforded because films were made cheaply and
efficiently enough, and frequently enough, to ensure a steady and more than
adequate income for each of the studios. We will see soon what happened
when this financial equation ceased to balance.

> [F]acilities created thirty to forty years ago no longer meet the current
> requirements and cannot be readily adapted to modern production methods. The
> giant shooting sets and supply departments were designed for the simultaneous
> production of a dozen or more medium- and large-budget features. Those days
> are long gone and nowadays a studio considers itself lucky having two or three
> films in simultaneous production . . . The maintenance of a studio with a dozen
> or more shooting sets costs annually around $3 million. The figure refers to a
> slack period, when administrative duties are reduced to hardly more than
> cleaning, opening and locking up.
>
> (Toeplitz, 1975; pp.31–2)

3

But while the production facilities were located on the West Coast of America, the headquarters and financial operations of the major film companies were, and still are, located 3,000 miles away, on the East Coast of the country, primarily in New York City. This is partly historical, because that is where the earliest film-making concerns grew up in the last years of the nineteenth century – for example, Edison in Orange County, New Jersey and Biograph on the East Side of New York City. It is also to do with closeness (both physical and psychological) to the financial heart of America, concentrated on Wall Street in New York. From the 1910s onwards, the film-making concerns operating out of Hollywood were fundamentally dependent upon the financial support of Wall Street. It made no sense at all, in such circumstances, to locate all aspects of a studio's operations, especially its financial management, several thousand miles away from the country's financial centre. This 3,000-mile separation between the organisational and financial base of America's film industry and its sites of production worked both ways, causing, on occasion, disagreement and tension, but also allowing each the space to do what it did best:

> *The movies were a 'vertical' industry in that the ultimate authority belonged to the owners and top corporate officers in New York. But the New York office couldn't make movies, nor could it dictate audience interest and public taste. And whatever the efforts to regulate production and marketing, moviemaking remained a competitive and creative enterprise. In the overall scheme of things, the West Coast management team was the key to studio operations, integrating the company's economic and creative resources, translating fiscal policy into filmmaking practice. This demanded close contact with New York and a feel for the company's market skew, but also an acute awareness of the studio's resources and heavy interaction with the top filmmakers on the lot, particularly the directors, writers and stars.*
>
> *(Schatz, 1989; pp.11–12)*

The studio was also a company that employed permanent personnel – stars, directors, producers and cameramen, as well as administrators, accountants and managers. During the main decades of the studio system, for example, Warner Bros. maintained a large number of creative and technical personnel on long-term contracts. Figures such as Hal B. Wallis rose up through the ranks over many years to achieve executive status. In 1953, when the studio finally terminated his contract under pressures to economise in the post-war period, Michael Curtiz had been with the studio for 26 years.

This permanent staff gave the studio a great sense of continuity. It knew that it could count on a particular director or star to be available if it chose to assign him or her to a new film project. It knew that if it wanted a certain look given to a film, its key cameraman could also be assigned to the production. And it knew that that cameraman had probably worked with the director and stars before on one or more of its previous films. This usually lent the whole production process a calm efficiency, with everyone knowing their place and role in the greater whole. Things had to run smoothly; the system could not work otherwise.

The five Hollywood 'majors' of the studio period – Warner Bros., Paramount, MGM, Twentieth Century-Fox and RKO – each made 40–60 films a year. This constituted around 50 per cent of the American film industry's annual output and 75 per cent of its class–A features, the remainder being contributed by the large and ever-changing army of independent film production companies. That is a considerable number, and indicates an impressive consistency and efficiency at the heart of the machine. The studio system could only achieve this level and continuity of production by maintaining efficient industrial methods, making best use of resources, spreading the risk and the financial load across a whole range of projects. As well as the Big Five, there were the Little Three – Columbia and Universal each had their own distribution system as well as a production arm, supplying smaller films to cinemas for frequent change of programme and double bills, while United Artists was solely a distributor for independent productions.

These films were released in the 23,000 cinemas open in the United States during this period. The majors owned or controlled only 3,000 of them, but they were the top 3,000, the largest and the best: the Paramount Publix chain of 1,200 cinemas or the Fox-Loew chain, which owned 800 cinemas. They were the first-run and premiere site cinemas, the flagships – the 6,250-seat Roxy, 5,450-seat Capitol or 4,000-seat Paramount, all on New York's Broadway – where major new films opened to great fanfare and, usually, a large box office. In a period when glossy, good-looking, starry feature films were what the cinema audience craved, this ownership of the prime cinema chains constituted a virtual stranglehold on the exhibition arm of the business. It allowed the big films to open well and securely, and forced the owners of the remaining, smaller, cinemas to accept whatever terms the majors dictated. Those terms were usually prohibitive, and included block booking, whereby weaker or less attractive films were grouped with the leading ones so the exhibitor had to take them all if it wanted the big ones. This situation of coercion would eventually run into problems of legality to do with monopolistic practices, and we will see shortly what effect its cessation came to have on the industry into the period covered by this book.

American film-making of the studio period also constituted a particular aesthetic. Defined by, amongst others, Bordwell, Staiger and Thompson (1985) as the Classical Hollywood Cinema, it is deemed to have a certain wholeness, and even purity, of form; a formal system with a set of aesthetic rules which

5

had been developed and honed through practice until they reached their fullest expression. The Warner Bros. production *The Big Sleep* (1946) is a good example. The first shot of the film establishes the location – the mansion of the Sternwood family – for the scene to come. Shot reverse shot sequences – in which a first shot shows one character looking off screen, and the following shot shows a second character looking off screen back, seeming to return the first character's gaze – clearly establish spatial relationships for the spectators as they watch the scene unfold. Directional and spatial cues are continually employed to reinforce this sense of a coherent space. For example, at one point in the opening scene, Humphrey Bogart's character, Philip Marlowe, gestures off-screen towards a drinks trolley. A cut to a new angle frames him as he rises from his seat. This 'match cut', with the edit timed mid-movement, deceives the eye into seeing the two shots as a single continuous action. The second shot then shows Bogart moving to the trolley towards which he had gestured in the first. These carefully timed edits between shots, together with the continual confirmation and reconfirmation, through gesture and look, of characters' spatial relationships to one another and the objects around them, create an 'invisible' filmstyle in which the audience watches, and is directed to look at, the action on screen rather than the formal processes.

Classical Hollywood films, taking their cue from traditional theatre play structure, also told a certain kind of narrative, which had a particular shape, number of 'acts' and a certain arch of action. Characters and significant events were carefully introduced. Clues and significant elements were 'planted' and then made to carry significance within the logic of the narrative. Even a famously convoluted narrative such as *The Big Sleep* observes these basic rules. The opening scene just described, for example, sets up the narrative premise: that one of the Sternwood daughters is being blackmailed and Philip Marlowe's private eye is being hired to find out who is doing it. At regular intervals throughout the narrative, Marlowe summarises the situation so far for one or more characters involved. All strands and loose ends are tied up by the end of the film: Marlowe solves the case, finds, captures or kills the villains, and falls in love with the heroine (the other Sternwood daughter) to form the couple by the film's end.

This classical form was intimately tied to production efficiency, to a process designed to get the film made in as quick, efficient and economical a way as possible. A hierarchy of production personnel was central to the efficiency of the system. The classic period witnessed a shift from what is termed the 'central producer system' to the producer unit system. Irving Thalberg at MGM, typified the former by 'believ[ing] that the producer was the pivotal figure, responsible not just for the creation of a single movie but ultimately for the entire style of film-making that conferred a distinctive character upon each studio' (Puttnam with Watson, 2000; p.141). David Selznick represented the latter, in which a producer was more directly involved with only one film at a time. The change occurred because it was felt that the former system, because it was essentially one man's vision and taste, led to too much similarity and uniformity. Having a range of producers each supervising a few films allowed greater range of style, genre and subject matter while maintaining overarching studio identity.

In terms of industrial economics, mainstream American film-making during the classic studio period is referred to as a 'mature oligopoly' – 'a group of companies co-operating to control a certain market' (Schatz, 1989; p.9). This understanding had been in place since 1930, by which time the countless interactions and re-formations of the companies forming the American film industry had become dominated by the five large studios. Although each of these studios was in competition with each of the others, there was also a fair degree of co-operation – lending of personnel, the exhibition of films from a rival studio in the others' cinemas. This symbiotic relationship between rival studios was designed to keep the industry in the hands of a few powerful interests. It was seen to be a better business strategy for the small number of dominant companies to share and exchange resources to a limited extent rather than to go head-to-head in an all-out competition where there was more risk of substantial loss for one or more parties. In this way the oligopoly became mutually supportive as a means of maintaining overall industry and market dominance.

Once a film was finished, it became a product in need of a market. During the studio period, each of the majors was vertically as well as horizontally integrated. What this meant in practice is that each studio was not only co-ordinated between its various departments on the production level (horizontally) but also between its production, distribution and exhibition arms (vertically). The major studios maintained virtually complete control over the film industry as a whole. They alone had the ability to regularly create expensive, mass attraction films. They could control their distribution from the place of production (studios) to the place of reception (cinemas). And they could ensure not only that they were guaranteed a showing in appropriate and attractive conditions, but also that much of the profit from these screenings was returned to the studios so that the money could be used to create more high-quality, market-leading product.

PARAMOUNT DECREES

All this changed with a legal action – United States vs. Paramount Pictures – which was initiated in the late 1930s and only settled over ten years later. It eventually reached court in 1948, where the Big Five were convicted of conspiring to run a monopoly on exhibition to the detriment of smaller exhibitors. Block and blind booking, the forcing of exhibitors to take films sight unseen because they had no other choice if they were not to lose out on the top-draw films, was a central issue, as was the degree of co-operation as a means of excluding others. The very industrial and economic structure upon which Hollywood had built its strength – vertical integration – was what began its unravelling.

The court case had several consequences. It forced the majors to abandon block and blind booking and thus to allow exhibitors to hire films on an individual, film-by-film, basis. Such a shift severely affected the stability of the old system whereby the strong films supported and protected the weak by allowing profits from all of them to be pooled to finance further production. With each film now having to stand on its own merits, the weaker films had far less of a chance either to succeed at the box office or to be subsumed in the money being generated by the large and more successful films. Risk was no longer spread across the entire output of the studio. A spotlight, stronger by the year, fell on each individual film and those who had created it. Exposure and accountability began to be the norm.

The Paramount decrees divorced the theatre chains from the production studios, making it impossible for the majors automatically to find an outlet for each new film they produced, and resulted in more open competition at the exhibition end. This opened up a gap for the independents; not so much the 'healthy' independents such as Selznick and Goldwyn, who had always maintained a decent position in the market but, more so, the smaller operators, such as Republic and Monogram, which had previously been frustrated by the stranglehold the majors held over the routes to exhibition. The new market allowed them to offer their product to exhibitors as an alternative to that being released by the majors.

Greater opportunity in exhibition meant greater opportunity in production as well. This situation benefited not only the Little Three, who had, up to this point, occupied a subservient position in the marketplace in comparison to their larger and more powerful counterparts, but also the myriad of smaller independents who were trying to exist on the peripheries of the business. The climate of expectation shifted. The old certainties were no longer in place, and in their place new gaps and possibilities arose.

The dismantling of the majors' vertical integration had a further effect which would impact directly on the kind of film being made as the period covered by this book begins in the late 1960s: the relaxation of censorship. As Tino Balio argues, with the loss of the first-run cinemas, 'the Big Five lost its power to enforce the strictures of the Production Code Administration' (Balio, 1985; p.405). The Production Code was a self-regulating censorship procedure originally initiated by Hollywood in the 1930s as a means of fending off external interference by industry, taste and religious watchdogs. It had worked, and had been responsible for a uniformly safe, and perhaps anodyne, quality to the films made in Hollywood during this period. The beginnings of the industry's inability to maintain this self-regulation, together with a decision in 1952 to include films in the First Amendment, giving them 'the same protected status held by newspapers, magazines, and other organs of speech' (Balio, 1985; p.405), opened up the movies for freer and more controversial expression than had been possible for several decades. This freedom was to lead to an explosion of hard-edged films which came close to then accepted boundaries of taste and decency: films such as *The Big Heat* (1953), in which Lee Marvin threw a pot of scalding coffee into Gloria Grahame's face, severely scarring her.

The ending of vertical integration was by no means an overnight event, taking almost 20 years from the initiation of the case in 1938 to the full effects of the results becoming endemic by the mid-1950s, for the shift to be complete. And even then, it is important to recognise the long-term effects on the industry. As Balio argues, '[a]lthough divorcement and divestiture restructured the industry, these provisions by no means reduced the import-ance of the majors. In 1954, the Big Five and the Little Three plus two minor companies collected most of the domestic film rentals, as did ten companies (not all the same ones) 20 years later' (Balio, 1990; p.6). So, while relations shifted within the industry as a result of the Paramount case, the actual power remained in the hands of more or less the same companies as had held it for the past few decades.

Moreover, there is a sense in which 'what goes around comes around'. The vertical integration, block booking, and so forth that the Paramount case was so adamantly trying to prevent, reappears at later dates in American film industry's history. The selling of films in blocks to television in the 1950s and 1960s, for example, contains echoes of the block booking arrangements of the studio period, where weaker films were bundled with the star-attraction films to ensure that exhibitors took everything the studios offered them. As Toeplitz, writing in the mid-1970s, comments: 'The old sales technique of "blind booking" . . . is gaining a new lease of life through television' (Toeplitz, 1975; p.31). Moreover, the Reagan administration in the 1980s enabled a form of vertical integration to return when it allowed the major film companies to reinvest in exhibition. MCA, for example, bought a 49 per cent share in Cineplex Odeon, while later Columbia Pictures were allowed to take over Loew's Theatres, and Paramount Communications, in partnership with Time Warner, own the Mann, Festival and Trans-Lux chains. It is one of the themes of this book that practices, strategies and phenomena do not occur just once. There is a strange cyclical aspect to the American film industry whereby certain lessons do not seem to be permanently learned. In its pursuit of massive wealth from such a fickle and unpredictable product as a feature film, the American film industry has proved to have a short memory. We will see this time and again as this book proceeds.

SOCIAL CHANGES

The ending of the Second World War ushered in changes in society – changes in leisure patterns, sexual relations and liberation, a valorising of the nuclear family – which were to impact upon the film industry in ways at least as dramatic as the divorcement proceedings just discussed. Initially, the ending of the war seemed to benefit the industry. Audience figures reached an all-time high in the year following the end of the war, as servicemen returned home to wives, families or new romances, and everyone went to the movies: some 60 million people a week in 1946. Over the next few years, however, audience figures began to fall as young adults got married and began having families. By 1951, the weekly attendance figure declined to 46 million (Cogley, 1985; p.487). People moved out to the ever-expanding suburbs to give their children the right space and fresh air, away from the large cinemas that had come to have such a central place in American cities. The industry could not afford to build new cinemas in the suburbs and the young marrieds were less and less inclined to travel back into the cities to see films. Furthermore, even though money began to be plentiful, what it was spent on changed so that the movies were no longer the automatic choice of social activity. New leisure activities competed with them – sports, bowling, travel both in America on the newly built highway system and abroad.

As this shift away from the movies occurred on the part of those more interested in settling down, becoming more focused on the home and intent on raising young children, the cinema-going experience gradually became identified with a previously underrecognised audience demographic: the youth. Teenagers became a phenomenon of the 1950s, given greater financial and social freedom than their parents and increasingly and explicitly addressed by the various media – music, magazines, television – as a recognisable, potentially lucrative, entity. With the film industry losing its recognised audience, the youth market became more and more attractive and important as the decade wore on. By the end of the 1960s, the youth audience was a central prop in the industry's survival plan, although the old guard within the industry felt they had no understanding of what the 'youth of the day' actually wanted or liked:

The old men who ran the studios were increasingly out of touch with the vast baby boom audience that was coming of age in the '60s, an audience that was rapidly becoming radicalised and disaffected from its elders. The studios were still churning out formulaic genre pictures, an endless stream of Doris Day and Rock Hudson vehicles; big-budget epics, like Hawaii, The Bible *and* Krakatoa, East of Java; *war films, like* Tora! Tora! Tora! *and* D-Day the Sixth of June.

(Biskind, 1998; p.20)

This incomprehension, this breakdown in communication between the industry and its audience, provided the context for the entrance into the industry – whether by wooing or force – of a new breed of film-makers, less interested in conforming to the mainstream norm. We will look in detail at these 'New Radicals' in Chapter 4, but it is necessary to stress here the degree to which there was felt to be a gap within the industry which urgently needed to be filled by something fresh and relevant to the industry's changing demographic.

A further important social factor was the anti-Communist witch-hunts that took place in the late 1940s and early 1950s. The House Un-American Activities Committee (HUAC) sought out suspected Communist sympathizers everywhere in American life. Its attempts to do so within the film industry were in many ways its most high-profile campaign. The film industry was badly affected, partly because its personnel were accused of Communism, thereby disrupting the smooth running of the studios. Moreover, the industry 'by monitoring those who worked and those who did not, . . . ruthlessly policed the post-Paramount decision workforce and as a result effectively stripped the various industry guilds and unions of their bargaining power', thereby forcibly effecting the reductions in personnel demanded by its falling audience figures and increasing financial problems (Lewis, 1998b; p.89).

More generally, HUAC created an atmosphere of uncertainty in which it was hard to know what was acceptable and what unacceptable. Touchy subjects – political or sexual – were strongly avoided for fear of subversive intentions being suspected. They were replaced with anodyne movies such as those starring Doris Day and Rock Hudson, or lavish big-budget musicals adapted from the stage, such as *Oklahoma!* (1955) or *Seven Brides for Seven Brothers* (1954), whose content was designed to offend no one. More generally, the efforts of HUAC caused widespread social anxiety and created a climate of apprehension and doubt, causing audiences to become less interested in going to the movies.

Between 1950 and 1953 and again between 1963 and 1972, America waged war against Communism halfway across the world, in Korea and Vietnam respectively, but representation of either of these armed conflicts was absent from the American cinema. The subject was studiously avoided throughout the decade, with a few notable exceptions, including *The Green Berets* (1968), a rabidly anti-Communist defence of America's involvement in Vietnam, starring, and directed by, John Wayne. Where people went to learn about it was their own living room, watching it daily on their own television set. Robert Altman's satirical comedy on the Korean War, *M*A*S*H* (1970), was turned into a long running (1972–1983) television series. Hollywood really failed to address the problem of Vietnam directly in major feature films until the mid-1970s.

Auster and Quart call this period of cinematic silence 'The War That Dared Not Speak Its Name' (Auster and Quart, 1988; pp.23–73). Perhaps film-makers needed a degree of distance from the events before they could properly address them on film. George Lucas' *American Graffiti* (1973) touches on Vietnam only in so far as it concerns itself with the effect of the draft on a group of teenagers. Martin Scorsese's *Taxi Driver* (1976) shows a Vietnam veteran, played by Robert De Niro, as a man whose experience of the war has left him psychologically scarred and unable to reconnect with civilian life. Similarly, Hal Ashby's *Coming Home* (1978) is a film about a Vietnam veteran, paralysed in the war, who falls in love with the wife of a serving officer as she helps him re-adjust to civilian life.

All of these films have the common thread of showing the effects of the war *in absentia*: characters are either just about to go out for a tour of duty, or are trying to come to terms with the physical and psychological effects of their experiences out there. The structural absence of addressing a war that is never actually shown on screen is telling. It took until the very end of the decade before, in *Go Tell the Spartans* (1978), a veteran of three wars, played by Burt Lancaster, was shown being heavily critical both of US Army Command's decision-making and America's continued presence in Vietnam. Michael Cimino's *The Deer Hunter* (1978) also showed the horrors and futility of war as, in the film's long central section, the main male characters are shown, in a somewhat racist manner, undergoing a hellish torture process. The following year, Francis Ford Coppola's *Apocalypse Now* (1979) was the last of the decade's significant attempts to address the subject, although its strange, drug-induced, dream-like tone and style allowed the film to avoid acting as a serious investigation of the real political issues involved. One could easily argue that it took until the latter half of the 1980s, when a batch of films about Vietnam, such as *Platoon* (1986), *Hamburger Hill* (1987), *Full Metal Jacket* (1987), *Casualties of War* (1989) and *Born on the Fourth of July* (1989), finally saw Hollywood seriously and fully engage with the horrors and consequences of the war.

Mainstream cinema found the issue of race similarly difficult to address; again, perhaps, because it appeared on television every day in reports of violence caused by growing resistance to segregation and to the murders of prominent Black people, most notably Martin Luther King in 1968. The race issue was also more contentious, certainly more problematic, than Vietnam,

Francis Ford Coppola directing Dennis Hopper in *Apocalypse Now* (Francis Ford Coppola, 1979)

because it was actually happening in American's own country. *Guess Who's Coming to Dinner* (1967) was an awkward attempt to address the issue of interracial marriage, and *In the Heat of the Night* (1967), a more serious study of racism in the South. The years 1969–70 saw a group of films about White–Black issues appear, all of which in one way or another externalised the difficulties American society was feeling as the rigid segregation between White and Black people was progressively broken down. *Change of Mind* (1969) is a bizarre science-fantasy film in which the life of a liberal White DA can only be 'saved' by transplanting his brain into the body of a dead Black man. *The Liberation of L.Q. Jones* (William Wyler, 1970), a fairly pessimistic film, shows the consequences of the murder of a Black funeral parlour owner by a bigoted Southern white cop, and the attempts of the town's White citizens to hush up the crime. In *The Landlord* (Hal Ashby, 1970), a tycoon's son buys a tenement in Brooklyn's Black ghetto, and undergoes a crash course in interracial relations. At one point in the film, a White female character responds to accusations that she's racist by saying: 'Of course we're liberal. Didn't we all go to see *Guess Who's Coming to Dinner?*' (quoted in Toeplitz, 1975; p.126).

Of course, part of the reason for this awkwardness and inability to freely address the problems of race and interracial relations in cinema during the 1960s and 1970s is that all of the heads of the major film studios were White, as were all of the major writers and directors working for those studios. Under such circumstances, the real experiences of America's Black population could not hope to receive accurate representation from White creative personnel who had little knowledge or real empathy with the realities of their lives. This lack of true understanding led to the emergence of the stereotype of the 'noble Black professional' on American cinema screens in the late 1960s. Sidney Poitier personified (and invariably played) this figure, for example as ramrod-backed, expert detective in *In the Heat of the Night*, doctor in *Guess Who's Coming to Dinner*, and teacher in the British production *To Sir With Love* (all 1967).

The relative lack of, or at least uncomfortable, engagement with racial issues on American screens during the 1960s and early 1970s was a major reason for the emergence of so-called blaxploitation films in the early 1970s. Films such as *Sweet Sweetback's Baadasssss Song*, directed by Melvin Van Peebles and *Shaft*, directed by Gordon Parks, both released in 1971, were films made by Black film-makers for Black audiences (although the latter, in particular, was popular with non-Black audiences too.) The success of the films persuaded the major studios, for a while at least, to finance a string of films by Black film-makers. As Toeplitz, writing at the time, observes:

> [T]he big studios, sensing in the black stories a new vein of profit, are getting ready to follow up. Sequels have already followed, such as Shaft's Big Score, and it is not without significance that Shaft is distributed by the once rigidly conservative and almost racist Metro-Goldwyn-Mayer . . . The board of directors, responsible for the shareholders' interests, have taken a realistic assessment of the market conditions. Population movement within the big cities has meant that the better-off, mostly white citizens have settled in the suburbs, far from the large cinemas . . . During the sixties 3.4 million blacks moved into the central cities and 2.5 million whites moved out. Glamorous movie palaces, prosperous twenty years ago, suddenly faced bankruptcy. Those cinemas can now pay their way only if they are supported by the new influx of city-dwellers, that is by the Negro proletariat and Negro middle-class. And black audiences are not likely to take to a gentleman hero like Sidney Poitier in Guess Who's Coming to Dinner.

> (Toeplitz, 1975; p.129)

TELEVISION

The growth of television has been widely blamed for the crises befalling the film industry during the 1950s and 1960s and, to a certain extent, this is justified. As the American public acquired television sets during these decades, they chose increasingly to watch moving pictures at home, on a small, black and white screen with appalling sound, rather than travel ever-greater distances to see films on larger cinema screens with generally far better sound quality. Some of the reasons for this, such as changing leisure patterns, and a greater emphasis on family and domestic lifestyles, have been discussed earlier in this chapter.

Although, as will be suggested shortly, the links between Hollywood and television began earlier than has conventionally been acknowledged, the film industry initially resisted television by refusing it access to its libraries of feature films. The television programmers urgently needed these collections of old films to fill up the large gaps in their schedules caused by their inability to produce television programmes fast enough and in large enough quantities to satisfy television's insatiable appetite for product.

Soon, however, the American film industry, in increasingly dire financial straits as its audience shrank, changed its position on this issue. It came to recognise the potential advantages of entering an alliance with television, especially in furnishing much-needed revenues and opening up vital new arenas of production. The turning point occurred on 25 September 1966, when David Lean's *Bridge on the River Kwai* (1957) was broadcast to an estimated audience of 60 million Americans on the ABC TV network. The deal cost the Ford Motor Company, ABC's main sponsor, $1,200,000 for a handful of screenings, to be interrupted by advertisements for the new Ford automobiles.

Towards the end of 1966 licence agreements were signed between the main television networks and the film production companies ABC and CBS concluded deals with Twentieth Century-Fox, Paramount and MGM. Ninety three million dollars were paid for the right to show 112 films. NBC paid Paramount $10 million for the right to show The Godfather *once, over two nights. The showing of* Gone With the Wind *cost NBC $5 million. CBS concluded an agreement with Metro-Goldwyn-Mayer for forty-five films for a sum total of $52,800,000, and – a point to note – eighteen of these films were still to be produced.*

(Toeplitz, 1975; p.30)

Toeplitz is right to emphasise his last point. With the pledging of money towards unmade films intended to be screened on television sometime in the future, the relationship between the film industry and television took a significant step forward. Henceforth, the two would be intimately bound together.

The big Hollywood studios, now over-manned and with empty studio space, began turning to the production of made-for-television films: feature length, cheaply made, with short shooting schedules, designed to fill large chunks of a television company's schedule. NBC's *Fame Is the Name of the Game* (1966) is generally credited with being the first made-for-TV movie (Schulze, 1990; p.351).

Most notable in terms of quality, perhaps, are Steven Spielberg's two feature-length television films, *Duel* (1971) and *Something Evil* (1972), which demonstrate how accomplished even this most denigrated of forms can be. Indeed, recognition of *Duel*'s quality led to it being given a theatrical release, proving especially popular in Europe, and eventually making $6 million profit (Baxter, 1996; p.84). During the late 1960s and early 1970s, the relatively sudden, and certainly massive, increase in production brought a need for creative personnel, easing the way for hopeful film-makers, such as Spielberg, to gain invaluable experience in directing feature-length productions.

Although television movies were seen as the poor cousin of the more expensive and polished theatrical feature film, and made for such a conservative medium as American television, surprisingly, they often took on difficult, almost taboo, subjects. *Something About Amelia* (1984), starring Ted Danson and Glenn Close, for example, dealt with the subject of father–daughter incest in an uncompromising manner.

The final phase in the increasingly intimate relationship between film and television came with the pre-planning of feature films for cinema release to acknowledge the potential revenues after the cinema-run of the film, from screenings on television. This assumption became an integral part of the budgetary and planning process, so that films began to be green-lighted only if it could be proved that they would secure healthy returns from television. In this way, television began to provide a safety net for film producers operating in an increasingly precarious market in which every film had to stand for itself, win its exhibition possibilities and attempt to break even or enter profit at the box office. With television as a known and dependable future source of revenue, the pressure to succeed at the cinema lessened considerably.

Most of the major studios developed an early vested interest in television:

Paramount immersed itself deeper into TV during the forties by operating the first experimental station in Chicago and the first commercial station in Los Angeles and by exploiting theatre television and subscription TV. Following Paramount's lead, Warner Bros., Loew's, and Twentieth Century-Fox also filed for stations in the major markets during the war and laid plans to buy into the young television industry.

(*Balio, 1990; pp.20–1*)

Ironically, however, the same divorcement proceedings that divested the studios of their exhibition arms and prevented their monopolistic control of their industry also prevented them from heavily investing in the television industry. To have done so would have opened them up to new accusations of industrial monopoly, creating a synergy between industries which would have shut out smaller operators in the same way as the independents had been contained within the film industry.

TECHNICAL DEVELOPMENTS

For almost 50 years, the shape of the moving picture on the cinema screen had not changed substantially. After an early period of experimentation in a plethora of image ratios – long and wide, tall and thin, circular, square – the now familiar 4:3 'academy ratio' was settled upon, ostensibly for reasons of industrial efficiency and optimum image quality. Coincidentally, the same ratio became the standard for television as it was developed, again for technical and aesthetic reasons.

Colour had been used in film-making since its beginnings, especially for dyeing the whole, or part of, the screen image in a certain hue to indicate mood or time of day (red for passion, or blue for evening, for example). However, technical limitations had always made it difficult to achieve consistent and acceptable results, at least in terms of producing lifelike colour and flesh tones When the industry made the shift to synchronised sound at the end of the 1920s, the issue of colour became of secondary technical importance to the need to perfect sound–image synchronisation. Research into colour stock went into abeyance for over a decade – a situation not helped by the advent of the Second World War, which further delayed serious developments. By 1950, therefore, both cinema and television had adopted and normalised a 4:3 academy ratio, black and white image and mono sound as their standard.

As the end of the 1940s witnessed the increasing rivalry between cinema and television – a battle which television was perceived to be winning – the film industry realised that it had to do something, to develop itself in ways against which television could not compete. The result was widescreen cinema, which appeared first as Cinerama, a cumbersome three-camera/three-projector system, in 1952 before becoming standardised in the far more technically efficient form of CinemaScope in 1953. Not only was the image considerably wider than the normal 4:3 academy ratio, but CinemaScope came complete with Technicolor and stereo sound; an audio-visual excess designed to show up television for the impoverished experience it certainly then was.

Big, colourful, richly aural films needed important, respectable, impressive stories to tell. 'Making them big meant investing in literary properties that were pre-tested and pre-sold, such as best-selling novels, Broadway hits, and even successful television dramas' (Balio, 1990; p.24). Spectacle began to be favoured over narrative as the central attraction of a film. Thereby, a technological development helped to usher in a shift in the way films were perceived in terms of their audiences' tastes. The period of the blockbuster had begun.

BLOCKBUSTER MENTALITY

The film industry had been here before, most notably at the end of the 1920s when synchronised sound provided a new and exciting reason to go to the movies. It was assumed that recovery in the 1950s required a return to the methods, styles and strategies which had proved so successful in the past: innovation, new features, but essentially the same product. Circumstances and audiences had changed, however. The public wanted something different; it no longer assumed cinema-going to be an automatic weekly or bi-weekly leisure activity. Going to the cinema had now become an occasional special event. The two decades between 1950 and 1970 saw the American film industry learn this painful lesson in an endless series of attempts to maintain aspects of the practices of the past while seeing the results too often fail at the box-office.

The audience expectation of an 'event' at the cinema resulted in a smaller number of large-budget films being produced to capture mass audiences at the box office. Average budgets rose over the 1970s from roughly $2 million to $9 million, averaging $11 million by the early 1980s (Balio, 1985; pp.440–1). Co-production deals could help to spread costs and risks, but not eradicate them altogether. The need to capture an increasingly distracted audience and persuade it that it wanted to make a special trip to the cinema, led to a progressive increase in advertising and marketing costs. By the end of the decade these could actually form a substantial percentage of the total cost of making and releasing a major feature film. 'With increased television advertising, costs for marketing the average film increased dramatically in the second half of the 1970s; by 1980, print and advertising expenses averaged about $6 million per film (at a time when the average negative cost – all production expenses before prints, advertising, etc. – was more than $10 million)' (Wyatt, 1998; p.82).

But the flaw in the strategy was that the risk of failure was increased on each film, and each film had a substantial portion of a studio's finances wrapped up in it. While it was trying to achieve a profit, that money could not be used elsewhere, to make new films. The studio had to wait until the money began returning from the box office before it could reinvest it in new product. And if any of the big-budget films failed, the money did not come back and could not be reinvested. The more films that failed at the box office, the less money there was to use in making other films. An atmosphere of constant anxiety and fear of failure was thus created throughout the industry. Writing as this was happening in the early 1970s, Toeplitz sums it up: 'the American cinema is now sailing between Scylla and Charybdis. You can make a fortune out of a single blockbuster, but in case of failure the spectre of bankruptcy looms large. To make, or not to make, blockbusters – that is the question' (Toeplitz, 1975; p.64).

One strategy for helping to cushion the financial risk of big-budget movies is through extensive merchandising. A considerable and supplementary industry producing allied materials – popcorn and soft drinks; lobby cards; souvenir booklets; fanzines and glossy magazines; jigsaw puzzles; soft toys; the list is endless – has accompanied the actual experience of viewing a film in a cinema since at least the 1910s. But however active this support industry may have been for any individual film, its products always constituted a second income layer, a (thin) icing on a cake which always consisted of the box-office returns of the film itself.

Disney was by far the most visionary of the companies operating before the period covered by this book, setting up Walt Disney Enterprises Inc. to handle a range of supporting product, including strip cartoons, comics, clothes, toys using Disney characters and images, and television shows. 'He christened this approach "total merchandising"' (Puttnam with Watson, 2000; p.185), the *pièce de résistance* being Disneyland, built in 1955 as a theme park to concretise the fantasy which was the Disney cartoon universe.

The rise of conglomeration during the 1960s, together with the emergence of the blockbuster movie with its ever escalating budget, intensified the concept of merchandising tied in to movie releases. The 'event' movie came to be used to sell a wide range of associated products, partly as a means of helping to recoup production costs and send films into profit. George Lucas and his film *Star Wars* (1977) fundamentally changed the balance between original film and supplementary spin-offs, by recognising that the money that could be earned from tie-ins and franchising could be more than that earned from the film itself. Lucas's career will be looked at in more detail in Chapter 4, while the specific economics of franchising in the age of the blockbuster will be explored further in Chapter 2.

THE 1969–71 CRISIS

The American film industry suffered a major crisis at the very end of the 1960s. The five majors lost over $200 million: UA $85 million; MGM $72 million;

Twentieth Century-Fox $65 million. Columbia almost went into receivership. The causes were several – as outlined above, film studios had, for the previous few years, placed more and more faith in a smaller number of high-budget movies, hoping that one or more of them every year would become a runaway hit, reaping massive box-office rewards. When they did not – and the late 1960s saw a glut of expensive box-office flops, such as *Camelot* (1967), *Dr Dolittle* (1967), *Star!* (1968) and *Hello Dolly* (1969) – the dire potential consequences of the blockbuster mentality were realised. The extravagance of road-showing – pre-release runs of a blockbuster in selected venues with higher ticket prices and on an unrestricted run which lasted as long as the film retained its popularity – prevented it from achieving a wide release to hundreds of cinemas where the real money was. Moreover, this flamboyant presentation of new films as something really special – events which should not be missed – could comfortably support only the very few films a year which warranted such attention. The others simply were not sufficiently large or impressive enough as productions, could not sustain the interest and had no hope of surviving in such an over-hyped atmosphere. As Twentieth Century-Fox vice president of sales Abe Dickstein observed in 1968:

> The Agony and the Ecstasy *was not successful. But who can say whether it was because it was wrong for roadshowing or because it just wasn't a good picture? I don't think you can make a silk purse out of a sow's ear, that is, give an ordinary film added prestige by going roadshow. If there's one thing that will kill the roadshow business, it's presenting films on a reserved-seat basis that just don't warrant this special attention.*
>
> (Beaupre, 1968; p.3)

For such films, the audience was often content to wait until the film had finished its road-show period and came into the smaller, cheaper and more convenient cinemas.

Consequently, after the disruption caused by the string of late-1960s big-budget box-office disasters mentioned above, a brief counter-reaction set in where studios retrenched by deciding to make smaller, lower-budget films. New directors such as Dennis Hopper (*Easy Rider*, 1969 – production budget, $500,000) and Martin Scorsese (*Mean Streets*, 1973 – production budget, $600,000) were allowed to enter the industry to make these films, which often dealt with subjects and genres which had not been catered for by major studios – horror, exploitation, drug culture. Even given this alternative culture emphasis, it was deemed less risky to invest in them because they were low-budget, and therefore, if they failed at the box office, they would only lose a modest amount of money, rather than the large sums lost by a big-budget box office flop. These films and their film-makers were given a space in which to prove that a different economic philosophy, whereby risk was spread by investment in a greater number of smaller films (each, hopefully, more in tune with the new youth *Zeitgeist*), would succeed where the blockbuster approach had not.

However, as we will see in the coming chapters, this optimism and this radically new strategy (very 'old Hollywood' in some ways) lasted only a few years. The film-makers who were entrusted with the task of saving the American film industry by producing a new and exciting kind of movie, were too often destructive, both personally and industrially. Furthermore, the identification of a new audience did not magically save the film industry from its mounting troubles. There was a growing realisation within the industry, as a direct result of the 1969–71 crisis, that worldwide attendance had levelled out and was not going to improve, and that therefore only so many films could be made a year if the market was not going to be glutted. Between 1969 and 1977, for example, the number of films made per year fell from 225 to around 110. During the same period, box-office gross rose steadily from $1.08 billion in 1967 to $2.16 billion in 1977 (largely due to rising ticket prices) and admissions from 553 million in 1967 to 942 million in 1972 and, finally, 1.12 billion in 1978 (Conant, 1985; p.539). Rising ticket prices and fewer films grabbing more of the box-office: this was the emerging scenario for the American film industry going into the 1970s.

The film which, somewhat paradoxically, helped prove the exhaustion of the new radical 'auteurist cinema' and the potentially massive profits that could be made from a single 'big event' film, was *The Godfather*. Made by Francis Ford Coppola in 1972, an epic film almost three hours long which did not cost a huge amount by blockbuster standards (about $6–7 million), *The Godfather* garnered considerable critical praise and massive box-office profits ($86.2 million in domestic rentals by the end of its first run [Biskind, 1998; p.163]). Its success directly led to a spate of ever-larger films capturing ever larger chunks of the box office throughout the 1970s – *Jaws* (1975); *Star Wars*; *Close Encounters of the Third Kind* (1977).

Following hard on the heels of *The Godfather*, the success of *Jaws* permanently hooked the industry on the promise of blockbuster windfalls. Saturation release, heavily reliant on television advertising supported by market research, led to high-sell, short-release patterns which buried all but the most resilient or overhyped film. 'The tremendous success of Universal's *Jaws*, which opened in 464 theatres during its initial release in 1975, set the pattern that the industry has followed since. Today it is not uncommon for a film to open in two thousand theatres' (Balio, 1990; p.30). In this mass-release marketplace, a smaller, more intimate film released quietly and using word-of-mouth to attract its audience, stood little chance of succeeding.

Such risk was increased by changes in exhibition strategy. The 'big picture' transformed the old pattern of release from a three-tier to a two-tier play-off. Typically, a pre-1970s blockbuster was released to a few select theatres for extended runs at high admission prices and only after its earning potential within this first-run scenario was exhausted, was it released to large numbers of theatres to capture broader-based revenues. The big picture also affected release schedules. Instead of distributing pictures at regular intervals through-out the year, companies started to release their important films during the peak seasons of Christmas, Easter and summer.

In a sense, this new/old strategy of the blockbuster attraction – with its con-centration of resources into a smaller number of films which were packed with special attractions: top stars, high action, spectacular locations – had been a growing phenomenon since the 1950s. The difference was in the nakedness and exposure now being suffered by each film as it made its way out into the exhibition arena. Risk of failure became more possible with each passing year.

The 1960s and 1970s experienced a general ebb and flow of changing industrial strategy and practice – from investment (economic and psycholo-gical) in big budget blockbusters (*Star!, Dr Dolittle, Hello Dolly*) to a seem-ingly radical retreat from this philosophy towards smaller, more personal statement films (*Easy Rider, Mean Streets*), in the early 1970s, and back to huge blockbusters (*The Godfather, Jaws*) by the mid-1970s. The phrase 'seemingly radical retreat' is used above, because at the same time as Holly-wood was financing and hyping the new wave of personal film-making, it was simultaneously maintaining its interest in bigger-budget action spec-tacles. The early 1970s saw the rise of the disaster movie, epitomised by *Airport* (1970) and *The Poseidon Adventure* (1972), showing that Hollywood was always careful to hedge its bets. Nevertheless, the focus at the time, the 'good money', was on the potential of the new generation of film-makers, and the fullest development of the disaster cycle came at the same time, the mid-1970s, as the 'new blockbusters' of Coppola, Spielberg, *et al.*

It is also important not to see it as a phenomenon of the past. As we will see, the blockbuster mentality is very much alive and well in our own age. In each case, the film industry, although at times exhibiting feelings of insecurity and uncertainty, reacted to changing circumstances as they appeared and survived to tell the tale. This chameleon-like resilience of the American film industry has been a feature of its survival over the past hundred years.

THE PACKAGE

During the studio system, studios invariably selected the ideas and stories they were to make into films.

*During the 1930s and 1940s . . . [t]he procedures for finding suitable story
material intensified. Studios embarked upon complete coverage of worldwide
publishing. East and west coast editorial departments hired up to fifty employees;
scouts talked to agents and famous writers, sometimes gaining access to a
manuscript or galleys before publication.*

(Staiger, in Bordwell, Staiger and Thompson, 1985; p.322)

They also selected the personnel who were to work together to make each
film – most of whom, whether stars, directors, or cameramen, were on the
permanent payroll. The only exception to this was the occasional star or
creative worker hired in or swapped from another studio. It was part of the
overall process of keeping everything under the studio's control so that all
profits eventually issuing from the project when it reached the box office
could legitimately be claimed by the studio.

This system began to change as the studios began to lose their absolute
control over their own industry following the Paramount case and the
divorcement of the theatres from the studios. In their reduced circumstances,
it made no sense for studios to maintain their punishingly expensive studio
complexes with their salaried personnel and capital possessions. As Balio has
argued, 'it made more economic sense to tailor-make individual pictures. An
expedient way to accomplish this was to finance independent producers who
had assembled "packages" of talent especially suited to a project' (Balio, 1990;
p.166).

What they also lost in this process was their role as overseer and promoter
of the acting talent which formed such a crucial part of their process. Talent
agencies – companies such as William Morris and MCA – began to take over
this role. With the weakening of the studio system after the Paramount decree,
agents began to assume a more prominent role, as initiators of film projects.
Leading examples would be Freddie Fields and David Begelman of Creative
Management Associates (CMA) who, in the mid-1960s, handled Henry Fonda
and Paul Newman amongst many others, and Sue Mengers of International
Creative Management (ICM). Later notable figures include Michael Ovitz,
who set up Creative Artists Agency (CAA) with four partners in 1975 and by
1980 handled many of Hollywood's leading stars, including Robert Redford,
Paul Newman and Dustin Hoffman.

Often these agents worked with their own clients, developing film ideas
that would suit the clients, especially the star actors or directors. In the
process, this ensured that they and their clients secured the maximum
amount of money for their involvement, not only in up-front fees, but,
more significantly, in post-release percentages of box-office take. A packager
assembled the main elements of a picture, but then typically took a secondary

position in the actual production. More often than not, the packager was also a talent agent, who drew directly from the ranks of his own clients – the writer of the script, one or several stars, the director – in forming the creative team which would head the project and woo the studio heads.

This development had several effects on the movie industry generally. Until the early 1950s, most of the people working at a studio were permanent employees, who could be assumed still to be working at the studio as every new project was developed. After the Paramount decrees, certain key personnel went freelance, and projects came to the studios from them, in association with their agents. Each film project therefore became a stand-alone entity, and all those working on the film worked on that film alone. When it was finished, they moved on, forming new relationships for other projects at other studios.

Take, for example, *The Big Country*, an epic western made in 1958 by United Artists, directed by William Wyler, photographed by Franz Planer and starring Charlton Heston, Gregory Peck, Carroll Baker and Charles Bickford. All four actors, and Wyler, were represented by the MCA agency, which packaged the deal. Wyler had previously directed *Friendly Persuasion* (1956) for AA (Wyler's own company), and went on to make *Ben Hur* (1959) for MGM, again working with Charlton Heston. Prior to *The Big Country*, Heston starred in *A Touch of Evil* (1958), directed by Orson Welles for Universal International Pictures, and went on to make *The Buccaneer* (1958) for Paramount. Co-star Gregory Peck's film before *The Big Country* was *The Bravados* (1958), for TCF. The film he made directly after *The Big Country* was *Pork Chop Hill* (1959), directed by Lewis Milestone for UA/Melville/Milestone. Lastly, the cinematographer Franz Planer had previously photographed *The Pride and the Passion* (1957), directed by Stanley Kramer for UA/Stanley Kramer, and went on to photograph *The Nun's Story* (1959) for Warner, directed by Fred Zinnemann.

As can be readily seen from even this brief example, all of the major talent involved in mainstream American film-making was, at this point in time, teaming up to work on single film projects before moving on to new projects with different sets of creative talent. While people might, as Wyler and Heston did, work together again, this was either by coincidence or personal desire, rather than because they had been told to do so by studios which held them under contract. The sense of continuity and security which had been a cornerstone of the old studio system was swept away.

A second effect of this way of making films was that the studio no longer provided in-house all the means of production for its entire output of films. Instead it subcontracted out a certain part of its work to independent and specialist companies. The growth of specialist firms servicing the major studios grew as the decade went on. 'In the 1950s, the studios began to use independent subcontractors to absorb the unstable part of their output and to differentiate the product' (Christopherson and Storper, 1989; p.311). This process, known as 'flexible specialisation', enabled the majors to concentrate their finances and labour on a small number of big-budget films, while arranging for smaller companies to provide either specialised input into certain areas of that production (special effects, sound recording), or to produce lower-budget and television movies to fill the studio's wider product commitment. One consequence of this shift is that it encouraged the development of independent and external production companies. Their growth might easily be seen as a direct threat to the dominance of the Hollywood majors:

> [S]pecialised firms and non-studio locations proved superior to the studios, not only for low-budget films and MFTs [made-for-television movies], but for high-budget and high-revenue productions as well. The studios could no longer compete against the independent production companies and specialised contractors they had helped to create, in the very market segments they had hoped to retain. Virtually none of the major studios today can offer the range of specialised services which are obtainable from independent firms; few can even carry out relatively routine tasks at lower costs than the independent supplier firms.
>
> (Storper, 1989; p.285)

Aksoy and Robins, however, have argued that this reorganisation of production procedures allowed the majors to retain control of the industry: '[O]gilopolistic control never ceased to be a distinguishing feature of Hollywood. The agenda was in fact always about the ways in which large corporations were manoeuvring and restructuring to consolidate their hold over the industry' (Aksoy and Robins, 1992; p.6). As we will explore in Chapter 6, on modern independent film production this process, whereby the majors enter into relationships with independent firms in order both to limit the threat posed by maverick film-makers and to provide the means by which the majors can increase the product they have to offer the market, fundamentally defines the contemporary independent film making landscape.

Perhaps most importantly, the advent of the package system, in giving power to the stars and directors as legitimate initiators of their own projects, foregrounded them as the real power-brokers in Hollywood. This move from salaried personnel to freelance movers and shakers in charge of their own creative teams, would have far-reaching effects on the industry. It directly affected the kinds of story that would be told, as actors, especially the image-conscious superstars, did not tend to want to be associated with anything too experimental or controversial. Robert Redford, for example, from his breakthrough film *Barefoot in the Park* (1967) through *Butch Cassidy and the Sundance Kid* (1969), *The Way We Were* (1973) and *All the President's Men* (1976), *Out of Africa* (1985) all the way to *The Horse Whisperer* (1999), has continually played blond, blue-eyed WASP-ish heroes. *All the President's Men* began Redford's explicit acquisition of properties in which he could maintain his specific screen image. Even slight exceptions, such as the coldly ambitious skier in *Downhill Racer* (1969) or his anti-social trapper in *Jeremiah Johnson* (1972) do not substantially compromise the continuity of that image.

With the dismantling of their vertical integration and the removal of their ability to initiate and maintain control over their own production process, the majors in effect became bankers and distributors. They put up the finance which allowed a film to be made, and then acted as mediators between the people behind the actual creation of the films and the exhibitors who showed them in their cinemas. The balance of power, or seeming power, shifted from studio to individual operator. The consequences of this in terms of the influence and control that actors and directors, especially, could hope to exert will be explored in later chapters.

INDEPENDENTS

It is a mistake to think that 'independence' is a modern phenomenon, the result of a rebelliousness against authority and the mainstream – in this case, against Hollywood major studio film-making. There have always been independent film production companies in the American film industry. Indeed, in the early days of cinema, there were nothing *but* independent companies because there was no mainstream Hollywood for any individual operator not to be a part of. And even when what has come to be known as Hollywood stabilised as a discrete entity in the late 1910s and early 1920s, there were still plenty of film producers working outside the mainstream. Companies such as Tiffany-Stahl and Gotham Pictures were significant players in the independent arena; others such as Rayart, eventually operated their own small exhibition networks (Seale, 1991; p.79).

The independent sector consisted of producers who chose to make films on the periphery of the mainstream, together with those who were forced to do so by the financial and economic stranglehold imposed on the industry by the majors. By making increasingly expensive films that exhibitors, either willingly or not, rented because they hoped their audiences wanted to see them, the majors evolved a market demand for lavish, star-laden films which the smaller independent companies could not hope to emulate. The existence of such independent producers was usually precarious, basically because they had to pledge the rights to their existing films in order to raise new finance through the banks, which lent them the money at punishing rates of interest. The perils inherent in this process were amply demonstrated by one of the biggest independent producer/directors of the silent period, D.W. Griffith. Having reaped massive rewards from his early feature-length films, most notably *Birth of a Nation* (1915), Griffith proceeded not only to lose all the box-office profits he had gained, but progressively put himself more and more deeply in debt to the banks as his films performed increasingly poorly at the box office. Each failure meant not only a loss of immediate profit, but the need to stake a greater, eventually total, percentage of the rights to his past films in order to persuade the banks to give him more money to make future films which looked less and less likely to break even. It is important to note that this process was not unique either to Griffith or to the silent period generally, but is a financial procedure still in operation today. We will look at its modern counterpart more closely in Chapter 6.

In terms of the studio period, however, Balio defines an independent producer:

[a]s generally understood by the industry, [to be] a small company that secured its own financing and arranged for the distribution of pictures made under its supervision. An independent might have a contract with a distributor, but no corporate ties existed between the two firms. Each was separately owned and controlled. In terms of output, an independent might produce a single picture or operate on a long term basis producing a few pictures annually.

(Balio, 1985; pp.412–13)

Some of the larger independents – Selznick, Goldwyn, Disney – made films which were often as big, expensive, glossy and popular as those of the so-called majors. Indeed, in some ways – the size and quality of their films, use of stars (albeit on loan from the major studios, as in the case, famously, of MGM loaning Clark Gable to Selznick for *Gone With the Wind* in 1939), their active relationship with those majors, the long-term consistency – they were major studios in all but name. But there were essential differences. Whereas the majors were geared up as a production line to produce many films a year, even the large independents produced only a small number annually. Each film produced by the large independents received personal treatment in terms of its handling, its marketing and selling.

All this is not to imply a total break between independents and the majors. This is not the case; in fact, there was a kind of productive symbiotic relationship operating between the two entities throughout the studio period. As Schatz argues, the independents relied on the majors, not only to lend them key personnel and production facilities, but also to help them into first-run cinemas when their films were released (Schatz, 1989; p.11). The studios depended upon the independents to produce 'high-end' product that would give the industry artistic credentials while also providing an alternative choice at the cinema.

The loss of major studio personnel to the armed forces and the re-focusing of studio facilities to other ends during the Second World War caused a significant shift in the fortunes of the independents. These factors, together with an increased demand from audiences wanting to be distracted from the horrors of war, resulted in a need for new film production companies making films to fill the gaps becoming apparent in the output of the major studios. Many new hopefuls entered the arena in an attempt to satisfy this demand. 'Most had fled the production ranks of Hollywood, men such as Hunt Stromberg, David Loew, and Lester Cowan. Some were stars such as Jimmy Cagney, and others were speculators of many stripes.' As Balio goes on to argue, '[b]y 1945, there were nearly fifty independents in business . . . The number burgeoned to over a hundred by the end of the decade' (Balio, 1985; pp.413–16). But independent production was a high-risk undertaking, dependent upon fickle audience tastes and loyalties, and as the 1950s wore on, many independents found it increasingly difficult to get financing for their film projects.

The higher-paid creative personnel at studios were badly affected by the high wartime tax limits. Perversely, they could improve their circumstances in this respect, by operating as a company which paid them as workers, rather than as private individuals. Many chose this option, swelling the ranks of independent operators. Although banks were still, even possibly increasingly, cautious about lending independent producers money to make films that had no guarantee of box-office success, the presence of a famous actor in the foreground of such a project eased the anxiety. If anything was designed to engender feelings of security and assurance of success, it was a popular actor who had a proven track record.

The effect of the Paramount decrees on the independent production sector, in terms of the abolishing of block and blind booking, gave the independents better access to, and opportunities in, exhibition in general. In the process, however, they lost their mainstream industry support mechanism which had enabled them to get their films into first-run cinemas, albeit mostly as second features on double bills. Now their films were forced to compete in a truly open market. Such was the scale of the threat to the independents' chances of survival that they 'now began to clamour for a reunification of the divorced majors so as to give the producer-distributors a new vested interest in theatre ownership' (Borneman, 1985; p.461). That is to say, having fought hard to dismantle the vertically integrated power of the majors, the independents now made an about-turn, in an attempt to reinstate the stable industrial model upon which they had previously, somewhat paradoxically, depended for their livelihoods.

As previously argued, the various crises that hit the mainstream industry in the 1950s and 1960s – the separation of cinemas from studio control, falling audience figures, the failure of big-budget movies, the consequent massive losses of 1969–71, and the shift to fewer films being produced per year – opened up a space into which the independents eagerly manoeuvred themselves. Operating on a single-film basis, independents found it easier to cope with a changing marketplace that was demanding fewer and fewer films. In the 1950s and increasingly in the 1960s, the majors, with their huge studios designed for continuous uninterrupted film production, and with all of the punishing overheads attendant on such an intensely industrialised process, found it far harder to deal with lessening demand for their product.

Consequently, the majors developed new relationships with the independents, both those such as National General and Allied Artists, which made mainstream films, or those, such as Roger Corman's New World, which specialised in more teen-oriented exploitation fare. By the 1960s, every major studio, Universal excepted, had formed alliances with independent companies, entering into active production with them. As a marker of this changing relationship, at the end of the 1940s, the independents made approximately a fifth of the 234 feature films released by the majors. Eight years later, according to Balio, this percentage had risen to well over half (58 per cent) (Balio, 1990; p.10).

In an important sense, the term 'independent' began to lose its currency in this growing intimacy between major and independent in the joint creation of movies. The independent producer was given considerable space in which to create his/her film, but the major studio oversaw the production of each film, aiding financially and maintaining a careful eye on that financial status as production proceeded. Control still ultimately resided with the holder of the purse-strings – in this case, the major.

The true meaning of the term 'independent', therefore, must be carefully considered. Does it mean simply a producer or film-maker operating outside of the small number of major studios (or now, more properly, conglomerate companies), providing product for them to exploit and distribute? Or does it mean something radically different: alternative, low-budget, maverick, raw, controversial or quirky; never meaning, or expecting to, appeal to a mass audience? Are independents identifiable by their use of low-weight, portable equipment, direct sound, and their emphasis on location shooting which gives the films a rough and immediate quality? Such questions should not be answered in a chapter that is mostly about other, more general, matters. We will therefore pick up these questions again in Chapters 4 and 6 on directors and independents.

FOREIGN FILMS

Foreign films have always had a part to play in the history of the American cinema. From the earliest days, when the French Pathé company dominated American cinema, they have been seen as a different product, as a threat to box-office maximisation and, therefore, as something to be fended off, resisted, and, where possible, stopped. America implemented trade barriers throughout the twentieth century to ensure that this is exactly what happened. The world has responded in kind, with Britain and France especially active, from the 1927 British Cinematographic Act through to the GATT negotiations of the late 1990s. As well as official trade sanctions, there have also been continual initiatives by non-American interests to co-operate in order to resist American hegemony. Between 1924 and 1928, for example, '[t]here had been much talk in the European, and especially the German, trade press . . . of the need to establish a pan-European cinema as the only coherent means of challenging the international supremacy of the Hollywood machine' (Higson, 1999; p.117). Film Europe, as it came to be known, remained an active initiative during the 1920s, although individual interests eventually caused its demise.

Within the boundaries of the period covered by this book, and the slightly larger context being sketched out in this background chapter, we must notice a changing of mood in the relations between America and the rest of the world in terms of film production. While trade restrictions undoubtedly remained, it was seen as politic and even economically advisable for the American film industry to foster more productive interactions with foreign film industries.

Despite the trough of despond into which the American film industry has been described as falling by the end of the 1950s, its domination of world cinema markets increased. Balio notes that before the Second World War approximately a third of revenues came from abroad, while post-war that figure rose to over 50 per cent (Balio, 1990; p.6). Foreign revenues had always been important for America's film industry. During the classical period, when films rolled off the production lines with ruthless efficiency, the global market provided a lucrative destination for Hollywood product. As production costs rose, world markets provided a means of generating the extra income that made the financial balancing act feasible. In the immediate post-war world, the flood of American films into long-denied foreign markets brought sudden and substantial profits into Hollywood's coffers. And finally, during the slumps of the 1950s and 1960s American film industry, foreign markets became all the more vital as uncertainty and instability gripped Hollywood in the face of a changing domestic audience profile that, at least temporarily, left the industry floundering and casting about for solutions.

In terms of domestic exhibition, the post-war period saw the greater accept-ability of foreign films playing on American screens, although only under tightly controlled circumstances. The reasons for this are various. The process of divorcement of American theatres from the control of the major studios and the decrease in the number of films made by the majors following the 1969 crisis caused cinemas to redefine themselves in order to cater for other audience needs. Art cinemas, such as those of the Cinema V company in New York (the Cinema I and Cinema II, as well as the Paris, Baronet, Plaza and Sutton), emerged as a significant feature in this new landscape. Less than 100 of these art cinemas existed in 1950; 15 years later that number had increased more than sixfold to over 600. They showed independent films to audiences wanting something new, an alternative to Hollywood's slick and glossy pro-duct, increasingly seen as out of touch and irrelevant to post-war social realit-ies. The art cinemas showed resurrected Hollywood classics and foreign films to new audiences of young people who had never seen them or, in the case of Italian neo-realism or French New Wave films, anything like them, before. '[Robert] Benton and [David] Newman [writers of *Bonnie and Clyde*, 1967] educated themselves by simply going to the movies at the art houses (the Thalia on 95th Street and Dan Talbot's New Yorker on Broadway between 88th and 89th), the New York Film Festival that burst onto the scene in 1963, and the Museum of Modern Art' (Biskind, 1998; p.26). Untethered by the Produc-tion Code that had provided such a straightjacketed set of moral guidelines for so long, they dealt with difficult subjects, harsh realities, controversial subjects, exploring them in unremitting detail. And because they had largely been made outside the necessarily streamlined production methods that typified the classical Hollywood system, they were often strikingly personal works. Some members of the audiences who saw these films will figure importantly in later chapters of this work. By absorbing the various histories and aesthetic influences, as well as the sense that film could be used to express a real personal vision of the world, those who came to be known as the film school generation – Scorsese, Coppola, Lucas, Friedkin, De Palma – were to prove vital to the changes that occurred in American cinema in the 1970s.

In general terms, foreign films also provided a much-needed expansion to the number of films from which exhibitors could choose as Hollywood retrenched and cut its annual production figures in the face of the various pressures outlined above. Indeed, as Balio notes, exhibitors 'faced with a product shortage and declining attendance ... were told in 1954 by an executive of United Paramount Theatres that "it might be wise for [them] to consider ways and means of popularising the foreign film" and "establish an audience where there had been none before"' (Balio, 1985; p.477). And as *Variety* reported in 1953, 'There is a feeling among film importers that, with a general product shortage in the offing, imports from abroad – in both subtitled and dubbed versions – are heading for a somewhat brighter future' (quoted in Wyatt, 1998; p.67). However, this opening of the American market to foreign imports was executed in highly controlled ways. Although it became attractive, and even necessary, to allow foreign films into the American market, this was only allowed via American companies:

> British, French and Italian interests tried to establish their own distribution chains in America, but American distributors were able to maintain a monopoly position in the domestic market, while simultaneously fortifying their worldwide distribution networks. As before, foreign films could profitably enter the U.S. market only by means of American companies, demonstrating that the situation had not changed in half a century.
>
> *(Guback, 1985; p.480)*

CONGLOMERATES

The conglomeration of the American film industry was the direct result of the various crises that hit the industry during the 1960s. The consequence of having their theatres taken away from them in the Paramount decrees was to force the majors to enter as many other media and leisure-time arenas as possible in an attempt to ensure and maintain alternative revenue possibilities. As Balio notes, 'Paramount was the first film company to take drastic measures to ensure its survival, but other companies in turn developed strategies to stay alive' (Balio, 1990; p.39).

The conglomeration of the film industry must be seen in the wider context of changes in American business practice in general during this period. After the Second World War American industry flourished and the general affluence of American society allowed people to buy the things it produced. This, in turn, led to an emphasis on the financial opportunities inherent in the combining of several industries under a single umbrella: economies of scale and production, interaction between parties, mutual advertising, and so forth. It was inevitable that the film industry, with its legendary potential to realise huge profits from a one-off product (the individual feature film) would come under the curious gaze of industrial giants of the business world. There was a range of different ways in which film companies became part of far larger multi-interest financial–industrial entities. They could be taken over by large non-film corporations, absorbed into entertainment concerns, or transformed into conglomerates themselves through expansion and diversification.

The trend was started in 1966 when Gulf and Western took over Paramount. The following year, Transamerica Corporation, a financial services organisation, acquired United Artists. In 1969, Kinney National Services, a conglomerate with a range of interests including funeral homes, car rentals and parking lots, took over Warner Bros., while the Las Vegas hotel owner, Kirk Kerkorian, acquired MGM. Gulf and Western started out in car and truck bumpers before expanding from 1957 onwards into zinc, sugar, fertilizer, real estate, musical instruments, and wire and cable, to name a few areas of activity. Acquiring a hold in one of the film majors was therefore just a small part of its much bigger game plan.

A question that immediately arises is: why would any hard-edged and conservative business concern want to buy into what seemed at the time to be a failing and crisis-ridden industry? There are several reasons, all of which centre on what film companies offer *other* than their ability to create new films. As Toeplitz summarises it,

> *Businessmen were motivated by the material, calculable advantages they saw in the film companies. William V. Frankel, explaining to shareholders of Kinney National Service the reasons for the acquisition of Warner Brothers, quoted the following factors determining the financial viability of the transaction: (1) publishes scores and records; (2) the potential value of equipment, installations, and the whole production capacity for cinema and television; (3) 110 hectares (250 acres) of ground in Burbank; (4) a well-stocked film library. Significantly, films currently in production in the studios were not included in the list.*

> *(Toeplitz, 1975; p.28)*

With hindsight, this description of the motives behind the takeover of one of the major film studios by one of the major conglomerates is a little chilling. It creates the image of a heartless and anonymous business giant, with no inherent feeling for film-making, absorbing a major Hollywood studio with a hugely nostalgic history attached to it (the fragility of early sound pictures, Fred Astaire and Gene Kelly musicals, Cagney gangster films, Errol Flynn's swashbuckling heroes, MGM's 'more stars than there are in heaven', and so on). And to a large extent this image is true. Conglomerate companies do react to the financial bottom line, and continue with, expand or contract, develop or sell off their holdings depending upon those holdings' performance in the marketplace. The majors themselves have a history of ruthlessness for anyone interested in reading about it. Film-making has always been a high-investment, high-risk endeavour, the risk minimised by the spread-bet strategies of the studio period, but never totally eliminated.

From a slightly different perspective, conglomeration could actually be seen as saving the film industry from financial ruin. Its essential business strategy did not allow the small number of large films made per year by the 1970s to stand out and attempt to win huge profits by themselves but, rather, surrounded those films with a range of activities which could partially absorb and cushion any losses accrued. As Balio puts it, 'on balance, the takeovers benefited the motion picture by reviving moribund managements, by stabilising operations, and by forcing the industry to adapt to new television technologies' (Balio, 1990; p.40). It is perhaps significant in this respect that the role played by film in Gulf and Western's activities grew from a few per cent in 1966 to over 30 per cent by the 1980s. Indeed, it restructured its operations, by getting rid of over 50 of its companies, to focus more fully on its entertainment aspects. And when Coca-Cola took over Columbia Pictures for $700 million in 1982, it was with the intention of modernising its operations by introducing the scientific marketing methods it had developed in its drinks division.

This introductory chapter has shown that the American film industry, exemplified by Hollywood, has seldom, if ever, been stable. Certainly, stability has been far from the norm in the last 30 years or so. The studio era is looked back upon as a period of great continuity and stability but even then, as Bordwell, Staiger and Thompson (1985) have argued, the great studios were continually in a process of development, innovation, absorption of rivals, and response to a constantly changing audience profile.

Those making films in the late 1960s and onwards found a very different reality. Unpredictable audiences could cause a film to become either a massive box-office sensation or an embarrassing box-office flop. Rival media threats could neither be ignored nor beaten. And changing industrial practices gave away control of the conditions of production, first to the ex-employees and later to impersonal businessmen for whom film-making was not a passion but simply a money-making operation. The means by which a mainstream feature film is conceived, planned, produced and sent to its audience, and the part played by those major figures involved in its creation, have changed significantly across the past three decades.

CHAPTER TWO

Show me the Money

The economics of contemporary American cinema

In 1980, United Artists released Michael Cimino's *Heaven's Gate* to an avalanche of critical abuse and minimal box office. From an initial budget of between $11.5 million and $15 million, the film finally cost $35 million to make, plus another $9 million to advertise and distribute. It took a mere $2 million at the box office. Its out-of-control writer/director and budgetary excesses, together with its critical and commercial failure, are seen to have at least substantially contributed to the downfall of its studio.

In 1997, Fox and Paramount released James Cameron's *Titanic*, widely reported to have gone wildly over budget in the hands of a similarly megalomaniac writer/director. A first budget estimate of $120 million soared to $200 million by the end of production. As its long and troubled production continued, its two studio financiers began to wonder if it could possibly ever make a profit when released: 'Tension had risen considerably between the partners, Paramount and Fox. There was an air of desperation in their dealings. The concern was not who would make more money, but who would lose less' (Parisi, 1998; pp.147–8). It was, instead, a massive hit, financially if not quite critically ($600 million domestic, $1,235 million overseas, making a worldwide total of $1.835 billion) and has become the emblem of high-risk, high-finance, high-return blockbuster film-making. Its makers, and their peers at other studios, have vowed not to make anything like it again. This chapter is at least partly about the shifts in the financial and industrial landscape of American film-making over the past two decades bookended by *Heaven's Gate* and *Titanic*, which allowed the first to fail, and the second to succeed, equally spectacularly.

Michael Cimino directs Kris Kristofferson in *Heaven's Gate* (Michael Cimino, 1980)
Courtesy of MGM CLIP + STILL

INDUSTRIAL STRUCTURE

The past 30 years of American cinema have been defined as the age of the conglomerate. Across the period, all of the major studios have been absorbed into large multinational companies to become the entertainment arm of diverse multi-industry concerns.

Paramount

Paramount was the first to undergo this process, having been bought by Gulf and Western in 1966. By 1971, Gulf and Western was seriously considering closing down its film unit (Paramount) because of disappointing results. Such a move dramatically illustrates the precarious future of a film studio within such a diversified operation, in which each branch was expected to justify itself with continual good results. By 1989, however, the inverse had happened, with Gulf and Western deciding instead to sell off its financial unit in order to allow it to concentrate its efforts on its entertainment interests. By 1980, Paramount Film and Television accounted for 11 per cent of Gulf and Western's annual revenues; by 1989, that figure had risen dramatically to 50 per cent. As a recognition of the importance of its film and television operations, Gulf and Western changed its name to Paramount Communications Inc. in 1989. Its holdings at that time were varied and substantial, and included Paramount Pictures and Paramount Television; Paramount Home Video; Madison Square Gardens (a major piece of New York property which included the New York Knicks and New York Rangers); publishing interests which included Simon and Schuster; and two major cinema chains: United Cinemas International and Cineamerica Theatres (co-owned with Warner Communications).

The conglomerate immediately showed its strength by making a hostile takeover bid for Time, in competition with Warner Communications. It lost the battle, having been out-manoeuvered by a series of boardroom and courtroom negotiations between Warner Communications and Time (Lewis, 1998; pp.99–103). In 1993, a battle for ownership of Paramount itself took place between Viacom (owner of MTV, Nickelodeon, Showtime pay-TV, television syndication companies and a range of television stations) and QVC (a home shopping network). Viacom won, buying the company for $8.2 billion. The following year, Viacom bought Blockbuster Entertainment, the world's largest video retail and rental chain, creating for itself an automatic distribution outlet for its product. It also owns six television stations (the Paramount Group), and co-owns, with MCA, the USA Network and TVN Entertainment (ten pay-per-view channels), for which it produces over 700 hours of original programming a year.

Warner Bros.

The Kinney Corporation took over Warner-Seven Arts in 1969 for $400 million. Between the late 1960s and late 1980s, it was known as Warners Communications Inc. In 1990, Time Inc. acquired its stock, creating Time Warner. The group now owns 25 of America's top 100 cable systems, including HBO, Cinemax and Comedy Channel. It owns Lorimar Telepictures

Corp., Warner Home Video and co-owns (with Paramount) the Cineamerica Theatres chain of cinemas. It produces 16 prime-time television network series (including *Friends*, *ER* and *West Wing*), and has branched out into the theme park business with Warner Bros. Roadshow Movie World in Australia and the Six Flags chain in America. In 1992 it restructured its film and cable businesses, creating Time Warner Entertainment in partnership with Japan's Toshiba and C. Itoh. In 1995, Time Warner acquired the Turner Broadcasting System for $7.4 billion, giving it enlarged programming and distribution capacity. Finally, in January 2000, Time Warner was bought by America Online (AOL), America's largest Internet on-line company. The purchase, an all-stock deal, amounted to more than $160 billion, the new firm having an estimated combined value of $350 billion (Junnarkar and Hu, 2000; p.1). The merger positions both parties to take advantage of the anticipated emergence of digital broadband services – the sending of audio-visual and textual material down high-capacity wires into homes.

> *AOL, the clear leader of dial-up Internet providers, has been positioning itself for the impending broadband explosion cutting deals with satellite delivery firms and telecommunications companies that offer digital subscriber line (DSL) services. AOL also has focused on gaining access to cable services controlled by AT&T and other cable companies. The Time Warner deal gives AOL access to those services.*
>
> *(Junnarkar and Hu, 2000; p.1)*

The future significance of this deal will be explored in greater detail in Chapter 9.

MGM/UA

Kirk Kerkorian purchased MGM from the Bronfman family (owners of the drinks empire Seagram) and Time Inc. in 1969, forming MGM/UA in 1981 when Kerkorian took over United Artists from Transamerica. In 1986 he sold it to Ted Turner, only to buy it back again a few months later, minus its studio acreage and film library (including such classics as *A Night at the Opera* [1935], *Random Harvest* [1942], the original *The Postman Always Rings Twice* [1946] and *Singin' in the Rain* [1952]), which Turner wisely chose to keep. In 1990, the Italian Giancarlo Parretti, of Pathé Communications Co., backed by Crédit Lyonnais Bank Netherland, bought the company for $1.3 billion, but had to inject another $145 million in 1991 and many millions more over the next year in an attempt to save it from bankruptcy. In 1992, Parretti lost control of MGM/UA to Crédit Lyonnais, which re-named the company Metro-Goldwyn-Mayer.

Universal

Allied to MCA, MCA/Universal was purchased by Matsushita in 1990 for $6.9 billion in an attempt to create a profitable 'synergy' (see detailed exploration of this later, p.45) or productive connection between software (films, television programmes) and hardware (Matsushita is an electronics giant, responsible for the VHS videocassette system through its JVC company, as well as owning Panasonic, National, Technics and Victor). It too owns theme parks – Universal Studios Hollywood and Universal Studios Florida. In 1995 Matsushita, disappointed by its lack of success in its attempts to marry the product coming out of its film unit with the audio-visual machines being produced by its electronics division, sold MCA/Universal to Seagram for $7 billion.

Twentieth Century-Fox

Twentieth Century-Fox was purchased by Rupert Murdoch's News Corporation in 1985 to become the Twentieth Century-Fox Film Corporation, consisting of Fox Film, Twentieth Century Corporation, CBS/Fox Inc video distribution and Deluxe Labs. It owns seven television stations in the US, and the Fox Broadcasting Company – Fox Network – is a network of 117 affiliates. Its prime time television series include the cult favourite *The X-Files*, of which a successful feature film version has also been made, based on its central characters and the ongoing government- alien conspiracy story which forms the backbone of the TV series' episodic narrative progress. In January 2001, Rupert Murdoch's News Corporation was reported as preparing to purchase DirecTV from General Motors for $40 billion.

> *DirecTV offers more than 200 television channels and has more than nine million customers in the US, making it the country's leading direct-to-home broadcaster. It also has a Spanish language service, DirecTV Para Todas, which offers Spanish language programming from the US, Latin America and Spain, and DirecTV Latin America, which provides television via satellite to more than 1 million customers throughout Latin America.*

> *(Williams, 2001; p.1)*

Disney

Disney is in some ways the original synergy company, with its legendary theme parks Disneyland and Disneyworld, its family-oriented television networks and programmes, and its range of merchandising sold in its own chain of shops. With the advent of cable television, Disney created its Disney Channel, which began broadcasting on 18 April 1983.

Having founded its name and reputation on wholesome family films and television shows, Disney found itself out of touch with a changing public taste in the 1980s. In 1984 it formed Touchstone Pictures to produce more adult movies, the first being *Splash* (1984). In an effort to boost its rating in the feature film production market, it expanded its output, releasing such hits as *Three Men and a Baby* (1987) and *Who Framed Roger Rabbit?* (1988). By 1988 it was commanding 20 per cent of the domestic theatrical market.

In 1993, in a blaze of publicity, Disney announced that it was buying the notoriously aggressive independent distributor Miramax, which had established a name for itself as a marketer of often difficult and risqué foreign and independent movies.

> As unlikely as it seems, the Walt Disney Company announced today that it planned to acquire Miramax as an autonomous division of Disney's distribution arm, Buena Vista Pictures . . . the independent company would continue to produce and release offbeat and arty movies and retain its artistic independence . . . 'We'll have complete freedom to operate as we always have,' Harvey Weinstein [head of Miramax] said . . . He said Miramax would continue to produce, acquire, market and distribute its own films and draw on Disney's support if necessary.

> Under the agreement, Disney will finance Miramax's future films and acquire video, cable, television, pay-per-view and all ancillary rights. The agreement also calls for Disney to acquire Miramax's library of more than 200 films, some of which may be remade for American audiences.

> (Weintraub, 1993; p.39)

The optimism of this announcement was to be short-lived, and the next six years would see Miramax progressively compromised and restricted in its choice of projects by an increasingly overbearing Disney Corporation.

Certainly, Disney's acquisition of the Capital Cities/ABC cinema chain in 1995 for $19 billion, which gave it an additional variety of outlets for its products, changed its working relationship with both Miramax and Touchstone Pictures. The increasingly troubled relationship, and eventual split, between Miramax and Disney will be the subject of a special case-study in Chapter 6, on independent American cinema. Tellingly, however, in summer 1998 Disney closed down Touchstone Pictures and reduced its number of releases.

Columbia

The conglomerate takeover of Columbia perhaps best illustrates the pros and cons of the way in which the major American film studios have been absorbed into global business interests. 1968 was a record year for Columbia, with profits of $21 million on $243 million in revenues. Three years later, in 1971, it suffered a loss of $40 million, and, on the verge of bankruptcy by 1973, was then bought out by Herbert Allen, a New York investment banker. Within two years it was brought back into profit with hits such as *Shampoo* and *Tommy* (both 1975) and the massive success of *Close Encounters of the Third Kind* in 1977 which, having cost $20 million to make, earned $116 million at the US box office.

Between 1982 and 1989, Columbia was owned by American soft drinks giant Coca-Cola, which had merged its two film-making operations – Columbia and TriStar – to create Columbia Pictures Entertainment in late 1987. But although the two were officially merged, they remained as two discrete production units, with separate, and distinctive, slates of films. In November 1989, the Japanese electronics giant Sony Corporation bought Columbia for $3.4 billion, plus $1.6 billion of debt that was then on Columbia's books, and which had to be repaid to Coca-Cola. Sony wanted the executive team of Jon Peters and Peter Guber to head their new film operation, and had to hand out another $1 billion, both to buy Guber and Peter's company and to recompense Warners, which had just appointed them as its new executive team, for letting them out of the contract. The total of $6 billion was seen as an alarming over-valuation of the 'goods' Sony was getting as a result. According to Griffin and Masters, 'a knowledgeable Sony insider says that Blackstone [an investment banking group which provided assessment of Columbia's financial worth] led Sony to be overly optimistic about the studio's earning power. "Where Ohga [Sony president] has frequently criticised Blackstone . . . has been in the quality of their projections . . . They put together high, medium and low [projections] and they blew it in all three areas. They simply didn't understand the business"' (Griffin and Masters, 1996; p.231).

Like Matsushita, Sony's explicit agenda in performing this operation was to acquire a company that could generate the audio-visual material that would make its range of electronic machinery appealing to consumers. Sony had already bought CBS Records in 1987, the first major Japanese purchase of an American entertainment company. Indeed, it must be remembered that Sony had had strong links with American business for some years before moving on Columbia: in 1960 it had set up the Sony Corporation of America. However, Sony was not just interested in future film product but also in Columbia's back catalogue of films and television programmes – over 2,700 films and some 23,000 television series episodes – which they saw as a valuable asset which could be placed on video cassette and sold to promote sales of the machines on which to play them. In this sense, the films which were the raison d'être of Columbia's operation, were simply a means to an end for the bigger company.

By 1990, Columbia's film activities accounted for only 2 per cent of Sony's net sales. In August 1991, Columbia Pictures Entertainment was renamed Sony Pictures Entertainment, but the change of name did not revive the company's fortunes. Although:

> *Sony Pictures Entertainment performed reasonably well until 1993, . . . the following year [it] took a $3.2 billion loss on its motion picture business, reduced the book value of its studios by $2.7 billion, and announced that 'it could never hope to recover its investment' in Hollywood. Nobuyuki Idei, the Tokyo-based president of Sony Corp., took direct control of the company's Hollywood operations and installed new talent to effect a turnaround. Sony's two Hollywood studios soon returned to profitability, but not to top-tier status. The reason: Sony had neither forged connections with cable television nor had it acquired theme parks or consumer product chain stores to extend the franchises developed by the studios.*
>
> *(Balio, 1998; p.69)*

Balio's summary contains a number of important elements that need to be teased out and explored, including the substantial sums of money involved in such deals; the frequency of personnel change, especially in top executive posts; and the importance of multiple-media ancillary markets in the overall economic equation by which modern mainstream American film-making operates. Each of these will be examined shortly.

THE CONSEQUENCES OF CONGLOMERATION FOR FILM PRODUCTION

It is evident from the potted histories of each of the major studios just itemised that most of them have been, and mostly still are, in the hands of non-Americans. Time Warner is currently the only all-American conglomerate. The new conglomerate owners were seen, correctly in many cases, to have no sincere love of films or the film-making process. Rather, they saw, and still see, films either merely as a product like any other, to be sold in the marketplace just like any other, and/or as a commodity which was a necessary step in the larger circuit of economic relay. Conglomerate owners, looking for production stability and predictability as a means of ensuring maximum profits, disliked what they saw as the inherent unpredictability and high-risk gamble of film-making and the movie market.

Although production methods in the making of films and any other major production process share some similarities, in that companies finance workers to make new product, there are substantial differences which make the imposing of one production philosophy on the other problematic. The end result of the film-making process is a unique product: no film is ever even remotely similar to any other, in that it consists of different shots, different combinations of actors in different locations. Moreover, until relatively recently, that product has not been sold to its audience, the *experience of viewing* it has; the audience comes, pays to watch a screening of the film at a specific time, and leaves at the end without taking the physical film with them. Conversely, a car, or a fridge-freezer, is produced in order to be purchased by someone; the money they offer for it gives them physical ownership of it. Perhaps it is not surprising in these terms that the conglomerate takeover of Hollywood has coincided with the advent of certain new distribution formats – videocassettes, DVDs – which *can* be sold for ownership to the public.

The problem of film companies trying to make films for their multi-industry parent conglomerates is that this distinction is not fully and persistently recognised, with the result that the film-making process is often forced to adopt industrial production methods adapted, or imported wholesale, from alien industries. For example Coca-Cola, when owner of Columbia, wanted the number of films produced annually to be increased from 12 to 20 as a means of increasing profits, on the assumption that the more you make, the more you can sell, as if films were identical to Coke cans. Unfortunately, such a scaling-up in the film-making business almost inevitably results in a sacrifice in quality. It is impossible simply to increase the number of films to be made, because there is always a scarcity of the top talent – writers, directors, actors, creative personnel generally – needed to create that high-quality and individual product. In the event, Coca-Cola sold Columbia to Sony before the strategy of increasing production could be put into operation.

In the classic studio period, studio heads – such as Louis B. Mayer, who was head of MGM from the mid-1920s to the early 1950s, and Harry Cohn, head of Columbia from the mid-1920s to the late 1950s – stayed in position for decades. This longevity built continuity within studios peopled by creative personnel who, because they were on long-term contracts, had a similar long-sighted commitment to the studio. As a result, there was a consistency in the production process and product style. In the post-studio period, executive turnover is far more frequent and far more rapid, with each new appointment expected to function in a hot-house environment where they are only as good as, if not actually their last film, then certainly their last *group* of films. As a measure of this difference, although Arthur Krim lasted as chairman of United Artists from 1951 to 1978, his successor, Andy Albeck, lasted just three years, resigning in 1981 after the massive box-office failure of *Heaven's Gate* (1980). David Puttnam, as chairman and CEO of Columbia Pictures, lasted an even shorter time: 16 months, from June 1986 to September 1987.

Each new appointment, partly to establish their own authority, partly to satisfy bosses who expect things to change, habitually instigates different production policies which overturn those of their predecessors. For example, when Joe Roth replaced Jeffrey Katzenberg at Disney, he swapped Katzenberg's policy of making many small-budget films, each earning respectable amounts at the box office, for his own which saw fewer, bigger-budget films with major ad campaigns to promote them. 'And by early spring of 1998, Roth left no doubt as to which would be his star summer attractions: *Mulan* and *Armageddon*' (Bart, 1999; p.33). Box-office figures would appear to confirm the success of this strategy. By mid-October 1998, after 17 weeks of release, *Mulan* had made $120 million in the US, $183 million overseas, for a total worldwide box office of $303 million; *Armageddon*, after 15 weeks on release, had earned $201 million in the US, $353 million overseas, making $554 million worldwide by mid-November 1998. But massive box office notwithstanding, the precariousness and impact of executive decision-making is neatly summed up by Peter Guber's comment on producer Ray Stark – 'He taught me, too, about the impermanence of executives, and the fact that although they are impermanent, they make permanent decisions' (Griffin and Masters, 1996; p.71).

The return of vertical integration

The growth of conglomerates during the 1980s and into the 1990s resurrected fears about an elite of monopolies coming to dominate the American film industry once again, as they had done in the decades before the Paramount decrees forced the studios to divest themselves of their exhibition arms. The 1980s, a decade dominated by Reaganite free-trade economic policies, saw the return, initially in a fairly limited way, of vertical integration. The second half of the 1980s saw MCA purchase the Cineplex Odeon chain of cinemas, Paramount and Warner Communications taking over the Cineamerica chain, and Sony Pictures Entertainment the 885-screen Loews cinema chain (Noglows, 1992; p.69). Co- and full ownership of theatre chains once again allowed the studios to control what was shown in cinemas and for how long. Other producers would have to strike deals with the majors in order to get their films onto studio-controlled screens. As the Noglows article argues, however, the cinema-ownership policy of the majors had turned sour by the early 1990s. 'Indeed, U.S. exhibs are experiencing tough times. Admissions last year hit a 15-year low, off about 8 per cent from 1990 . . . "Paramount and Time Warner would both like to get out of Cineamerica, but they can't find a buyer," says a source. "The same is true of MCA with regard to Cineplex Odeon"' (Noglows, 1992; p.69).

Horizontal integration

But the period was not only marked by the return of vertical integration; it also brought *horizontal* integration, the interaction between film and other media such as television, video games, books, and so on. This interaction is referred to as *synergy*. As noted above, two of the biggest conglomerate purchases of American film studios – Sony's of Columbia and Matsushita's of MCA/Universal – were engineered explicitly in order to forge a productive relationship between software and hardware, between films and the machines on which to view them.

A wider definition of the term includes the re-purposing of material generated primarily and initially for feature film production into other media forms, or material generated in other media being re purposed to help create new film product. It is important to note that this kind of interaction and symbiotic production of different media products is not unique to the modern period of American mainstream film-making. American movies have frequently had tie-ins and supporting materials, whether lobby cards, innovated by Kalem and Vitagraph in early 1910 (Staiger, in Bordwell, Staiger and Thompson, 1985; p.101); press books; toys or fan magazines. The latter were also begun around 1910 – for example, with the *Motion Picture Story Magazine*, started by J Stuart Blackton, owner of Vitagraph (Staiger, in Bordwell, Staiger and Thompson, 1985; p.99). Plenty of fan magazine pages have been filled with such products; many more pages of film trade papers have instructed those concerned how to use such materials to help boost interest in certain films.

It is the scale of supplementary product and the level of interaction that differentiate the modern period of American mainstream film-making from its predecessor. Film subjects are now chosen and developed specifically because of the diversity of their possible connections to other media forms. This synergy was pioneered in the modern era by *A Star is Born* (1976), when the soundtrack of the film, performed by Barbra Streisand and Kris Kristofferson, became a best-seller, as did the accompanying novelisation, posters, and other paraphernalia. It is perhaps best exemplified by a film like *Batman* (1989). As Jon Lewis has noted:

> *The film grossed in excess of $250 million domestically. But for, Time Warner, the domestic gross was just a very small part of the film's overall worth to the company. Batman is a DC comic Comics character, licensed by LCA. The merchandising subsidiary has taken its cut from the profits of every T-shirt, cup, book, or action figure sold (at a Warner Bros. store and elsewhere). The film has appeared on HBO and Cinemax and has been delivered into homes across*

the country by means of cable systems owned by Time Warner. When the film was released on video and laser disc, it bore the Warner Home Video label, and the popular soundtrack CD [by Prince] came out in two versions, both from companies owned by Time Warner. Coverage – constant reminders about the film (as an event, as a franchise) – appeared in Time Warner magazines like Time, Life, *and (at least in time for the first sequel)* Entertainment Weekly.

(Lewis, 1998b; p.103)

Such explicit interconnection between media producers is a natural result of the conglomeration of the entertainment industry over the past two decades, both in terms of connections made between existing divisions within a conglomerate, and as a result of the purchase of new companies by those conglomerates in order to fashion such connections in the future.

Although synergistic activity has come to almost define the modern conglomerate-controlled entertainment industry, many observers note that it has not been as complete or as successful as has been thought. Certainly, Sony found that the desired synergy did not happen after its takeover of Columbia. As Griffin and Masters note, by the end of 1991 the 'synergy was not yet anywhere in evidence . . . In fact, as some observers had predicted, tensions started to fester between Sony's electronics and entertainment divisions. The hardware side began to resent the software unit for extravagant spending and lavish executive salaries' (Griffin and Masters, 1996; p.306). Investment banker Herb Schlosser is even blunter on the subject: 'The synergies are overrated. For $500 million you could license all the software in the world for a new system' (quoted in Wyatt, 1994; p.90).

THE FINANCIAL IMPLICATIONS OF CONGLOMERATION

The important thing to understand about the economics of modern American mainstream film-making is the scale of it. Billions of dollars are bound up in each conglomerate-owned film studio; hundreds of millions of dollars are involved in the production of a small number of films each year. These films are expected, required, to make huge sums of money when they are sold in the marketplace: the cinemas in America and around the world. Further huge sums of money are expected to be generated when those films are released into ancillary markets: video, cable, television.

In general, concentration is focused on the (rising) costs of feature film production over the past ten years or so. The industry and popular press revel in tales of outrageous salary demands of the leading actors, of out-of-control budgets, of productions haemorrhaging money until it is difficult for them to recoup costs. Tom Cruise, for example, reportedly took home:

about $70 million for his work on the first Mission: Impossible, *on which he also worked as a producer, bringing him a whopping 25 percent of the gross, a sum he shared with his partner, Paula Wagner . . . On the sleeper hit* The Sixth Sense, *Willis netted $50 million from the $600 million-grossing film . . . with a combination of his $20 million salary, 17 percent of the gross and his share of video revenues.*

(Natale, 2001; p.1)

Such stories make up the stuff of legend; they are shocking because of the obvious excess, sexy because they involve larger-than-life characters and famous actors. The majors, certainly up to 1996, took the scatter gun approach that it was better to push out more and more high-budget films, on the assumption that some of them would make so much money at the box office that they would offset the failure of the majority of films to cover their costs. This philosophy eventually grew so expensive and insanely risky that it threatened to stall production altogether.

But the financial insecurity of the modern American film industry is equally due to the financial state of the companies themselves. Several of them are valued at much more than their actual worth. This is, in part, a consequence of the difficulty of pricing the component parts of film studios. While some of these – real estate of studios and cinemas, for example – can be fairly accurately priced, most cannot, such as library back catalogues which are capable of earning untold sums of money in the future depending on future trends and tastes, and films that are about to be made or are in production at the time of the costing. As Griffin and Masters note in their analysis of Sony's purchase of Columbia:

Setting a value on Columbia required some sophisticated analysis and some educated guesswork. What was the value of projects in the works? Would Flatliners, *a movie about medical students doing life-after-death experiments, be dead on arrival or would it earn millions? Kevin Costner in a picture called* Revenge – *wouldn't that be a sure bet?*

(Griffin and Masters, 1996; p.217)

This overvaluation of film studios has been partly the result of financial over-optimism typical of the 1980s, and came partly as a result of corruption on the part of certain industry players whose desire to maximise their own fees for negotiating certain multi-billion dollar deals led them to distort the economic reality of the studios they were representing. One such was Michael Ovitz, head of the Creative Artists Agency, who had an active role in brokering the deal whereby Sony purchased Columbia Pictures. Ovitz was interested in framing the deal in the best possible terms – not only to ingratiate him, and his agency, with Columbia's new owners but, as things developed, to secure himself a top executive post in the company. Griffin and Masters report that: 'Greenhill and Ovitz made their presentation to Sony. The Japanese were stunned by its dimensions. For Ovitz, nothing would do but the deal of deals – a deal that reflected Ovitz's position in Hollywood. He would ask for everything: huge compensation, total control of the company, a significant amount of stock, and enormous acquisition fund to buy new businesses' (Griffin and Masters, 1996; p.219). As it transpired, Ovitz was not considered for a top executive job, but '[a]ccording to two Sony sources, Ovitz received an $11 million fee. And shortly thereafter, he was retained by Matsushita to broker its acquisition of MCA' (Griffin and Masters, 1996; p.233).

The consequence of this overvaluation is that the studios now carry huge debt loads that permanently disable them from operating freely in the marketplace. 'In 1989, with a second wave [of conglomeration] clearly underway, it seemed highly possible that companies involved in these mega-mergers and acquisitions might take on so much debt that they would stop producing new movies altogether' (Lewis, 1998b; p.101). Given this situation, each new big-budget release threatens to add substantially to the huge, continuing debt should it fail badly at the box office. As Griffin and Masters note in reference to Sony's position in 1991: 'Its overhead was now steaming along at $300 million a year. While the film unit's losses were offset by profits in television and music, the entertainment operations were struggling to break even. Meanwhile, the company needed to produce about $500 million in cash flow just to cover its debt' (Griffin and Masters, 1996; pp.320–1). Perversely, however, these huge debt loads can act to fend off threats of takeovers from rivals, who are discouraged from such attempts because of the debt they would have to assume should they take over the company.

As noted at the beginning of this section, the financial excesses of the leading stars and directors fill countless column inches of the trade and popular press every week. The equal, even more grotesque, avarice of the studio heads, however, goes largely unreported, at least to the general public. Two examples will suffice to illustrate a bigger picture. In 1979, Kirk Kerkorian sold 297,000 shares in MGM and used the money to secure a $38 million loan, which he in turn used to buy 24 per cent of publicly trading shares in Columbia. Several months later, he sold them for $137 million. And, as mentioned earlier, when Peter Guber and Jon Peters were invited to head the new Sony-owned Columbia pictures, they insisted Sony buy their company for $1 billion, so they could operate through it.

There is a curious paradox at the heart of the American film industry in terms of short and long-term financial return. The obsessive focus is on the box-office performance of each feature release, especially the top package projects featuring top talent and boasting mega-budgets. Such is the intensity of this focus that it has now zeroed down to the opening weekend – the first two or three days of a film's ability to earn money in its marketplace. Industry watchers can tell whether a film is going to be a success or failure by the returns from this short time frame alone. An atmosphere of fear and loathing is built up as a result of this overdetermination.

At the same time, it is universally acknowledged that it is virtually imposs-ible for a film these days not to go into profit, however small, at some point in its multi-format release. Take the greatest example of high-risk, big-budget film-making of recent years, *Titanic*. James Cameron, perhaps understand-ably, always thought his film would go into profit: 'His guess was about $400 million in box-office receipts worldwide, which was certainly a healthy sum. When you factored in home video and TV rights, he thought the film would be profitable, though not wildly so' (Parisi, 1998; p.147). However, his financiers were less sure, certainly for the majority of the production period. Eventually, after a series of successful test screenings, they came round to thinking they had a potentially profitable film on their hands, if not in the short term, then probably in the longer:

> On a business level, who knew? While it didn't appear they'd get hurt badly – no Waterworld-sized writedowns of $60 million – there didn't seem to be much financial upside either. And that, after all, was the reason they were in business. Still, in twenty years, people wouldn't be judging whether it made or lost $10 million, they'd be watching the movie. If at any point in the future News Corporation decided to sell Fox, he [Bill Mechanic] could see someone buying it just to own Titanic, like Ted Turner who bought MGM for Gone With the Wind.
>
> (Parisi, 1998; p.210)

The important point to note here is the shift from considering the film *Titanic* simply as a short-term box-office success or failure, to seeing it as a film whose significance lies firmly in the longer term, both as a reaper of revenues from other markets, and as a significant asset on the company books; an asset which will continue to be financially attractive for years to come.

It is this long-term financial capability which makes the focus on opening weekend box-office revenue more than a little skewed. What that skewed focus does illustrate, however, is the overdetermined need for film companies to make massive and immediate profits if their costly operations are going to be able to sustain themselves onward to the next production cycle. Waiting for films to eventually make a profit – or not – is too slow a recuperation pro-cess for companies that regularly need massive sums of money to finance new productions.

There are distortions in film history regarding the expense of certain films, as if the industry needs a scapegoat whenever it is periodically accused of excess and profligacy. In 1980, it was *Heaven's Gate*, pilloried for costing over $40 million with negligible box-office return at a time when the industry was becoming concerned with runaway budgets and out-of-control directors. Two years later, *Annie*, directed by John Huston, cost virtually as much (not helped by the $9 million it cost to obtain the rights to the original theatre show), and received a similar critical and box-office response. But it is *Heaven's Gate* that is remembered and asked to represent the hedonism and megalomania of late–1970s big-budget film-making; *Annie* has simply been forgotten. Similarly, at the same time as *Last Action Hero* (1993), starring the world's then biggest star Arnold Schwarzenegger, was being savaged by critics and shunned by audiences, the film *Geronimo: An American Legend*, starring Jason Patric, Robert Duvall and Gene Hackman, cost $50 million and made only $13.7 million (Griffin and Masters, 1996; p.409). Although on a substantially bigger scale, a similar fate potentially awaited *Titanic*, whose production masked the culmination of a period of increasingly massive budgets. Perhaps it was fortunate that *Waterworld* (1995), another epic adventure-romance staged on the open seas, had beaten it to the post. It got the flak and *Titanic* got the plaudits and the financial returns.

FILM PRODUCTION

Conception

The creation of a feature film usually begins when a studio, a production company or an independent producer acquires the rights to some form of literary material – a novel, a play, a short story or an original screenplay. These rights can be expensive: $9 million, as just mentioned, to acquire the rights to the stage musical *Annie* (1982); $3 million paid to Joe Eszterhas for the original screenplay of *Basic Instinct* (1992). Finding material of sufficient quality on which to base an expensive production is of vital importance. Those involved must actually believe in the quality of the source material if they are to sustain themselves through the long creative process of making the film. For this reason, the major studios invest heavily in material gathering operations. 'Each studio has between two hundred and three hundred screenplays in development at any given time. This represents an investment of hundreds of millions of dollars and is a major contributor to the roughly $300 million-a-year overhead that is run up by each major studio' (Bart, 1999; p.68).

Even when that material has been found, and a screenplay written, rewrites often continue to be carried out throughout the production process. These rewrites need not necessarily be done by the original writer. Indeed, it is a bone of contention with many writers in Hollywood that their original work is given over to other writers who, in adding their own ideas to the original, distort its intention. Some film-makers habitually employ teams of writers, each of whom is hired to contribute a specific element to the final mix. Steven Spielberg is noted for his unsentimental hiring and firing of writers who work on his scripts, but he is not unique:

> *Hensleigh [original writer of* Armageddon*] understood the Simpson-Bruckheimer formula for dealing with writers: Work them hard for a few drafts, then bring in hired guns to handle specific scenes and incidents. Never mind if the voices of characters would vary from scene to scene. This was an action movie and, by the time it had been edited, sliced and diced, not that much dialogue would remain anyway.*
> *. . . Bruckheimer's road company of body-and-fender men moved in, one by one. The ubiquitous Bob Towne, who'd been doing this sort of thing since the days of* Bonnie and Clyde *[1967] and had worked on Bruckheimer's* Crimson Tide*, was brought in to develop a mutiny scene. Scott Rosenberg, who had worked on* Con Air*, made a cameo appearance to rewrite lines for some of the supporting cast, while Ann Biderman* (Primal Fear) *spruced up Liv Tyler's dialogue. Tony Gilroy* (Extreme Measures) *focused on devising a new beginning for the script because no one bought the original setup in which two kids first saw the satellite, then were quarantined by the police so their story wouldn't leak out. Writer J.J. Abrams contributed an overall dialogue polish, since Michael Bay liked his snappy phrases. Meanwhile, still other craftsmen like Paul Attanasio and Shane Salerno breezed in and out, as the script budget soared past $2 million.*

> (Bart, 1999; pp.87–8)

Pre-production

Another factor that adds to the costs of making films in Hollywood is the often long development time of some projects. *Deep Impact* (1998) took 20 years to move from the initial idea to being green-lighted for production, partly because the writers variously chosen to develop the basic idea, such as the intellectually inclined Anthony Burgess, produced screenplays which the studios considered uncommercial. *Godzilla* (1998) took ten years, partly because of resistance from the Japanese company Toho, which had made the original series of Godzilla films in the 1950s, and partly, as a result of these, because the whole Godzilla concept was seen as overly camp. Final approval of the film that we now know as *Godzilla* would have to wait until advances in computer-generated imagery were sufficiently developed to allow the film-makers to create a photo-realistic, and genuinely impressive, monster which would be able to shake off its associations with the rubbery Japanese version of the 1950s.

More general reasons for these delays are numerous. Interest on the part of a studio executive can be cancelled when he or she is replaced in the reshuffle that the managements of major studios now regularly undergo. Scripts can be put into 'turnaround' (allowed to go to other studios) because the new executive doesn't really believe in the subject. The time might not be right for particular subject matter because of social or political events or simply because it does not quite fit the *Zeitgeist*. The desired stars might not be available because of prior commitments. Those stars might lose their popular appeal before the project can be sufficiently developed. Each delay, each further purchase of rights by the next interested party, adds to the initial costs of a potential movie project.

There are two basic models for setting up a production based on the literary material which is to form the story to be told: the package deal and the assemblage of talent method. The package deal has already been covered in the previous chapter: a producer, a script (or an idea for one), a director and possibly one or two leading actors form a 'team' which presents a strong front to a studio which might finance the film the team are proposing. The second model involves the hiring of major personnel – director, stars, artistic and technical personnel – after the project has been given approval. The first tends to be the model for high-concept films – those with high-profile stars, or sequels to proven successes. A typical example is *Armageddon* (1998), which originated as a story idea by Jonathan Hensleigh who, with his producer/fiancée Gale Anne Hurd, interested Michael Bay as director. With this team in place, the idea was pitched to Joe Roth of Disney, who readily approved it. The major star – Bruce Willis – was then approached and signed up. The second tends to be the model for lower-budget, more personal projects, such as *The Truman Show* (1998), which began as an idea developed into a script by new screenwriter Andrew Niccol.

Niccol sent it to literary agent Lyn Pleshette who, in turn, tried to interest various producers in the idea. Scott Rudin eventually won out, and Paramount, where Rudin had a producing deal, put up the finance. Rudin then went in search of a director. Several directors expressed interest in the project, including Brian De Palma, but Peter Weir eventually agreed to direct. As Bart notes, Weir's attitude to film-making was the reverse of the 'package' mentality, because for him, 'A-list material was all "cut and dried". It was calculated commercial fare, material designed to attract a top star and build the groundwork for an expensive Hollywood movie. "I wanted scripts from the bottom drawer," Weir said. "I wanted scripts that were broken"' (Bart, 1999; p.75). Weir, during the inevitable rewrite period, even insisted on continuing to use Niccol as writer in order to retain the original vision, rather than bringing in the habitual team of 'script doctors'. The final stage was the casting of Truman, a process solved when Jim Carrey, who had been sent the script by Rudin, expressed interest and agreed to accept significantly less ($12 million) than his usual $20 million fee. Although the film's final agreed budget – $60 million – might hardly seem 'low-budget', it is when compared to many of the blockbuster 'package' projects, costing $100–150 million or more, that are representative of the first model described above.

Once the personnel have been selected, salaries and point profits have to be negotiated. In many of the big-budget films currently being made these costs can become prohibitive: major stars now demand $20 million for a film, and/ or a percentage of gross profits. On *Saving Private Ryan* (1998), both Spielberg and Tom Hanks took minimal up-front salaries, but received 20 per cent of the gross. As the film was being made by the world's most successful director and starred the world's leading male star, it was expected to be a big hit and the potential pay cheque from percentage points was huge; in the end, both men made tens of millions of dollars on the deal.

Pre-production also involves the development of detailed budget break-downs, so that, as far as possible on something as unpredictable as a film shoot, every possible eventuality – fire, accident, injury to main star – can be predicted and accounted for, both financially and logistically. And because of this constantly present threat of accident or failure, arrangement must be made for special risk insurance and completion bonds.

Production

As the project moves to the shooting stage, sets must be designed and built, locations scouted and day-by-day production schedules planned. The shooting of the film's main scenes (principal photography) as well as second unit photography – shots not requiring lead actors – can take several weeks or even months for a large-scale film. But in many ways it is not the most expensive phase of a production: that will often be either before (script rights, star salaries) or afterwards (complex and costly effects work). Of course, this is not always the case: the extraordinarily large and mechanically complex set of *Titanic*, for example, meant that every setup and take was extremely expensive.

Post-production

The post-production phase of a film's creation has expanded over the past decade or so with the advent of digital special effects technologies and the popularity of effects-laden action-adventure narratives. In some cases post-production can take longer than the period of shooting the film. *Titanic* took six months to shoot (18 September 1996 to 22 March 1997) and at least (preliminary post-production having started before shooting had finished) seven months (late March through to late October 1997) to post-produce. Editing, special effects work, dialogue replacement, music scoring and recording are all tasks which are painstaking in their detail, adding significantly to the total length of a film's production time.

The total cost of making the film to this point is called the *negative cost*. If the film has been made by a major studio, a percentage or set fee will then be added to the negative cost by the studio to cover overheads and general expenses incurred by the running of a permanent site and staff, which cannot all be charged to any one film.

We can look at a typical example of a recent mid-budget film, *Captain Corelli's Mandolin* (2001), to see this process in action. Producer Kevin Loader bought the rights to the book shortly after it was published in 1994. He took it to Working Title, the British film production company. Distribution was arranged with Universal Pictures (USA) and Miramax Films (UK and Australia). Between late 1998 and early 1999, Loader, original director Roger Michell and screenwriter Shawn Slovo prepared several drafts of the script. The fourth draft was submitted for approval in mid-May 1999. By autumn 1999, Nicolas Cage had been signed to play Corelli, and sets had begun to be built on the Greek island of Kefalonia, with construction finishing in late April 2000.

In November 1999, director Roger Michell suffered a heart attack and had to withdraw from the project. John Madden was hired to replace him, and initiated a major rewrite of the script to suit his own vision of the story. Between March and May 2000, the other principal actors – Penelope Cruz, Christian Bale and John Hurt – were all signed to the production. Shooting began on 22 May 2000, and wrapped in early September. The next five months were given over to editing and post-production work, a troubled time which prompted the announcement, in Febuary 2001, of a delay in the release date because more time was required for editing and the preparation of marketing materials. This delay was later rescinded, and the film was finally released on 4 May 2001.

Distribution

A distributor licenses the exhibition of a film, generally for a period of several years. The distributor is responsible for advertising and supplying exhibitors with prints and supporting materials. These days a policy of saturation release – initiated with the release of *Jaws* in 1975 – has become the norm; certainly for the big films of the year, but also, increasingly, for every mainstream release:

A mere twenty years ago, it was common practice to open a movie in a few theatres across the country, build word of mouth, adjust advertising strategies to audience response, and then slowly expand to an ever broader audience. Today a movie is unveiled, not with a quietly orchestrated build, but with a cosmic paroxysm, a global spasm of hype involving giant marketing partners like McDonald's and a profligate network on the Super Bowl or the Olympics. A new film is thus machine-tooled to become either an instant blockbuster or an overnight flop. There is no room for adjustment or strategic change. There is no shelf life available for the weak or infirm in the bold new Darwinian economics of the nineties.

(Bart, 1999; p.3)

Major releases can expect to open in 2,000 screens on their first weekend. As this requires 2,000 prints to be struck, one for each screen, at a cost of $2,000 per print – $4 million total print cost – opening a major movie is a considerable expense for distributors. It is no wonder, in this context, that other ways have been sought to get a film into cinemas which do not involve this cumbersome and costly physical print method. We will consider one method now being touted as the next significant development in exhibition – digital cinema – in Chapter 7.

Furthermore, there are established seasonal differences in box office, with Christmas and summer identified as the two most lucrative periods. Beginning around the time of *Die Hard* (1988), summer has accounted for some 40 per cent of the annual box office. Such seasonality determines the release dates for the major films each year, as well as which type of film gets released at what point in the year. 'Typically, family films like *Mrs Doubtfire* (1993) and *The Addams Family* (1991) had done well in November, opening on Thanksgiving and playing through to Christmas' (Bart, 1999; p.180). Action blockbusters tend to be released in summer. This was certainly the original slot intended for *Titanic*, until its production ran long and made this impossible. Also important, however, is the manner in which the major releases jostle for space within those seasonal periods to ensure that they don't cancel one another out:

When Titanic *vacated the July 4 weekend, it created a wake that rocked every major release through the end of the year. Fox, sensing* Speed 2 *might not live up to its original high expectations, moved the release up to June 27, when the only real competition was Paramount's* Face/Off. *Thus, Columbia's* Men In Black, *directed by Barry Sonnenfeld, had the field pretty much to itself.*

(Bart, 1999; p.180)

Finally, the establishment of firm release dates within this seasonal logic has the effect of placing additional pressure on film-makers to complete their films in time for the release window chosen by their studios. This window can be determined by one or more of several main factors: the need to qualify for that year's Academy Awards, an appearance at one of the world's leading film festivals, the need to show the film to the press or exhibitors in order to stem rumours of a troubled production, or because the window is one of the year's main release periods (namely, Easter, summer and Christmas). This policy of predetermining the release date can give film-makers little room for error, so that when something unexpected occurs during a production, any slack can immediately evaporate. Take as an example this somewhat fictionalised, but nonetheless representative, account by Peter Bart:

> Meanwhile, across town at the Armageddon editing rooms, the crews were red-eyed and bleary, looking more like hostages than artisans as they struggled to meet their dates and, at the same time, compress the overlong movie into a tenable running time.
>
> All the while, on one project after another, the almost identical dialogue was taking place between the film-makers and the studio suits. 'We need to see the film,' the suits pleaded relentlessly.
>
> 'We'd be glad to show you something, but the effects aren't ready,' the director or producer responded.
>
> 'We have to show it to our distribution people, our marketing people, our publicity people.'
>
> 'What can I tell you? It's a complicated process.'
>
> 'The exhibitors think we're hiding it from them. So do the long-range critics. We promised them . . .'
>
> 'We can show them the film without the effects . . .'
>
> (Bart, 1999; pp.167–8)

The payoff

The exhibitor (generic, not singular) collects the box office for showing a film on its screens. This is the *gross box-office receipts*. It then retains a percentage of these receipts – anywhere from 10 per cent to 90 per cent, depending on the deal struck with the distributor (the more popular the film is expected to be, the lower the percentage kept and the higher the percentage returned to the distributor). This remainder is termed the *gross film rentals*. The distributor then deducts its distribution fee (anywhere from 15 per cent to 35 per cent) plus operating costs, expenses, etc. The remainder of the gross film rentals is then returned to the producer to cover the actual costs of making the film (its *negative cost*). After the negative cost is deducted (plus any interest charged on loans taken out to finance the film) what is left is called the *net profit*. Out of this come the percentage points given to stars in deferral of salary. The rest is divided up by the financing parties.

So, as a hypothetical example: say a film costs $100 million to make and the studio charges another $15 million in overheads. The negative cost of the film will be $115 million. It costs the distributor $35 million to strike prints, create advertising, and get the film out into cinemas. The film makes $175 million at the box office. Exhibitors take $52.5 million out of that for their 'cut'. The distributor deducts another $35 million for its fee, plus another $35 million to recover costs. That means $52.5 million is returned to the producer, out of which he/she has to give the star(s) $30 million in percentage points. That leaves him/her with $22.5 million. If the film costs $115 million in negative cost and makes only $10 million at the box office (not uncommon), the equation and the percentages claimed by the various parties radically alter and the sums simply fail to add up. This is why modern American mainstream, big-budget film-making is such a high-risk activity, at least as far as box-office success is concerned.

However, as noted earlier, films do not rely on box office alone these days. They rely instead on what is known as a film's 'release cycle'. This takes the film through a sequence of release windows and environments/formats. It is first released into cinemas, simultaneously with, in many cases, substantial merchandising operations: promotions with burger chains; soundtrack release; toy, accessory and T-shirt manufacture; perhaps after a slight delay, a computer-game version of the story. These mechandising tie-ins can often earn as much as the film itself does at the box office; sometimes they earn more. The international theatrical market is the next phase of the cycle; sometimes occurring simultaneously with a film's US release (this is often the case with films felt to be in danger of failing at the US box office and/or getting negative criticism: such things could severely damage a film's chances in the foreign markets if it was released at a later date).

Next come domestic videocassette/DVD/laserdisc rental and sales, the former often some time before the latter in order to maximise moneys earned. Video has been an important market since the mid-1980s. In 1980 only 2 per cent of American homes owned a VCR; by 1990 that figure had risen to 66 per cent. In 1989, while $5 billion came from the US cinema box office, $10 billion came from video sales and rentals. In Europe, in 1978, there were 500,000 domestic machines; by 1989 there were 40 million, generating $4.5 billion in video sales. More recently, the Asian-Pacific rim has opened up new possibilities. In 2001, the majority of homes are assumed to have at least one video recorder; a massive potential market for films on cassette. The video market is especially significant for the mini-majors and independents, a proportion of whose product is tailored specifically for the video market. The majors now have in-house video distribution divisions, while the smaller studios and mini-majors license films to external video distributors.

Once the video market has been exhausted, the next phase of the release cycle is pay-per-view cable, which charges a fixed fee – $3–$5 – for a single viewing in the domestic space. HBO in the 1980s was the first and most powerful cable operator to charge premium rates for movies. The conglomerate control of both film studios and cable channels has brought accusations of monopoly abuse. For example, in 1979, some of the majors (Columbia, Twentieth Century-Fox, Paramount, MCA/Universal, plus Getty Oil) combined to develop the 'Premiere' cable network, but it was prevented from operating by monopoly anti-trust laws (Hilmes, 1990; p.404).

Then follows the US domestic television network showing of the film, worldwide pay-television, worldwide videocassette/DVD/laserdisc, foreign TV rights and, finally, syndication: selling to a network for multiple screenings several years into the future.

This planned distribution to all media is designed to ensure maximum coverage and return on investment. Phasing the release into the various markets allows the film to maximise profits in each before moving on to the next. As Sydney Pollack commented in a television debate about the state of the American film industry on PBS television's *Think Tank*, 29 April 2000:

> *A whole technological revolution has happened in the after market. Pictures that were four years old or more ten years ago were non-revenue producing assets, essentially, unless you sold the library. Pictures that are four years old today, between DVD, and high definition television, and syndication, and the Internet, are real income producing assets. So, in total, motion picture companies have more sources of revenue than they had before, and that's producing higher quarterly reports, and that's what you're reading. But, I still say what Peter says is right, are more people going to movies today? I don't know.*

> (Think Tank, *2000*)

It demonstrates, further, how the film industry has learned its lesson from its reaction to the threat of television in the 1950s: that is, not to fight and resist, but to buy into and thereby partially control potentially rival distribution channels. Such a strategy ensures that no film really makes a loss these days; it just takes longer to recover its costs.

Again we will briefly look at an example, perhaps the best of recent years: *Titanic*. The film's cinema release date was 19 December 1997, although it had undergone a series of preview screenings to gauge audience reaction since

Kate Winslet and Leonardo DiCaprio flee the sinking ship in *Titanic* (James Cameron, 1997)

17 July of that year. In 12 days, it grossed over $100 million; after 25 days, that figure had passed $250 million; by 23 February 1998, it topped $1 billion. By April 1998 *Titanic* had been released across the world, including China, where it was a massive hit. The saturation release of the video was scheduled for autumn 1998, to maximise sales in the run-up to Christmas. As Ed Hatch, an analyst at UBS Securities, commented, the 'video should add probably another $800 million of gross sales'. The film's cable premiere was both on HBO in America in mid-April 1999 and on the pay-per-view Sky Box Office channel on 21 April 1999, before moving to the subscription channel Sky Movies at the end of October 1999. The DVD was released in November 1999. Its surprisingly modest production values – few extras, considering the infamy of the production and the number of 'making-of' documentaries that had been shown on television during its production and release – prompted speculation as to the possibility that a feature-laden, special edition, 'director's cut' DVD might be released several months later (it has not, as of July 2002), thereby almost doubling the potential revenues from DVD sales. The film's US terrestrial premiere was on NBC over Thanksgiving weekend 2000. Finally, the UK terrestrial premiere of the film took place on Christmas Day 2000, on BBC1, the corporation having paid $6 million for the privilege.

CO-PRODUCTION

The exponentially rising costs of mainstream American film-making have encouraged, even made necessary, the sharing of the financing of feature film production. This co-financing can take a variety of different forms. Budgets, and subsequent profits, can simply be shared. Split rights on movies have become a common scenario. For *True Lies* (1994), Fox entered a partnership with Universal, which had the lion's share of foreign distribution rights through its UIP subsidiary. Fox and Paramount co-financed *Titanic*, with each contributing $60 million (at the start of production that was 50 per cent of the proposed budget). Paramount's involvement was capped so that it could not be asked for more if the production ran over budget (which it finally did by some $80 million, to finish at $200 million). In return it was given domestic distribution rights; a profitable arrangement as it transpired, when *Titanic*'s domestic box office eventually reached $600 million.

> The movie [Titanic] *didn't have to be as successful for Paramount to make money since their breakeven was lower, which was kind of ironic. If* Titanic *was wildly successful, Fox stood to gain more; a little eleventh hour addendum they added when Paramount capped. Revenues would be split evenly until Paramount recouped its investment, at which point Fox would begin drawing sixty percent of the profits in perpetuity. But in order for Fox to see any upside,* Titanic *would have to be a monster, one of the top grossing films of all time.*
>
> *(Parisi, 1998; p.186)*

Companies can also have part-involvement in the distribution of movies made by other studios; for example, Disney winning the foreign distribution rights to *Air Force One* (1997), which was released domestically by Sony. Similarly, Disney agreed an international split-rights deal with Paramount on *Face/Off* (1997).

Co-production deals are endemic in Hollywood, and indicate the now-prohibitive costs of financing major motion pictures. No single studio can realistically envisage financing a big-budget ($100–150 million) production alone, certainly not in the high-risk marketplace as it now exists. A single failure, a box-office flop, would spell catastrophe for that company. Better to invest smaller, though still considerable, sums in a wider range of films, any of which are capable of substantial box-office profits. The loss on a failure is consequently lower, but the returns on a massive hit are greater.

CHAPTER THREE

Foreign Relations

ECONOMIC RELATIONS

American cinema has, almost since its inception, had a complex relationship with the film industries of the rest of the world. The earliest years of cinema were marked by a healthy competition between the American film industry and other film industries; so much so, in fact, that some of the latter, most notably the French Pathé company, dominated the American market until the advent of the First World War. The story since that date, however, has largely been one of foreign industries fighting off an increasingly invasive American cinema.

There has always been a two-way traffic of films: into America and out of it to the world. Of the two, obviously, for America the latter is more important as a means of maximising profits from any film, while the former has always been heavily controlled: 'There was an asymmetry: non-Americans seeming far more ready to see films from exotic Hollywood than were Americans to see films from or about the old countries, especially if they were not in English' (Jarvie, 1998; p.39).

America was effectively aided by two world wars, both in closing off exports from foreign countries to America and in the disruption of film industries in countries occupied by war. During the Second World War American films were prevented from being imported into foreign markets. But after the war, a glut of American movies – films such as *Young Mr Lincoln* (Ford, 1939), *Citizen Kane* (Welles, 1941), *To Have and Have Not* (Hawks, 1944) – flooded world, especially European, markets. 'People wanted to see colour films like *Gone With the Wind* [1939], still not released. For cinephiles there was *Citizen Kane*, also not released, but which Jean-Paul Sartre, among others, had seen in America' (Jeancolas, 1998; p.48). This, in turn, created an appetite for American films and, importantly, provided the subjects for many of the formative auteurist criticism of the French writers (and future New Wave directors) of *Cahiers du Cinéma* in the following 10 to 15 years.

In the aftermath of the Second World War, Europe was financially dependent upon America, desperately needing American support for rebuilding and American produce to feed and clothe European populations. In such circumstances, it was difficult to impose any kind of economic restrictions on imports. Further, as Jarvie (1998) argues, at the end of the Second World War the American film industry had at least five distinct advantages over all potential rivals in international trade. It had extensive European investments, which it aimed to reactivate. Foreign exhibitors and distributors were favourably disposed towards American films because of their reliability and popularity. Blocked foreign currencies encouraged American companies to invest in European location shooting, co-operation deals and talent. America aimed, as the dominant military, political and economic Western post-war power, to promote free international trade. And, finally, Hollywood was the pre-eminent maker of popular entertainment films (Jarvie, 1998; p.44).

America in many ways needed this advantage. After the Paramount decrees, the reduced number of films being made in Hollywood, together with the increasing loss of the cinema audience to television and other leisure pursuits, caused uncertainty in the exhibition sector about the regularity and numbers of films that could be expected from the American film industry. This uncertainty continued until at least the end of the 1960s. When the 1969–70 crisis hit the American film industry, Al Howe, of the Bank of America, reported in the journal of the Producers' Guild of America, in March 1970 that '[there is] a probability that the product shortage will be filled largely with pictures from abroad' (quoted in Puttnam with Watson, 2000; p.210). Tax law changes offered incentives to companies making movies in America. One such tax incentive enabled anyone investing directly in film-making to claim 100 per cent tax exemption. This financial cushioning made it easier for small independent producers to finance new directors to make more adventurous films, such as *Five Easy Pieces* (Rafelson, 1970); *One Flew Over the Cuckoo's Nest* (Forman, 1975); and *Taxi Driver* (Scorsese, 1976) (Puttnam with Watson, 2000; p.212). In using these benefits to the fullest, the American film industry surmounted the 1969–70 crisis, but the situation and balance between American and European films would continue throughout the 1970s and into the 1980s. In this context, also, foreign markets became important as a means of retrieving lost domestic income.

However, this concerted attempt by the American film industry to monopolise foreign markets was resisted vigorously by those markets, especially in Europe. Indeed, since 1949, the French cinema had more or less achieved parity with Hollywood in the home market. Out of 387 million attendances in that year, 42.4 per cent had been for French films, against 44.5 per cent for American. This resistance was maintained throughout the 1950s and 1960s, protected by Aid Laws and by co-production agreements. In 1956, 48.6 per cent out of 399 million French spectators saw French films, as opposed to 33.4 per cent for American. By 1967, when the number of spectators had dropped to 211 million, the proportions were 52.2 per cent for French films, and only 29.6 per cent for American. Throughout the 1970s, the percentages of American and French films being seen in France remained consistent, hovering around 46–50 per cent for French films against some 20–30 per cent for American.

Into the 1980s, the situation began to reverse itself. As North American theatre admission declined in 1991, and video, cable and television revenue has been flat since 1989, growth in the foreign market has been a vital factor in continued profitability. By 1995, 'the European Community ran an audiovisual trade deficit with the United States of some $6.3 billion, a 15 percent increase from the previous year. At the present rate, it could grow to $10 billion by the turn of the century' (Puttnam with Watson, 2000; p.281). That is to say, the revenues from European films are now some $10 billion less than those being gathered from American films shown in Europe.

Hollywood now vitally needs world markets in order to make its budgets balance. Such has been the exponential rise in budgets over the past decade or so as a result of the blockbuster mentality that has gripped the American film industry, that the domestic market is no longer lucrative enough to recoup the huge costs of making the blockbusters favoured by Hollywood. 'Lately, the importance of the international film market has been attributed to the higher expenses of American film-making . . . "The costs of doing business are so high these days that we need to be involved in every possible profit centre"' (Wasko, quoting an unidentified studio executive 1994; p.223). Currently, worldwide markets account for a significant 60 per cent of total sales.

According to figures compiled by BIPE Conseil in Paris, the American share of the European (EU) film market has risen from just under 50 percent in the early 1980s to over 60 percent in the 1990s. The shift is most dramatic in Europe's premier film-producing countries, France and Italy. In France the share of the market held by indigenous films has dropped from 47 percent in 1980 to 32 percent in 1994, while the American share has risen from 35 percent to 58 percent. Comparable figures for Italy show the indigenous share dropping from 43 percent to a measly 15 percent, the lowest figure since 1945, and the American share rising to 73 percent. Of the major countries, only Britain has to some extent bucked the general trend. Over the same period (again according to BIPE) the indigenous share has gone up (from 15 percent to 20 percent) while the American share has dropped from 80 percent to a still massive 75 percent.

(Nowell-Smith, 1998; p.1)

Between 1985 and 1990, the percentage of revenues earned from American films shown in Europe rose from 64 per cent to 77.4 per cent. In 1991, 68 per cent of all films shown in Italy were American, as were 58.7 per cent in France, 91.5 per cent in Ireland and 93 per cent in the UK. In ten years, between 1983 and 1993, the French cinema lost 15 per cent of its share of the market, while the American cinema gained 20 per cent. At the same time, 60 per cent of European film distribution companies were in American hands; that is to say, US companies were not only distributing American films, but many European films as well, operating a stranglehold on the foreign market. As Jeancolas has commented, 'The *cinéma d'auteur* cannot compete with the dinosaurs of *Jurassic Park*' (Jeancolas, 1998; p.57).

This situation is repeated in the increasingly important Asian markets. From dominating 80 per cent of its domestic market in 1992, Hong Kong had slipped to 40 per cent by 1999/2000, a figure echoed in Singapore (30 per cent of its own market), Thailand (12 per cent of its domestic market), and Indonesia (down from a figure of 50–60 per cent in the mid-1980s to only 10 per cent by the beginning of the 1990s). However, some other Asian markets are holding a better, although still largely subservient, position. Malaysia, for example, has a roughly equal share (45 per cent), split between indigenous and foreign (largely American) films. South Korea's share of its own market has grown dramatically across the latter half of the 1990s, from only 10–15 per cent in the early to mid years of the decade, to 32 per cent in 2000. Japan has fought an aggressive campaign to protect its own film industry. 'The number of foreign films distributed in Japan has fallen 56 [per cent] since 1990, while Japanese films displayed an 11.5 [per cent] improvement over the same period' (IDATE 2001, p. 266).

From these global statistics, it is evident that American control of the world's film markets continues to grow and consolidate with every year. However, there are some significant battles still to be won. Although China is one of the leading film markets in the world, heavy state control (a maximum of 20 imported films a year, with the expectation that the actual figure will be far lower) and low ticket prices make it an uneconomical arena, earning only $250 million in 2000. 'The majority of films shown in Chinese cinemas are domestic (around 70 per cent) with only a few Hollywood films deemed suitable for screening every year. However, those western films released in China tend to do very well' (Informa Media Group, 2001; p.119).

1995 was the first year in which the American studios' net receipts from overseas theatres overtook the amount earned from cinemas in North America, with countries such as Germany, Japan, France and the United Kingdom generating the largest proportion:

With domestic box office now regularly accounting for only 20 percent of a film's total revenue, foreign theatrical revenues, averaging 15 percent of the total, and often much more, can frequently exceed the domestic box office. Rocky V, Pretty Woman *and* The Little Mermaid *all had higher grosses in Europe alone than in North America, while* Gremlins 2 *took $69 million in Europe but only $46.4 million domestically, and* Look Who's Talking Too *took $70 million in Europe and $46.4 million domestically. Revenue from Europe increased from $403.3 million in 1985 to $983.3 million in 1989, accounting for over half of all foreign earnings, and the market shares for American movies have increased still further (85 percent in Spain and Germany, 70 percent in Italy, around 80 percent in Britain).*

(Hillier, 1992; pp.32–3)

More significant, perhaps, has been a shift in audience tastes not so much away from the big-budget, high-action blockbusters that have proved so popular with foreign audiences over the past decade but also towards the smaller, more quintessentially American mainstream and independent production. As Peter Bart commented during a televised debate on the state of the American film industry in April 2000:

there was a time when the American pictures that dominated the world scene tended to be very simplistic action pictures, you had Stallone, and you had Schwarzenegger, and you had a plot of the hero, the protagonist wins. Today, the American pictures that dominate overseas are things like American Pie, *and* There's Something About Mary, *even American teen pictures now are extraordinarily predominant around the world, for reasons that escape me. But, I think now what's happening is this very heterogeneous, niche-oriented film making in the United States is the next part of the domination of the world markets.*

(Think Tank, 2000)

It is this dual-pronged movement that has enabled American film to recover its dominant position in world markets. In the aftermath of the terrorist attacks on America in September 2001, and the shift of interest away from high-action, explosive blockbusters and towards smaller, more intimate dramas, the global balance between the two will inevitably alter. Time alone will tell whether that changed relationship will be permanent or whether, as the immediate horror felt at the atrocities recedes and something resembling normality returns, the balance between blockbuster and small drama will return to its former level.

The battle to regain control of the international marketplace has been waged partly in terms of international trading organisations and agreements, such as GATT (General Agreement on Tariffs and Trade) and WTO (World Trade Organisation). Essentially, the Americans have argued for a free trade agreement, an open market, because they knew their product was dominant: foreign audiences wanted to see American films more than those of their indigenous film industries.

Part of the force and weight of this drive to occupy and dominate foreign markets has come as a result of the conglomeration of the American film industry. It could be said now that every major American company is global, with a corresponding need for its product to appeal to the greatest possible worldwide audience.

> *The potential for international expansion was cited as a major factor driving the Disney/ABC deal [1995]. 'More and more I have noticed that our company's expansion is outside the US,' observed Eisner at the time the deal was unveiled. 'We think the combination of ABC and its assets, particularly outside the US . . . gives us the ability to grow.' As the cost of making and marketing films rises, the studios need to keep expanding their audience and that is why India and China are becoming ever more important to them. The expansion of commercial television in Europe also promises to provide rich dividends; according to one estimate, the Hollywood studios will earn over $7.5 billion during the decade from film deals they have recently made with German television stations alone.*

> (quoted in Puttnam with Watson, 2000; p.228)

Moreover, the conglomerate takeovers of American film studios have resulted in the acquisition of film libraries of old movies which have proved to be a lucrative asset in sales to the newly deregulated foreign television networks which have been proliferating in the last few years. Billions of dollars have been earned in sales. 'It has been estimated that in 1986 the US [film] industry received around 30 percent of total revenues from film, pay cable, TV and video from foreign markets. By the early 1990s, that amount had increased to 43 percent. The industry received an estimated $11.5 billion from all these markets in 1991' (Wasko, 1994; p.219).

There are a number of reasons for this growth in the 1990s: privatisation of the media, which has resulted in the escalation in the number of television stations wanting to show feature films; the unification of the European market, bringing an audience of over 300 million; revolutionary changes in Eastern Europe opening up new, previously untapped markets desperate for 'progressive' American culture; and the development and proliferation of new technologies: satellite, cable, video, offering new distribution opportunities. Europe boasts the single biggest concentration of television sets in the world with some 260 million. During 1991–92 the number of broadcast channels increased from 83 to 105; broadcast output expanded from 325,000 hours in 1988 to 483,000 in 1989. By the mid-1990s, some 250 million videocassettes were sold annually, earning over $2 billion from international video sales and rentals; and by the end of the 1990s, there were over 70 satellite-delivered channels in Europe, many wanting to show American feature films as part or all of their output. All of these statistics indicate how important an element the dramatic growth in earnings from these sources is in understanding the American film industry in the 1990s; indeed, as will be seen, these revenues are now more significant than those earned from cinema box office.

INTELLECTUAL PROTECTIONISM

The fight between the American film industry and the rest of the world has not simply been in terms of economics. Europeans, especially, are seen as regarding film as an art form far more than the Americans, who see it mainly as a commercial product. The Europeans, and particularly the French, therefore want to protect their film industry as much against cultural aggression as against financial monopoly. The battle is over a combination of economic and cultural issues, the financial and intellectual domination of foreign film industries. 'Though the competition from the United States affected European countries very differently, and the domestic industries themselves were neither originally conceived as "national " nor unified in their business strategies, intellectuals immediately categorised the shift in trade terms exemplif[ying] the influx of American movies as the opening of a life-and-death struggle between two competing civilisations' (de Grazia, 1998; p.20).

ARTISTIC INFLUENCE

This intellectual and artistic battleground is more complex than a simple polarity between American capitalist versus European artistic integrity. It is more a two-way street in which European film-makers are influenced by American cinema and culture and American film-makers, certainly the late-1960s new generation of American film-makers – Coppola, Scorsese, Hopper

– are similarly influenced by European art cinema, especially the French New Wave. In many of his films, Jean-Luc Godard quoted American iconography: gangsters, guns, and trench-coats in *A bout de souffle* (1960) and *Alphaville* (1965), and the Western in *Vent d'Est* (1969), which David Sterritt has called the first Marxist Western (Sterritt, 1999; p.130). In turn, Francis Ford Coppola expressed his admiration for Bertolucci in the early 1970s: 'He's an extraordinary talent. I look at two reels of *The Conformist* every day. He's my freedom therapy' (quoted in Lev, 1993; p.70).

> *[I]f there is a hegemonic influence of American film on European film, there is also an influence in the other direction. First, the success of the European art film in the 1960s had a broad influence on how American film-makers conceptualised cinema and on the films they produced. It was a fairly common sentiment in the 1960s that the new ideas in film were coming from Europe.*
>
> *(Lev, 1993; p.70)*

Scorsese has repeatedly acknowledged the influence of the French New Wave film-makers on his own development as a director:

> *What I loved about those Truffaut and Godard techniques from the early sixties was that the narrative was not that important. You could stop the picture and say: 'Listen, this is what we're going to do right now – oh, by the way, that guy got killed – and we'll see you later.' . . .*
> *The use of freeze frames was partly influenced by* Jules et Jim . . .
>
> *(Thompson and Christie, 1996; pp.151–2)*

The late 1960s and early 1970s were marked by a number of socially critical and artistically innovative works by American directors: *Bonnie and Clyde* (Arthur Penn, 1967); *Easy Rider* (Dennis Hopper, 1969); *M*A*S*H* (Robert Altman, 1970); *Carnal Knowledge* (Mike Nichols, 1971); *Five Easy Pieces* (Bob Rafelson, 1970); which had been explicitly influenced by European cinema. The co-writer of *Bonnie and Clyde*, recounts that 'within two months, I saw *Jules et Jim* twelve times. You cannot see a movie that often without beginning to notice certain things about structure and form and character' (Biskind, 1998; p.26). Robert Benton and co-writer David Newman had sent Truffaut the script for *Bonnie and Clyde*, but he had declined, passing it on to Warren Beatty. One can see Truffaut's influence in the film, in its playful style, shifts in generic reference, and sense of doomed romance, although certain elements of the original script, such as Clyde's homosexuality, had to be toned down for American audiences. As Benton comments, 'We were trying to make a French movie, and those were issues that never bothered

Truffaut' (Biskind, 1998; p.32). The influences were numerous: French auteur theory; Paul Schrader's critical studies of three art-film directors, Ozu, Dreyer, and Bresson; Woody Allen's avowed appreciation of Ingmar Bergman in films such as *Love and Death* (1975) and *Interiors* (1978); Coppola's similar 'naming of names' of directors who have influenced his work: Bertolucci, Antonioni, Godard.

This influence has carried through to the current day, when American independent film-makers, similarly, look to foreign film-making practices as a way of differentiating themselves from the increasingly anonymous, homogenised blockbuster cinema. Harmony Korine, writer of *Kids* (1995), and director of *Gummo* (1997) and *Julien Donkey-Boy* (1999), cites Fassbinder, Godard and, especially, Alan Clarke as influences:

> *If someone said to me who is the greatest director or my favorite, I would say Alan Clarke without hesitation. His stories, without ever being derivative, and without ever having a simple ABC narrative are totally organic, precious and amazing. It was nothing but him. In a strange way I don't even like talking about him in the press or to people because he is the last film-maker or artist that is really sacred. But especially in America no one knows who he is, even in England there is very little attention*

> *(Hack, 2001; p.1)*

HOLLYWOOD SWALLOWS UP RIVAL CINEMAS

This two-way influence represents the positive aspect of the relationship between American and world film industries. The negative aspect has to do with absorption and disempowerment. This process has been a regular part of Hollywood's strategy in dealing with the potential threat to its business that foreign cinemas and, more specifically, foreign film-making talent pose, by absorbing that talent. Many film-makers come because of the greater technical expertise and funding for projects that Hollywood offers, others, because of the greater access to worldwide distribution systems which will allow films to be seen by a far wider audience. Furthermore, foreign directors generally come to America after significant success in their own country; Hollywood is careful to import only the best – or at least the most successful.

Historically, it has always been this way. Many of the earliest film-makers in the American film industry, as is entirely right for the 'land of opportunity', were foreigners. There have been several phases of importation across the past 80 years. The first, in the 1920s, was explicitly concerned with nullifying the perceived threat posed by the developing film industries of certain European countries: most notably Germany, Scandinavia, France and Italy. Directors such as F.W. Murnau, Mauritz Stiller and Victor Sjöström were invited to Hollywood to make films, with varying degrees of success. The second wave occurred in the late 1930s and early 1940s, as a result of political changes taking place in Europe: namely the rise of Nazism. This wave brought over such directors as Fritz Lang (*Fury*, 1936; *You Only Live Once*, 1937); Otto Preminger (*Laura*, 1944); Robert Siodmak (*The Suspect*, 1944; *The Killers*, 1946); Max Ophüls (*The Exile*, 1947; *Letter From an Unknown Woman*, 1948) and Billy Wilder (*Double Indemnity*, 1944; *The Lost Weekend*, 1945). The third, in the late 1960s and early 1970s 'was in a sense a combination of both its predecessors, on the one hand attempting to lure some of the figures responsible for the remarkable revival of interest in European cinema that occurred during the 1960s, and on the other, bringing film-makers like Roman Polanski and Milos Forman who were unable to work freely in their native countries' (Petrie, 1985; p.1).

A fourth wave of foreign émigrés can be identified, moving to America during the early to mid-1980s. The Dutchmen Paul Verhoeven and Jan De Bont, as director and cinematographer respectively, teamed up to make a series of films in Holland, including *Turkish Delight* (1973) and *The Fourth Man* (1983), before moving to America to work on *Flesh and Blood* (1985). Thereafter, they separated, although they teamed up again for *Basic Instinct* (1992). Verhoeven made a reputation for himself as the director of graphic examinations of fascistic violence (*Robocop*, 1987; *Starship Troopers*, 1997) and explicit sex (*Basic Instinct*, 1992; *Showgirls*, 1995). De Bont continued as director of photography on many films, including *Die Hard* (1988) and *The Hunt for Red October* (1990) before directing his first feature, *Speed*, in 1994, followed by *Twister* (1996); both high-action, special effects movies which had major box-office success.

Andrei Konchalovsky worked on a number of films in Russia, co-writing the script for Tarkovsky's *Andrei Rublev* (1966) as well as directing his own features: *The First Teacher* (1965); *Asya's Happiness* (1967); *Uncle Vanya* (1971) and *Siberiade* (1978). It was perhaps the long suppression by the authorities of *Asya's Happiness* that contributed to his decision to leave Russia for America in 1980. Since then he has had a chequered career, including *Runaway Train* (1985), which fared better on video than at the cinema, and the Sylvester Stallone/Kurt Russell vehicle *Tango and Cash* (1989).

Finally, Ivan Passer was a noted Czech film-maker and screenwriter (he wrote many of Milos Forman's Czech films), and a key member of the Czech New Wave, before moving to America in 1968. His first success there was with the cult film *Cutter's Way* (1981), a melancholy and uncomfortable examination of three complex characters: a crippled Vietnam veteran, his best friend and the former's wife, who is in love with the friend.

The motives behind the relocation of this fourth wave of foreign directors are twofold: Verhoeven and De Bont came to America because of the better facilities and bigger budgets, which would allow them to make more ambitious films. Konchalovsky and Passer made the move for political reasons: Konchalovsky because of the suppression of some of his work in Russia, Passer because of the Soviet invasion of Czechoslovakia in 1968.

By welcoming these film-makers, Hollywood effected a two-pronged victory: getting major talent to make its films while depriving a foreign film industry of that talent, thus reducing the number of significant films capable of being made in that country. It is important to recognise how often the particular sensibility of any foreign film-maker coming to make films within the American film industry is altered and nullified in some way. Sydney Pollack, talking on a television debate on the state of American film-making, notes the peculiar Americanisation of foreign film-makers and conversion of foreign perspectives to American cultural values:

> The whole country is immigrants, anyway. So we're making sort of homogenised European movies, re-conceived by some sort of commonality that is partially dictated by the fact that it doesn't require a culture to understand it, it doesn't require a tradition to understand it. You can't understand a lot of Japanese movies unless you understand Japanese culture. You don't have to understand American culture to understand our movies.

> (Sydney Pollack, speaking on Think Tank, 2000)

In most cases a European film-maker is not signed to make a strictly American film. An Antonioni or a Wenders is signed because of an affinity between director and material and is expected to add a personal slant to the film. Often the director has written or co-written the script, with English-language filming called for because of budget or subject (or both). And the films made in this way are often cross-cultural in subject as well as in production conditions.

Of course, this process is never completely successful. Many foreign film-makers have unhappy experiences making films in Hollywood and choose to return to their own countries. Jim Hillier observes that the

> [f]ilm industry émigrés of the last thirty years have rarely established long, stable Hollywood careers. More typically, they come to the United States to make one or two films and then quickly depart. Some examples of this pattern are Jacques Demy, Model Shop; Agnès Varda, Lions Love; and Paolo and Vittorio Taviani, Good Morning, Babylon. These films retain an outsider's perspective; they are Euro-American rather than Hollywood films.

> (Hillier, 1992; p.163)

This notion of the outsider's perspective is a useful one. Hollywood has always imported foreign directors partly in order for them to create films which are distinctive and different while remaining within the broad boundaries of formal construction that typifies the American film-making style. Product differentiation has always been one of the driving forces behind American film production. Foreign film-makers therefore offer a different take on the familiar: American culture and society. Werner Herzog's *Stroszek* (1977), for example, is a critique of the failure of the American Dream, typifying Herzog's general engagement with American culture. Perhaps even more representative is Wim Wenders, whose films are also often reflections on America. His work in the United States between 1977 and 1984 included *Hammett* (1982), a troubled production made in association with Francis Ford Coppola; *The State of Things* (1982), a semi-autobiographical film about the troubled making of a film, made during hiatuses on *Hammett*; and *Paris Texas* (1984), the pinnacle of his off-beat studies of the American Dream, whose images recall the epic landscapes and emotional density of John Ford.

STARS

Hollywood has always been interested in foreign stars as well as foreign directors. And, as with tempting directors away from their national film industries, importing foreign actors also largely prevents them from starring in indigenous films. Once again, the foreign film industry is weakened, and its capability to compete with American films, now starring those very actors who were once a feature of the national cinema, is reduced.

A few examples will help to demonstrate this tendency. Greta Garbo came from Sweden in the 1920s to become one of the biggest stars in Hollywood during the 1930s. Conrad Veidt began his acting career as the somnambulist in *The Cabinet of Dr Caligari* (1919), before fleeing Nazism to come to Hollywood to make the appropriately titled *Escape* (1940), and thereafter specialised in playing villains such as his evil Nazi commandant in *Casablanca* (1942). Maurice Chevalier was a major French star of stage and film when Paramount signed him in 1929, allowing him to make a number of successful American films throughout the 1930s, including *The Love Parade* (Paramount, 1929) and *Folies Bergère* (Twentieth Century Pictures Co., 1935). Finally, following their collaboration in Germany on *The Blue Angel* (1930), Marlene Dietrich came to Hollywood with Josef von Sternberg, the beginning of a short but brilliant partnership for them (*Shanghai Express*, 1932 and *The Scarlet Empress*, 1934), and a long, if uneven, American film career for her, *Destry Rides Again* (1939) and *Rancho Notorious* (Lang, 1952) being among the best of her American films.

Anthony Hopkins and Antonio Banderas draw swords over Catherine Zeta Jones in *The Mask of Zorro* (Martin Campbell, 1998)

Foreign actors therefore help to give American films their global appeal – an appeal increasingly necessary in today's hyper-expensive production environment. A good example is perhaps Antonio Banderas, who began his career in Spanish films, most notably Pedro Almodóvar's quirky and erotic films, *Women on the Verge of a Nervous Breakdown* (1988) and *Tie Me Up, Tie Me Down* (1989). His move to America, first starring in *The Mambo Kings* (1992), where he had to recite his lines phonetically because he could not, at that point, speak English, has culminated in his playing Zorro in *The Mask of Zorro* (1998). That particular film is significant for its largely foreign cast – in addition to Banderas, the film stars the Welsh actors Anthony Hopkins and Catherine Zeta Jones, as well as co-starring the English actor Stuart Wilson. The international cast was necessary to maximise the chances of the film succeeding on a global scale; a strategy that seems to have been successful: while domestic box office was $93.8 million, the film's international box office was $139.6 million.

Perhaps more interesting is Gérard Depardieu, the French actor with many well-respected films to his name made in his native country. Indeed, the respect he had accrued working in his native film industry was, inevitably, one of the reasons why he came to the attention of American producers. Thoughts

Andie MacDowell and Gérard Depardieu sitting comfortably in *Green Card* (Peter Weir, 1990) © Touchstone Pictures

of bringing him over to America had been in play for some years before Peter Weir, an Australian writer/director, wrote *Green Card* (1990) especially for him. As with Banderas, Depardieu had to speak his lines phonetically due to poor English, but this was seen only to add charm to his performance. Having appeared in his first American film, however, Depardieu returned to France to make a number of French films, including *Mon père, ce héros* (1991), which he subsequently remade three years later, in English, in America as *My Father the Hero* (1994). Most recently, Depardieu has appeared in the sequel to *101 Dalmatians* (1996), imaginatively titled *102 Dalmatians* (2000), as an outrageously stereotyped French fur dealer. His appearance is explicitly designed to widen the international appeal of the film:

> *For producer Edward S. Feldman there was only one man who could play this role, 'I never wanted to have an Englishman or an American doing a French accent. I wanted a true Frenchman and when you think of a true Frenchman, you think of Gérard Depardieu. As with the American–foreign relations issue generally, therefore, foreign stars, for American audiences, lend exoticism to the American films in which they appear, while also adding international appeal for the film's global release.'*

> *(Walt Disney Pictures, 2000; p.1)*

This model of foreign stars retaining relative autonomy, of being able, at least partly, to decide how and when they move between Hollywood and their native industries, is certainly a common model in contemporary world cinema. Indeed, it can be seen as a variation on the independent star/package-unit system that has been in place since the demise of the studio system at the beginning of the 1950s. But it is important to recognise that, to some degree, it has always been the case with foreign stars and directors. Even during the studio period, most of those individuals cited over the last few pages, and many more besides, were able to split their time between America and Europe. The modern version of this is an intensification of, rather than a break with, the past.

REVITALISING THE WORLD EXHIBITION SECTOR

One area in which the American film industry has openly intervened in order to engineer a situation to its own advantage is that of international exhibition. Since the mid-1970s, an American programme to revitalise Europe's exhibition sector has been in process. This was begun largely as a response to the decline both of the American exhibition sector in response to falling audience numbers, and to the reduction in European audience share being experienced during the 1960s and 1970s, as noted above.

By the early 1970s, European cinemas were in a poor state – shabby decor, tiny screens, and the sound from one auditorium bleeding through to the one next door. 'The situation was especially bad in the U.K., where the owners of two leading chains, Rank and ABC, had consistently refused to make any serious investment in upgrading their existing sites, let alone building new venues' (Puttnam with Watson, 2000; p.252). Such a decline in standards of comfort and quality of presentation had discouraged people, who were beginning to be disinclined anyway, from going to the cinema; they stayed at home and watched television instead. A vicious circle was set up in which declining audiences meant less maintenance of cinemas, whose falling standards put yet more people off attending them.

The renaissance in cinema standards began in America itself, with the development of multiplexes, led by AMC, and then taken up, when the logic proved successful, by other indigenous exhibition chains. At the same time as the growth of conglomerates in the American film industry was beginning to lay an emphasis on global reach, it was realised that there was a huge gap in the European exhibition sector waiting to be filled. American multiplex companies, presenting cinema-going as a special event to be experienced in comfort, moved in to take advantage of the possibilities this gap opened up:

75

European theatre construction (especially multiplex set-ups) is on the rise, with active participation by some of the US majors. Britain has been the forerunner of such activity, with American Multi Cinema, National Amusements, MCA and others adding 350 new screens in the UK during the last few years. More new theatres are planned for other European countries. Specifically, United Cinemas (MCA and Paramount) plans outlets for Germany and Spain, while Time Warner is looking to build new theatres in Germany and the countries of the former Soviet Union.

The general consolidation of European cinemas also favours US distributors. According to one report, 'They have fewer exhibitors to deal with and can more easily control release patterns.' And, of course, the more theatres, the more pictures are needed. As the head of Warner Brothers International's theatrical division reports, 'Business has improved tremendously. Before, you'd be in line to get your films into the two theatres in town. Now you can get them out much earlier and feed off a lot of the publicity coming out of the United States.' An MCA spokesman claims that 'the multiplexing of Europe will enable us to release twice as many movies'.

(Wasko, 1994; p.234)

This programme of European multiplex construction had the added, and hardly unintentional, effect of creating an exhibition environment in which American films could be easily shown. Those films – by the late 1980s/early 1990s, increasingly expensive blockbusters – needed large global audiences to break even. If enough cinemas could be made to exist in order to show them to that audience, the rest of the world would provide the market that would make the figures add up.

Over time, it has meant that American companies have gained substantial control of exhibition circuits in Europe, and eventually across the world, and great influence over the kinds of film that get shown in those multiplex screens; a natural and unavoidable pressure to accept American films over foreign. In this movement, we see a return, or at least an echo, of the vertical integration of the studio system so dramatically dismantled with the Paramount case in 1948. The threat that it poses to indigenous markets is indicated by the French resistance to the building programmes; in 1996, for example, the French government introduced legislation designed to curb construction of new venues.

Together with the increase in cinema building in Europe, other markets are now opening up to American control, largely as a result of the changing political situation in certain countries, such as Eastern Europe and China. In the year 2000, China's cinemas were permitted to screen only about ten US films a year, but those ten films dominated the market. In contrast, Chinese film studios produced only about 50 films that year, representing a reduction of over 60 per cent on the number they made four years previously. The reason is partly political: China has granted concessions to foreign film-makers in exchange for China's inclusion in the Geneva-based trade body; a move that will inevitably make things even harder for Chinese film-makers:

> *Under a deal worked out with the Clinton administration last year, Beijing promised to double the number of foreign movies shown in China to twenty in the first year of China's membership in the WTO. Over the following three years, the total would rise to fifty. That may seem like a relatively small number in the United States, where a single theatre may screen that many films in less than a year, but in China it's a terrifying prospect.*

> *(Chandler, 2000; p.E01)*

Titanic made an estimated $47 million from exhibition in Chinese cinemas, making it the highest-ever grossing movie in China. The central problem appears to be persuading the population to go to the cinema in the first place, due both to cultural resistance and the poor quality of theatres. The China–WTO deal has set up a revenue-sharing provision that gives Chinese distributors a generous cut of future ticket sales from foreign films, in the hope that authorities in Beijing will allow that money to be reinvested in the local industry to produce better movies and renovate ageing theatres (Chandler, 2000; p.E01). This deal, therefore, shows both America's continuing development of strategies to break into, and hopefully dominate, new foreign markets, while adapting to the specific demands and pressures of those markets, even if that means striking deals that actually help the indigenous film industry.

AMERICAN FINANCING OF FOREIGN FILMS

The American financing of foreign films has been a feature of the American film industry since the 1950s/60s and into the 1970s. The foreign film stars could stay in Europe to make the films, which featured international casts and exotic foreign locations. In such circumstances, there was not so much traffic of creative personnel to Hollywood; they preferred to stay in their own countries while taking full advantage of American financing and facilities. The interest in World Cinema shown by the new generation of American film-makers emerging from film school from the late 1960s onwards, together with the increasing global conglomeration from the mid-1960s onwards, provoked an interest in making American films with international casts.

Indeed, the European cinema boom of the 1960s was bound up with the decline of the US market. As the American film market hit problems, American companies began expanding their foreign operations, taking advantage of subsidies for European partners. An increasingly archaic and moribund American studio system, hampered by escalating production costs and a fragile and dissolving audience, saw the European cinema, with its cheap labour, pools of talent, and still significant local markets, as an appealing alternative, especially when tax benefits were factored into the equation.

By the mid-1960s, the Italian film industry was one of the most attractive to American film companies wanting to work abroad. 'For the film to qualify for a subsidy, only the director of its original Italian version had to be Italian. A number of American companies saw that this gave them a loophole for access to state support. They began to appoint "straw directors," who were credited as directors on the Italian version of the film, but were in reality nothing more than local assistants to American directors' (Puttnam with Watson, 2000; p.205). *El Cid* (1961), directed by Anthony Mann but credited to another director in Italy, is one such example of a subsidised, American–Italian, dual-version feature film. The example of the Italian film industry was not an isolated one. American financing of foreign productions generally grew throughout the 1960s and 1970s. 'At one time in the 1960s the Americans were contributing nearly 90 percent of the finance for the production of films in Britain' (Walker, 1974; p.16).

But such a situation was a precarious one for a European film industry increasingly reliant on the American dollar. Eventually, European overproduction caused considerable damage to European industries. The British film industry had also been overtaken by American investment and British branches of American majors. But the eventual realisation that such operations were unprofitable caused the major American studios to close their foreign branches at the end of the 1960s. '[W]hen the Americans withdrew at the end of the decade, we were left with practically no resources to fall back on' (Walker, 1974; p.16).

Beginning about 1970, American investment in European production gradually declined, for two basic reasons. Firstly, the American studios decided to invest instead in a new generation of American film-makers, many of whom incorporated European sensibilities into their film-making style. Secondly, there was an abrupt shrinkage of European theatrical markets for motion pictures. From 1975 to the late 1980s, motion picture audiences in Western Europe declined significantly, partly as a result of the growth in the number of European television channels.

Recently, however, American financing of foreign films has been expanding again. This has a number of causes. Partly, it is to do with the success of some American blockbuster films, such as *Pretty Woman* (1990) and *Terminator 2:*

Judgement Day (1991) at the foreign box office, fuelling feelings that a huge untapped audience lay waiting for new films. Partly, somewhat ironically in face of the point just made about the growth of European television channels, the proliferation of media outlets – cable, video, and so on – has opened up huge new markets to American companies; this market wants indigenous films as well as American ones. Thirdly, it is a result of the internationalisation of the film production business through conglomeration, as the Warner Communications Annual Report of 1982 noted:

> *Though motion pictures produced and distributed by the Hollywood studios continue to attract the largest world-wide audiences, there has been a substantial increase in foreign independent film production around the world in the past few years. Warner Bros. becomes involved in the production of foreign features – particularly those with an English language version – when there appears to be a significant international market for a specific project. One result of such activity was Warner Bros.' involvement in Australian director George Miller's two Mad Max films, which were originally acquired for foreign distribution only. Both films have been successful internationally, and The Road Warrior, the second of the Mad Max films, ultimately proved very popular in the US as well. Warner Bros.' international operation not only distributes domestic feature films on a world-wide basis, but also is on the lookout around the world for new sources of product for the US market.*

> *(quoted in Balio, 1985; p.597)*

This financing strategy can currently be seen to be paying dividends with the success of the Chinese-produced Ang Lee film, *Crouching Tiger, Hidden Dragon* (2000). Sony Pictures Entertainment (SPE), which had originally bought only the North American and Latin American rights to the film, took on a much bigger role following the closure of Far Eastern financing due to the collapse of the Asian money markets. SPE, together with the New York-based Good Machine International, financed the film's $15 million budget, partly due to its previous relationship with Ang Lee, who made *Sense and Sensibility* (produced by Good Machine's James Schamus) for SPE in 1995.

AMERICAN RELEASE OF FOREIGN FILMS

Although American audiences are usually regarded as insular and unwilling to regularly watch more adventurous European art-films over American-produced action films, there is some evidence that that is too monolithic a picture:

Some foreign films, English-speaking or not, do get shown extensively in the United States, and not only in the art house ghetto; witness such diverse examples as the Hercules/Maciste films, spaghetti westerns, Bruce Lee and other kung fu films, Mad Max, Das Boot, La Cage aux Folles, Nikita, Crocodile Dundee.

(Jarvie, 1998; p.41)

However, the potential box office of even the most successful of foreign films released into the American market pales before the top American money-earners. *Like Water For Chocolate* (1991), for instance, with distribution by Miramax, one of the most successful and aggressive of independent distributors, took more than a year to earn $20 million. This made it, at the time, the most successful foreign-language film in American cinemas. In only four days, on its opening weekend, *Hannibal* (2001) earned almost twice as much ($35.5 million). This is why the success of *Crouching Tiger, Hidden Dragon* is so significant, because its box-office success signals the possibility that foreign-language films can make huge profits at American cinemas. By the end of June 2001, the film had made $127.65 million at the US box office alone, making it both the first Sony Pictures Classic and the first independent feature to go over the $100 million mark. It is equally, if not more, significant that *Crouching Tiger, Hidden Dragon* was financed with American money. In this way we can see American film companies returning to financial investment in foreign film-making as a means of controlling competition and maximising profits.

FOREIGN INVESTMENT IN THE AMERICAN FILM INDUSTRY

The American film industry, symbolised both physically and psychologically by Hollywood, can too easily be seen as a hermetically sealed entity: self-financing, re-absorbing its profits. It is important, however, not to forget that for several decades at least, it has made its movies only by entering into financial arrangements with foreign film companies, whether in production, distribution or exhibition. As David Puttnam notes, during the 1980s and 1990s, European companies alone poured several hundred million dollars into Hollywood production. Some – Cannon (the Israelis, Golan and Globus); DEG (Dino de Laurentiis); Carolco, etc. – set up new companies within the American film industry itself. Indeed, MGM/UA, as noted in an earlier chapter, came to be bought by the Italian Giancarlo Parretti, financed by Crédit Lyonnais. Many of these smaller foreign production companies were set up to exploit the booming video market of the mid-1980s onwards, because worldwide sales of videocassettes were seen to be on the verge of substantially exceeding theatrical revenues.

Co-productions have long been seen as an area in which America and Europe could combine interests, both financial and artistic. European co-productions were a feature of the European cinema in an attempt to rebuild it after the Second World War. Some significant films were produced as a result – for instance, *The Third Man* (1949), co-produced by David Selznick and Alexander Korda's London Films, and starring an international cast which included Americans Orson Welles and Joseph Cotten, the British actor Trevor Howard and Italian actress Alida Valli, and *Stromboli* (1949), an RKO/Roberto Rossellini co-production which caused a public scandal when its 'American' star Ingrid Bergman became romantically involved with Rossellini. Overall, these films were seen as a means of re-establishing a European film-making practice and creating a body of European films which could compete against the American product then beginning to flood into the continent.

However, simultaneous with these attempts to control the import and export of films between countries, and especially between America and the rest of the world, were moves to encourage co-operation with American companies, especially in the area of production. Although European film industries, for example, were entering into co-production deals in an effort to build up European resistance to American domination of their markets, steps were also taken to forge links with American companies:

> *Contemporary [1950s] with the move towards European co-production, however, producers in various European countries, notably Italy and Britain, began in the post-war years to explore various forms of co-operation and collaboration with American companies . . . [Italy in the 1950s] not only attempted to export Italian films to the United States but opened up film-making facilities to American studios and independent companies.*

> *(Nowell-Smith, 1998; p.6)*

The second half of 1980s saw a new phase of Euro-American art-film productions. *The Name of the Rose* (Annaud, 1986; financed by Cristaldfilm [Italy], France 3 Cinema and Les Films Ariane [both France], Neue Constantin Film and Zweites Deutsches Fernsehen [both Germany], and distributed by Twentieth Century-Fox); *'Round Midnight* (Tavernier, 1986; Little Bear and PECF [France], distributed by Warner Bros.) and *The Sheltering Sky* (Bertolucci, 1990; Aldrich Group, Film Trustees Ltd, Recorded Pictures Co. [all US], Sahara Co. [Gibralter], TAO Film [Italy], distributed by Warner Bros.). *The Last Emperor* (Bertolucci, 1987; AAA, Hemdale [GB], Recorded Pictures [US], Screenframe [US], TAO Films [Italy], distributed by Columbia) is perhaps the best example of international co-production: an English-language film, produced by an Englishman (Jeremy Thomas), shot in China by an Italian director and a primarily Italian crew, financed by a consortium of European banks, based on distribution guarantees from European and Japanese distributors. Such productions become very difficult to identify as being the product of any one national film industry.

From the early 1970s onwards, American film studios benefited from money generated by tax shelters overseas. One British financier, John Heyman, raised some $2.5 billion of new money for the studios, much of it from Japan. Walt Disney and Columbia Pictures also raised significant amounts of new capital from these same Japanese tax shelters. Throughout the 1980s and 1990s, Hollywood became ever more dependent on foreign money.

This financial arrangement has now become a dangerous situation in which Hollywood faces a disastrous withdrawal of foreign investment. Hollywood has been seen as becoming too dependent upon foreign money, whether in co-productions or pre-sales. The rising costs of production and the consequently higher risk of not recouping that money or, at least, of not making the kinds of profit that such high-risk investment requires to make it worthwhile, have led many foreign investors to think again, or at least to proceed with more caution.

The Europeanisation of the American film industry developed to such an extent that an Englishman, David Puttnam, was hired by Columbia Pictures to bring a European sensibility and knowledge of non-domestic markets to its film production process:

> In part, I was hired because the owner of the studio, Coca-Cola, was hoping to increase the revenue that Columbia's films earned abroad; Coca-Cola's managers believed that a European with extensive experience of the international market would be ideally placed to achieve this goal. Because the company had been so successful in expanding its exports to Europe and elsewhere during the postwar period, some 65 percent of Coca-Cola's total revenues came from abroad, compared with only 30 percent of Columbia's.

(Puttnam with Watson, 2000; p.270)

Puttnam was considered by the American film industry to have failed because he produced a string of, to American eyes, unwatchable movies. One of the most notable was *Me and Him* (1987), which remains unreleased (some inside Columbia, and elsewhere, would say it was unreleasable), and was the story of a talking penis. Although one could see that such a topic could conceivably become the subject of a quirky European art film, it is hard to imagine it working on any level with the Hollywood of the time (one could imagine it working better in the juvenile, 'gross-out' comedies of more recent years, such as those made by the Farrelly Brothers [*Dumb and Dumber*, 1994; *There's Something About Mary*, 1998]). It epitomises the problems inherent in trying to fuse together American and non-American sensibilities.

FOREIGN PRODUCTION OF AMERICAN FILMS

Hollywood has found it attractive to film productions outside the United States. Exotic locations, perhaps demanded by the film's subject matter, add production value to a film. But making films outside America offers lower costs for, amongst other things, unions, in-front and behind camera talent, and studio overhead charges. Non-American expenses are generally cheaper, labour regulations more flexible, and currency rates usually favourable. In addition, substantial subsidies can significantly reduce the amount of money a studio has to put up front to make a film:

> *Producer Doug Claybourne* [Rumblefish, Wars of the Roses] . . . *recently priced a motion picture two ways: As a U.S. shoot, he says, the budget was $44 million; in Canada, it was $39 million. 'The actual saving was 26 per cent in the production period, below the line,' he says.*
>
> *(Madigan, 1999; p.9)*

All of these factors have made the use of foreign countries, their locations and facilities attractive to film-makers who are seeing their production costs rise year after year, especially if the production in question is a big-budget, special effects-laden, action blockbuster:

> *Given a stable exchange rate, Europe has consistently offered something like a 30 percent cost advantage over the United States, so all other things being equal there is a considerable incentive to shoot offshore. Europe's studios and technicians, as well as its actors, have been essential ingredients of many of the movies that seem to encapsulate the very essence of Hollywood.*
>
> *(Puttnam with Watson, 2000; p.278)*

Such arrangements have not always proved popular or beneficial to the American film industry in the longer term. Certainly, they came to be seen as a problem in the 1950s and 1960s, when overproduction in non-American locations caused both a glut of stodgy, similar-looking films with bloated budgets – film such as *Ben Hur* (1959), *El Cid, Cleopatra* (1963), *The Fall of the*

Roman Empire (1964) – and a shortage of work for American-based crews. This is one reason why, when a new generation of film-makers emerged from film schools and elsewhere at the end of the 1960s, American studios were willing and eager to give them a chance rather than continue to make films out of the country.

However, such a situation is once again concerning many of those who work within the industry, and has become a political issue in the past few years. 'Runaway productions', as they are known, are films shot in foreign countries with foreign workers, usually receiving huge tax incentives in the process. A report commissioned in 1998 by the Department of Commerce found that domestic production of made-for-TV movies had declined by 33 per cent in the preceding six years, while production at foreign locations rose by 55 per cent, resulting in either almost $3 billion or over $10 billion lost in direct expenditures, wages and taxes. The wide gap between lower and upper estimates depends on whether the entire production costs are counted, or just that proportion of the budget shot in the foreign country. Canada is the largest host, with over 80 per cent of the share of American productions shot outside the US. Its 1999 haul of American productions included Disney's *Mission to Mars* (2000), *Reindeer Games* (2000), starring Ben Affleck, and Sylvester Stallone's *D–Tox (2001)*.

While big-salaried stars and directors can afford to work out of America for long periods of time, crew members cannot. Consequently, up to 80 per cent of crew workers get hired at location. The threat posed by 'runaway production' is perceived to be so great that the FILM US Alliance has been formed to fight it. This initiative includes all of the major film and television industry unions and bodies, including the Screen Actors' Guild, Academy of Television Arts and Sciences, Directors' Guild of America and Producers' Guild of America.

Other observers see the loss of income as a self-inflicted phenomenon, caused by studios cutting back on their production numbers while increasing the budgets of the films they do make, as well as wanting to dominate and manipulate global film markets through attracting foreign finance for American productions. 'Hollywood's output was not financed entirely by American dollars. It was financed in part – often a third or more – through export sales. And people who depend on export sales should be the last to complain if, on occasion, there are a few imports' (King, 1999; p.1). Runaway production is therefore being seen as an inevitable part of a new global economic landscape:

> *'It's part of the globalisation process that production is moving to different places depending on prices,' says S. Abraham Ravid, a professor of finance at Rutgers U who has studied the entertainment industry. 'This is similar to what happens*

in other industries. There are going to be more centres than just Hollywood for making films.'

(Madigan, 1999; p.9)

REMAKES

Why should Hollywood want to remake foreign films? What are the specific impulses and rationales behind doing so if, as is often argued, the two are like chalk and cheese, crassly commercial and fastidiously high-art, respectively? This section examines the various reasons behind this now fairly common activity.

The first is perhaps straightforward. Hollywood has a voracious appetite for new ideas that will furnish new product for its ever hungry, proliferating distribution channels. Hollywood is interested in finding that material wherever and whenever it can. In this context, story ideas originating from anywhere in the world are as potentially acceptable as those generated from within the American film industry itself.

And here lies the first problem, neatly summed up earlier in this chapter by director Sydney Pollack: 'You can't understand a lot of Japanese movies unless you understand Japanese culture. You don't have to understand American culture to understand our movies' (speaking on *Think Tank*, 2000). Foreign subject matter usually has to be 'Americanised' in order for it to appeal to an American audience, or even every other audience except its original one. In this sense, Americanising the material, giving it American cultural values and references, levels it to the widest global common denominator. Just as every foreign worker has had to adapt to fit the values and philosophy of film-making by which Hollywood operates, so does the story material which Hollywood acquires from world cinemas:

> *The remake phenomenon throws some light on both film and television. In the movies* 3 Men and a Baby, Cousins *or* The Vanishing . . . *we see clear evidence that the Americans judge the European original to need modification to suit American tastes.*

(Jarvie, 1998; p.42)

In a sense, what is happening here is 'a synthesis . . . a recognition of the intelligence and emotional power of European film-making, and an effort to reshape that intelligence and power into a format accessible to American audiences' (Lev, 1993; p.71).

The traffic has by no means been only one-way. European film-makers have borrowed themes, plots and narratives from American films as much as vice versa. Lucy Fischer, for example, has argued that the Spanish director Pedro Almodóvar's *High Heels* (1991) is a postmodern remake of Douglas Sirk's *Imitation of Life* (1959) which, by circulating in European art cinema circles, allows an ironic play to be made of mainstream American social and cinematic values. Similarly, Andrew Horton notes that Kusturica's *Time of the Gypsies* (1989) is a remake of Coppola's *Godfather I and II* (1972 and 1974). Such reworkings have a significantly different agenda from their American counterparts, in that they allow non-American film-makers to explore pertinent issues within their own societies, often dominated by American hegemonic values, by changing or even inverting the original elements. For example, Kusturica's film, Horton argues, takes the heavily patriarchal *Godfather* trilogy and transforms its values by placing its narrative within a gypsy culture which is strongly matriarchal: 'The gender implications that radiate from such a makeover of Coppola's crime classics are profound.' But the remake also has an overt political agenda, as Horton concludes:

> *The perpetual state of making over cinematic texts and allusions, with Coppola's* The Godfather *and* Godfather II *being the primary object of plundering, locates Kusturica in the 'unfinished' state of being a Bosnian-born film-maker who has gone beyond the borders of geography, politics, language, and regional culture (though he does strongly represent these as well) to 'steal' from the international currency of cinema.*
>
> *(Horton, 1998; pp.187–8)*

Such end products have been referred to as 'cross-cultural makeovers' and, by Leo Braudy, as 'unfinished cultural business'. In other words, they are expressions of an ongoing cultural exchange and debate between America and the rest of the world, in which two sets of values, two sensibilities, are brought into direct contact, even direct conflict. The unsatisfactory or problematic resolution of that conflict is what frequently makes American remakes of foreign originals fascinatingly rich as film texts.

While picking up foreign hit films as story material for remakes has the added benefit that the story has already been proved to work with a public, there are two inherent problems with this move. Firstly, the material might not translate well, might not 'Americanise' well, resulting in a confused and unfocused remake. Secondly, the finished film might seem too similar to the original and audiences might not find the prospect of seeing the same story slightly differently told a sufficient incentive to go to see the remake.

A further reason to remake foreign films in American versions is the problems American audiences have in watching foreign movies. Subtitling of dialogue is actively resisted by American audiences, who find the effort of constantly glancing down from the action on screen to read condensed lines of dialogue too distracting and difficult. Foreign films, concerned, as they often are, with observing everyday life and human relations rather than fantastic action and adventure, are seen as having too slow a narrative pace for audiences used to visceral action and relentless, quick-cutting, film style. Remaking a foreign original can inject the subjects with the necessary 'American pace', as well as removing subtitles by having actors speak their lines in English. Such was the case with *Breathless* (1983), Jim McBride's remake of Godard's *A bout de souffle* (1960). Godard's film includes lengthy sequences, most notably when the two main protagonists just sit and talk on a hotel bed for 15 to 20 minutes, which would be unacceptable to American audiences. Therefore, they were replaced with shorter scenes, and a greater emphasis on trashy visual qualities and snappier editing on Richard Gere's strutting character.

Finally, there is a certain kudos in being attached to serious 'art' subjects more normally associated with non-American cinemas. In a marketplace which still operates according to the principle of product differentiation, this difference from standard escapist product means that the 'serious remake' might catch more of the potential audience's attention in an overcrowded market. This desire for Hollywood to be seen to be treating film as a serious art form rather than a simple commercial product has intensified in recent years, and is reflected in the increasing tendency for the Academy to choose foreign films in the Best Picture, Best Director and Best Screenplay/Adapted Screenplay categories on Oscar night. The sweeping success of such films as *The English Patient* (1996) and *Life is Beautiful* (1997), and the multiple Oscar success of *Crouching Tiger, Hidden Dragon* (for Foreign Language Film, Art Direction, Cinematography and Music Score) in 2001 is evidence of this focus.

Hollywood's foreign relations therefore have a long history, and an extremely complex set of contemporary issues. The American film industry has perpetually found itself both needing and resisting the film-making potential of other countries. While desiring a complete control of world markets, it has recognised that that is neither possible nor even sensible. Instead, it has instituted a policy of selective co-operation, making connections with foreign operators whenever and wherever this has seemed prudent, while resisting or absorbing the threat when necessary. By so doing, it has sought to maximise its control over the global situation while permitting pockets of foreign operation if they ultimately benefit Hollywood. Foreign co-productions, foreign filming of American productions, and carefully negotiated distribution deals, are all strategies by which Hollywood hopes to retain dominance in the world's film markets. In the age of media conglomeration, it is perhaps no surprise to find it thus.

CHAPTER FOUR

The Talent I

The directors

During the Classical Hollywood period, and even by the early 1960s – some time into its aftermath – the film director was not unduly foregrounded as the main artist involved in the creation of a feature film. Certainly, he was seen as an important member of the creative process. Indeed, there were many directors who were known by name by the film-going public: Orson Welles, John Ford, George Cukor, Alfred Hitchcock. But the main spotlight was on the stars appearing in the films – stars like John Wayne, Clark Gable and Bette Davis. Ten years later, that situation had significantly changed. Why should this be so? What had happened in the intervening decade?

Investigating the sequence of events and the range of influences which caused this shift, and the subsequent redefining of the director within the framework of the film-making process, is the purpose of this chapter.

INDUSTRIAL CHANGE AND THE ROLE OF THE FILM DIRECTOR

As noted in the background chapter, during the decades of the Hollywood studio system the director was only one category of employee among many who were permanently employed by studios. However, the decline of the studio system from the end of the 1940s onwards, and the emergence of the 'package', recast the film director as someone who could also be used to lend a legitimacy to a proposed film project. Along with the always-favoured star actors, the director came to be given a significance, and attendant price-tag, which altered the industry's perception of him/her as a 'player' in the industrial and economic make-up of the film business.

The crisis which gripped the industry at the very end of the 1960s and beginning of the 1970s crystallised a situation which had been developing for several years, in which the old-time studio executives found themselves increasingly divorced from changing public tastes. In their anxiety and desperation to find a solution to the perceived chasm between the film studios and their audiences, those studios allowed a new breed of film-makers – directors, rather than actors, or writers – through the hallowed studio gates. These directors – Francis Ford Coppola, Martin Scorsese, Brian De Palma, Dennis Hopper – because they were young, fresh and rebellious, were presumed to be more in touch with the new audience than the 'old-timers' who had been responsible for producing the films that had satisfied studios and audiences alike for several decades. The new status enjoyed by the film director, which had taken on prominence with the emergence of the package system of the 1950s, combined with a serious crisis of purpose for the American film industry at the end of the 1960s, foregrounded the director as a potential saviour.

Any discussion of the changes that the identity of the film director of the late 1960s and early 1970s underwent in America, must take account of a European intellectual theory that was developed in France and imported into America a few years later. Originally labelled *la politique des auteurs*, and renamed for America as the auteur theory, it argued that, rather like a writer (hence the auteur/author slippage) or artist, the film director was the main creative force propelling forward the creation of the film text.

The theory was initiated partly due to the influx of American films into Europe following the reopening of trading relations, after the Second World War. In this glut of films, writers, critics and fledgling film-makers, especially in France, had the opportunity to view, in rapid succession, significant percentages of the work of key American directors such as Howard Hawks, John Ford and Alfred Hitchcock, amongst many others. Under such circumstances it became possible, even easy, to spot stylistic consistencies, thematic preoccupations and narrative continuities.

Interestingly, a parallel process occurred in America, where the selling of back catalogue libraries of films to television and their frequent screening to fill empty schedules allowed American film critics to do the same. The business of selling libraries of old films to television began in 1955 with the RKO back catalogue of 740 features being sold by C&C Television Corporation, which had bought RKO from Howard Hughes earlier that year for $15 million. C&C then licensed single features to television networks, earning $25 million in revenues in two years. Between 1956 and 1958, all of the other eight major studios had joined RKO in off-loading their old films onto television, with Columbia receiving $9.7 million, and Warner Bros. $15 million for their back catalogues (Boddy, 1993; p.138). By 1956, WOR-TV New York was showing features films for 88 per cent of its schedule, in the form of series such as the *Million Dollar Movie* (Barnouw, 1990; p.198).

It is important to appreciate the degree of difficulty experienced by students and film-makers in seeing older American films in the days before television, organised film archiving and, lastly, video. Cinema was seen as a thing of the moment: films were shown and then withdrawn, often even destroyed. To get to see any of them at a later date was virtually impossible. The sudden release of new Hollywood films onto the European market after the Second World War, the purchase of back catalogues of American mainstream movies in order to fill long hours of broadcasting, and the ease of use and access which came with the advent of the videocassette, must therefore all be seen to be of crucial importance. Access to a wide body of the past classics of Hollywood cinema centrally influenced the development not only of serious film criticism during the 1950s and 1960s, but also of the cine-literacy of a generation of new film-makers emerging from film schools during the 1960s and 1970s.

The agenda, certainly for the French, and in a different way for the American critics, was to 'rescue' the popular American cinema, so often dismissed by high-art intellectuals as crass, commercial fodder. Whilst somehow seeming to portray that cinema as restrictive and potentially stifling of artistic expression, it also erected the notion that the 'Old Hollywood' had actually been a directors' cinema, and that those directors who were gifted or determined enough managed to carve out a personal style in spite of the restricted and prescribed circumstances in which they made their films. This interesting tension between the individual and the system within the auteur theory, formed by criticism and academic opinion, helped to shape the reaction to Hollywood during the late 1960s. It also allowed the new film-makers to work *against* something (the moribund and out-of-date Hollywood) while simultaneously recognising kinship with their Old Hollywood counterparts. The focus of auteur theory was therefore, in many ways, retrospective, assessing the great films and film-makers of Hollywood's past and assigning value to them. One of the issues considered in this chapter is how that process of looking towards, and finding value in, the past was both taken up and made to work in their own time by the new directors of the 1970s.

It is in some ways one of the ironies of this period in American film-making that this reappraisal of the studio period was taking place at the moment when that system was being systematically dismantled, not only legally and industrially, but emotionally and psychologically. It is an irony which we will look at shortly, directly in terms of the new wave of American film-makers coming into the industry as the 1960s ended.

It is important to recognise also that the *politique des auteurs* was also conceived within a specific cultural and film-industrial context: that of postwar France. France had obviously always been a film-making country. Indeed, in the early years of cinema, it had been one of the foremost film-making nations of the world. But since then, while its film industry could not exactly be described as 'cottage', it simply did not compare in size and ambition with the American studio system. In some ways there was a mismatch between systems. Auteurism was always more problematic within large industrialised film-making systems such as that operated in America where it is difficult to assign sole authorship of a film which is the result of the labours of large groups of creative people.

European methods were smaller-scale, almost intimate in comparison. Colin Crisp notes that there were significant early parallels in the development of French and American cinema but the partial collapse of the industry following the First World War 'left a complex and fragmented industry, which throughout the twenties and early thirties made sporadic attempts to organise itself into larger production units' (Crisp, 1997; p.269). The eventual result was the emergence of the package-unit system, which took two forms: the director-package and the producer-package, depending on which figure assumed the responsibility for assembling the package.

As Crisp goes on to argue, the French system was a diverse and multifaceted one in comparison to the more industrialised American studio system. As a result, the products of the French system was smaller and more personal, and established film as an artistic form of expression more than an economic object:

> In effect, by preserving an artisanal and 'intimate' mode of production, the fragmented industrial structure contributed to the maintenance of a consciousness among all concerned in making the films (and specifically in the producers who were the central decision makers) of being involved in an exhilarating enterprise with national cultural responsibilities. Their representation of cinema and of French cinema, not to mention their own self-representation, was markedly different from that of their American counterparts. In effect, the lack of ongoing contractual relationships engendered constant personal negotiations, such that film-making could not escape seeming a highly personalised and adventurous undertaking.
>
> (Crisp, 1997; p.283)

Moreover, within this flexible, artistic environment, creative personnel could take on multiple roles. Crisp notes that:

> of the 530 directors active between 1929 and 1958, some 100 were not content with just directing, but aimed to control most or all major decisions in the areas of scriptwriting, acting and/or the technical practices of filming (set design, cinematography, editing and music composition). A smaller number aimed at an even greater degree of independence permitted, at least in theory, by the director-package system.
>
> (Crisp, 1997; p.316)

Within this perspective, the New Wave directors such as Godard and Truffaut represent a continuation and development of, rather than a radical break from, past film-making practices in France. For example, the production of *A bout de souffle* (1960) saw Godard directing, Truffaut scripting and Chabrol offering technical assistance. On another film, the roles might easily be reversed or swapped.

The debt owed to the French system of film-making – not only the New Wave but its predecessors – by the new generation of American film-makers who were emerging in the late 1960s must be explicitly acknowledged. The flexibility of roles each film-maker played in French film-making was something Hollywood film production did not copy, but the new, young film-makers certainly did. In part this was because many had come through film school, where they were not only exposed to French cinema, but were also taught a range of different specialisations. In part, also, it was because some had made their own independent films, on which they were forced to perform many, if not most, tasks, before moving up to feature film direction. So, for example, we see Coppola acting as producer on writer/director George Lucas' *American Graffiti* (1973), and Lucas producing Coppola's *Tucker: The Man and His Dream* (1988).

Methodologically, also, the French were more used to the idea that directors might frequently be the writers of the films they made – René Clair, Jean Renoir, Jacques Tati, often or always wrote their own scripts. Hollywood directors did not tend to write their own scripts, as the writing process was controlled separately from the production process. Many, however, unofficially made important contributions to scripting as the production process went on. Significantly, as we will see, many of the new American film-makers, from the 1960s/70s to the present day – Coppola, Lucas, De Palma, Scorsese, Milius – were/are writers as well as directors. This does give them a greater chance of producing that personal vision which is so central to the auteur theory. Such a philosophy could, however, be abused in the interests of self-promotion, as Biskind notes of Robert Altman, for example: 'If he was truly going to be an auteur, he had to write the script as well or, since he wasn't a writer, at least derogate the contribution of the writer . . . Although he had initially praised Lardner's script [for *M*A*S*H*] in interviews, Altman now implied that he had discarded it and started from scratch' (Biskind, 1998; p.97).

Culturally, the French had always revered 'the artist' as an important figure in the psyche of the nation. It was possible within the smaller, more personalised environment for film-making offered by art cinema to see the director as more individual, and as more of a controlling force, than perhaps was the case within the American culture of mainstream cinema. The theory split film directors into two camps. In the first camp were the 'true artists', the *auteurs*, those artist-directors who put forward a coherent world-view in their films. In the second were the competent and accomplished film craftsmen: the *metteurs-en-scène*, the 'putters-in-the-scene', who were seen as having less of a personal view, and who simply displayed a mastery of cinematic technique and an ability to stage events efficiently for the camera.

There were several other reasons why the auteur theory had particular resonance within American film at the end of the 1960s. As mentioned in the opening chapter, the industry suffered a crisis between 1969 and 1971. Desperate studio executives looked to the new, young, film-makers alluded to earlier to rescue the industry. In this atmosphere of overreliance, of directors being given carte blanche in the hope that they would produce something new which would rejuvenate the industry, the belief in the director as the central governing force in the film-making process had to be foregrounded.

Many of these new writers and directors had graduated from the relatively new film courses springing up in colleges and universities across the country, such as New York University, the University of Southern California and the University of California. Although this phenomenon is considered in greater detail later, here I just want to flag that it was almost inevitable that the auteur theory, an intellectual, academic – certainly by the time it was imported into America – educated way of looking at films, would take hold within the arena of the emerging film courses. And therefore, it was also inevitable that the graduates of that environment would be centrally informed by the theory; they would see themselves and their future, in such terms. Again, they were being primed to enter the industry with a certain attitude which signalled change and a new order.

In many ways it is not surprising that the auteur theory succeeded in America in the late 1960s and early 1970s. It had originally been developed in post-Second World War Europe, in the face of a range of social and political systems that were seen to be no longer working and with an emphasis on the need for a new social world founded on the individual. These values seemed to touch a nerve, both politically and culturally, in the America of the late 1960s, beleaguered as it was by a set of increasingly insupportable political, social and economic crises. The war in Vietnam had caused increasing social unrest and protest throughout the decade, culminating in the killing of four protesting students at Kent State University by National Guardsmen in May 1970. Similarly, the civil rights protests against racism challenged American social values during the 1960s; resistance to the campaign resulted in the assassination of Martin Luther King in April 1968. Against this background, America looked increasingly towards individual expression and action as countermeasures to this apparent institutional corruption. Artists such as Andy Warhol (especially in his serious protest artworks such as *Birmingham Race Riot* [1964]), Bob Dylan (with his protest songs such as *The Times They Are A'Changin'*), Norman Mailer (*Why Are We in Vietnam?* [1967] and *The*

Dennis Hopper, Peter Fonda and Jack Nicholson being filmed on the road for *Easy Rider* (Dennis Hopper, 1969)

Armies of the Night [1968]), and Dennis Hopper and Peter Fonda in *Easy Rider* (1969), became the recognised voices of youth dissent. Certainly, the new American film-makers of the late 1960s and early 1970s were not slow to take on this mantle.

But the auteurist tendency in American film-making should not be seen as a monolithic entity. It has undergone phases of development and redefinition, partly defined by the changes and redefinitions of the economic and industrial reality of the industry in which it functions. It is almost possible to periodise it, though one must be careful in doing so not to become restrictive. Within this periodisation, an experimental phase might be identified between the late 1960s and the early 1970s, when new directors were given substantial artistic freedom because of the state of the film industry. Here we find Hopper and Fonda in *Easy Rider* (1969), Hopper in *The Last Movie* (1971) and, later, Henry Jaglom in *Tracks* (1976), playing with narrative structural and stylistic norms to produce films which refuse to adhere to the rules of mainstream film-making.

With the collapse of this idealistically radical film-making initiative by 1973 – partly because of industrial recovery and partly because the new directors of a few years before had become interested in making a larger kind of film – we move into a period which might be called the 'blockbuster with personal vision'. In this category we might list Coppola's *Apocalypse Now* (1979) and Michael Cimino's *Heaven's Gate* (1980), both huge films in every way – thematically, in terms of artistic ambition, in terms of budget (and overspend: *Apocalypse Now* eventually cost $25 million, *Heaven's Gate*, $36 million) and in production schedule (and schedule overruns). The advent of what might be termed the 'auteurist blockbuster' seemed to imply a direct clash of systems. Auteurist films are, almost by definition, small, intimate, personal; the blockbuster, again by definition, is large, usually epic, and involves large production crews.

Given this tension, it has proved very difficult to make such films succeed. A few directors, as we will see shortly, managed to forge a coherence between the two: Francis Ford Coppola, Steven Spielberg, Michael Cimino. But the return, and especially the massive success, of such auteurist blockbusters – *The Godfather* (Coppola, 1972); *Star Wars* (Lucas, 1977), *Close Encounters of the Third Kind* (Spielberg, 1977) – had severe repercussions within the industry, producing an ideology whereby big was always beautiful. Across the decade, average budgets rose from $1 million in 1971 to $11 million by 1980 (Puttnam with Watson, 2000; p.220). The result was fewer films, more money spent on each of them, more debt to the banks in order to do so, and more pressure on the director to come up with a sure-fire hit. From auteur to buck-stopper, the director became ultimately responsible for the winning or losing of millions and millions of dollars. The shift of emphasis, from the expression of an artistic vision to the garnering of massive financial return on a sub-stantial investment, as the main focus of a director's role during this period would result in a new kind of blockbuster emerging in the following decade.

The 1980s saw the emergence of the 'blockbuster without personal vision'; again, large-budget films but now lacking any intention of examining serious issues or subjects. In this category we might list the kind of film made by Don Simpson and Jerry Bruckheimer – big, loud, stunt-filled, action-dominated films designed to bludgeon their audiences into submission. Here, *Top Gun* (1986) and *Days of Thunder* (1990) spring to mind. This kind of film is certainly being maintained to the present day: *Con Air* (1997), *Armageddon* (1998) and *Pearl Harbor* (2001) are heirs to these films.

Two final points need to be raised on this issue. The first is that, as films grew bigger, more expensive, and more technologically complex, the leading directors were increasingly required at least partly to adopt the identity of managers of huge production complexes: Lucas's Industrial Light and Magic, Spielberg's Dreamworks, or Cameron's Lightstorm Entertainment and Digital Domain. The precursor to these director-led production houses is Francis Ford Coppola's Zoetrope Studio, a then technically cutting-edge facility, set up in 1980 to give the director total freedom to make his films, such as *One From the Heart* (1982). It is questionable whether this extra responsibility resulted in the additional loss of any remaining personal vision in their films or actually increased such vision, because they were now able to realise the images in their heads by more directly controlling the means of their creation. This will be considered a little later in the section on the director as studio head.

The second point is the argument that auteurism must inevitably be compromised by the conglomeration that is swallowing up the independent identity of the film industry as a separate entity. With films now being designed to function in many different, often contradictory arenas – cinema, television, video game, book, etc. – the decision making process which determines the shape and content of any given film can often take place at management/corporate level rather than at artistic/director level. In these circumstances, it is very hard to argue for a film being the expression solely of its director's vision.

In the past year or so, however, we may have been witnessing an end to this cycle of film-making. Peter Bart has charted the relative failure of the super-spectacle films, such as *Godzilla* (1998), and an audience shift towards smaller, more personal films, such as *The Truman Show* (1998), once again. Ben Affleck, one of the stars of the big-budget spectacular *Armageddon*, might appear in another big-budget spectacular action movie such as *Pearl Harbor*, but he also appears in *Bounce* (2000), a small film about love and personal relationships.

In the early 1970s, films – such as Lucas' *American Graffiti* (1973), Scorsese's *Mean Streets* (1973) and *Alice Doesn't Live Here Anymore* (1974), and Coppola's *The Rain People* (1969) and *The Conversation* (1974) – started to become smaller, more personal, more experimental. By the mid- to late-1970s, the demand was for bigger, more spectacular films, but dealing with serious issues: Spielberg's *Close Encounters of the Third Kind* (1977), Coppola's *Apocalypse Now* (1979), even Scorsese's misjudged *New York, New York* (1977). By the mid-1980s, a more visceral, escapist tendency was beginning to become dominant. The *Rambo* films, starring Sylvester Stallone, graphically chart this latter shift. The first of the series, *First Blood* (1982), while an action film in many ways, focuses also on Rambo's damaged psyche. By the third, *Rambo III* (1988), however, Stallone's character has been reduced to a cartoon killing-machine.

Such shifts are not determined by the directors alone. They are the result of the complex interaction between several interested parties: industry, audience and film-maker. The film industry undoubtedly requires periodic renewal in which the creation of a different kind of product is offered to its audiences as a means of increasing interest in the process of attending the movies. Certainly, also, audiences do get jaded with current fashions and styles and seek out the new. To take a very recent example:

[n]ot so long ago, the runaway success of American Pie, Road Trip, *and the slasher spoof* Scary Movie *seemed to show the more moronic a movie could be, the more money it made.*

Teenagers, who make up nearly half of all cinema audiences, could not get enough toilet humour or the kind of wince-inducing visual jokes in which a sperm sample is mistaken for hair gel.

There seemed to be no end to the trend . . . Until the past few weeks, when American adolescents have suddenly grown tired of politically incorrect comic gore, bouncing breasts and single entendres about Viagra that President George Bush has admitted he finds so amusing.

(Gibbons, 2001; p.5)

The idea that the director alone determines this is unacceptable within the realities of modern film-making, although it would also be an error to under-estimate his/her determining influence on the film's final visual and aural texture. Ultimately, however, it is important to recognise that it is at least as much the industry's response to the economic realities of the marketplace, as it is the director/artist's vision, that drives the creation of a new kind of film.

What is finally important about the auteur theory and its influence on the directors making films within the American film industry over the past three decades is not so much its long-term credibility within intellectual circles, nor its validity and believability within the American film industry generally. Its real significance lies in its continued hold on the minds of studio executives, the financiers, and the directors themselves, such that all believe the hype surrounding the role of the director as someone whose talent can make or break a film. This illusion of importance was created around 30 years ago and has been in place ever since, whether the film is big or small, emotionally real or special effects-laden. In an interview in *Wired* magazine in February 1997, George Lucas commented that: 'The problem with film is – who is the artist? Who is the author? Writers claim authorship; the director claims authorship; the producer claims authorship. Ultimately, somebody should be designated as the author' (Kelly and Parisi, 1997; pp.77, 102). It is perhaps significant that the context for his comments is the clarification of copyright ownership for financial purposes (i.e., who gets the royalties) rather than any marked sense of the film-maker as artist.

Perhaps we should take a step back from considering the complexities and influences of the auteur theory to explore the various routes via which the leading American film directors have come into the role. Although such routes are many and varied, the most important and prevalent are: theatre, television, writing, film school, and, as a more modern phenomenon, advertising and the pop promo.

ROUTES INTO DIRECTING

Theatre

Links between the role of the director in the American film industry and legitimate theatre have existed almost as long as cinema has. As Staiger points out, in the 'director' system of production, which took over from the cameraman system around 1907:

> one individual staged the action and another person photographed it. Moreover, the director managed a set of workers including the craftsman cameraman.
> The historical precedent for this system was the legitimate theatre and its stage director . . . Many of the early film directors came from stage acting experience: G.M. Anderson (with Selig from 1903), Hobart Bosworth (with David Belasco until hired by Selig in 1909), D.W. Griffith (with Biograph in 1907), Herbert Brenon (with IMP, 1909), Al Christie (with Nestor, 1909), and Sidney Olcott (with Kalem, 1907). When the 1907–8 shift to fictional narratives occurred, film production was able to take as a model the stage director who controlled the choices of scenery, and used a script as an 'outline' of the narrative.
>
> (Staiger, in Bordwell, Staiger and Thompson 1985; p.117)

As the American film industry entered its 'studio era', the theatre became an important source for directors who were being asked to maintain control over dramatic narratives which were unfolding over increasingly long performance lengths (eventually 'normalising' at between 90 minutes and two hours by the late silent period). Equally important, as films began to tell more complex, emotion-based stories, was the experience of theatre directors in working with actors to develop the psychological depth of characters demanded by the naturalistic style of play which had begun to dominate American theatre from the 1890s.

This became especially prevalent with the advent of synchronised sound cinema, when the ability to handle dialogue, as well as the dramatic flow of action, became an important and valuable skill in Hollywood. Scott Eyman notes, for example, that Paramount's B.P. Schulberg 'began importing theatre directors from New York to work side-by-side with experienced film-makers. The idea was that the veteran moviemakers would direct the camera, and the *arrivistes* from New York would handle the actors and the dialogue . . . Some of these dialogue specialists that Schulberg hired (George Cukor, John Cromwell) would go on to considerable careers of their own, although none would ever be noted as a visual stylist' (Eyman, 1999; pp.191–2). Throughout the studio period, figures who had gained a reputation for their theatre productions were invited by Hollywood to make films, with variable results.

Orson Welles, for example, who had run his own theatre company, the Mercury Theatre, before being invited to Hollywood, made films – *Citizen Kane* (1941), *The Magnificent Ambersons* (1942), *The Lady From Shanghai* (1948) – which were both cinematically and dramatically exciting.

The emergence, during the late 1940s and early 1950s, of a new style of theatre acting – Method – pioneered at New York acting schools like the Actors' Studio, also brought a new generation of directors interested in directing these method actors, in both theatre plays and movies: directors such as Elia Kazan. 'As the principal liaison between the students and techniques of Actors' Studio and the American cinema, Kazan's contribution and influence have been decisive; apart from "discovering" James Dean . . . Jack Palance, Lee Remick and Jo Van Fleet, among many others, he has directed some of the best performances ever recorded on film' (Rosenbaum, 1980; p.538). This emphasis on the naturalness of an actor's performance was taken a stage further by John Cassavetes, who trained as an actor at the American Academy of Dramatic Arts, where Stanislavskian and Method acting techniques were also taught, before appearing in TV drama series (Kraft Theatre and Lux Playhouse) and small film roles. He is famous for developing an improvisational acting style which, in turn, informed his cinematic style: 'Because his camera is so supple, and his characters and actors express themselves so imaginatively, Cassavetes' films give the impression of being improvised. But, in fact, except for *Shadows* [1959], all of his work is scripted. He filmed only after extensive rehearsals in which actors were encouraged to bring up suggestions' (Margulies, 1999; p.287).

The final figure I want to focus on is Sam Mendes, a British theatre director who became known through his productions with the Royal Shakespeare Company and *The Blue Room* at the Donmar Warehouse, which starred Nicole Kidman. The producers of his New York theatre production of *Cabaret* mentioned the production to Steven Spielberg, who asked to meet Mendes with a view to him directing *American Beauty* (1999), which Spielberg's Dreamworks had just picked up. They saw Mendes as having a very cinematic sense in the way he staged and composed action in a theatre space. In an interview, Mendes recounted that, as preparation for the film, he 'watched a lot of films . . . I imagined the movie and storyboarded it very thoroughly. Then I basically described what I wanted to see to as many people working on the film as I could, and it was their job to find a way of doing it' (Cercel, 1999; p.1). Mendes description of his entry into film direction is strongly reminiscent of the descriptions of the learning curve Orson Welles underwent in preparing to film *Citizen Kane*:

> *[Welles] assumed it was his job to set the lights – after all, wasn't that how he had worked in the theatre for the Mercury [Company]? No, it wasn't; people*

like Abe Feder had placed the lights there. But in New York Welles had picked up a reputation – deserved – for stage productions that were uncommonly cinematic in their lighting schemes.

But, as Welles told the story, Toland tactfully indulged that vanity, while quietly making adjustments behind the director's back to ensure that his wishes were fulfilled.

(Thomson, 1996; p.159)

Such was Mendes' inexperience that the first two days of filming on *American Beauty* had to be completely redone. In fact, when asked whether the production's script advisors had been helpful, Mendes replied: 'They stand next to you and tell you when you are about to make a terrible mistake. They dig you out of so many holes I can't tell you. They tell you when you are crossing the line or when continuity is threatened. They're also there to make sure you cover every scene and that you cover them well' (Anon, 2000a; p.1).

It is evident from Mendes' comments that theatre directors like him are assigned to direct feature films because of their skill in staging the physical action, and exploring the emotional relations between actors, rather than their technical film-making knowledge. We can see a continuity here between modern theatre directors such as Mendes who move into directing feature films, and their counterparts, like Welles, from previous periods of American film-making, as well as a recognition that the mechanics of film-making are to be retained by those specialists working wholly within the industry. In this way, the disruptive potential of non-professional creative personnel is absorbed and made to work to Hollywood's advantage. Finally, it is a possible marker of Hollywood's need for directors who are readers of human emotion rather than stage-managers of grand-scale, but emotionally empty, action. In this way, not only will product differentiation (something for everyone) be maintained, but the wildest excesses of the dumbing-down process with which Hollywood is so constantly charged in this age of the blockbuster action film, will be avoided.

Television (1950s–60s)

As mentioned in the first chapter, television posed a serious threat to cinema from the early 1950s onwards. The two were essentially different media, especially in those early years. Film-making, now that it had become standardised, industrialised and was expected to have high production values, was a painstakingly slow process, with each shot separately set up and filmed. Furthermore, the whole work was recorded onto film, and was therefore a past event by the time it came to be watched by audiences in the cinema. Television, in contrast, and certainly at that time, was almost invariably live: the actors actually playing their parts and saying their lines as the audience watched them on their television sets at home. This production-reality demanded of television directors a different set of talents and values from their colleagues in film: ability to work under intense pressure, speed of planning and decision-making during production and broadcast, the ability to improvise when things went wrong, which they often did.

> *The structure of these plays related to circumstances under which they were produced. Such problems as costume changes and ageing were unwelcome. This encouraged plays of tight structure, attacking a story close to its climax – very different from the loose, multi-scene construction of films.*
>
> *Ingenuity could ease the limitations. An actress could start a play wearing three dresses and peel them off en route between scenes. Colour lighting could make painted wrinkles invisible in one scene, emphasise them in the next . . .*
>
> *When a play involved a number of sets, these were generally arranged around the periphery of the studio. In the middle the cameras – three or more – wheeled noiselessly from set to set, each tended by its cameraman, and each trailing behind it a long, black umbilical cord leading to the control room. Each camera had a turret of several lenses, so that its cameraman could, in a second or two, switch from close up to medium or long shot.*
>
> *(Barnouw, 1990; pp.160–1)*

Television also differed in the amount of product it needed to satisfy its audience. Even in its early years, television broadcast several hours a day, every day. For a long while, there was a serious shortage of programmes and creative personnel to make them. This gap opened up all manner of possibilities for newcomers to enter the business and to get a foot in the door of directing, and many of the most prominent directors of the period covered by this book took this route into the film business. Indeed, as television drama developed, more and more of it, as with some of the examples listed below (for example, the *Hitchcock Presents* and *The Alfred Hitchcock Hour* episodes and the Western series), came to be recorded on film rather than played live. In this way, television *explicitly* became a training ground for directors wanting to enter the film industry.

Arthur Penn, John Frankenheimer, Sydney Pollack, Robert Altman and Sam Peckinpah all came through this route. Penn worked both in theatre and live television in the 1950s, directing many single television plays such as *Tears of My Sisters* for Gulf Playhouse in August 1953, *Man on the Mountaintop* for Philco TV Playhouse in October 1953 and *Invitation to a Gunfighter* for Playhouse 90 in March 1957. John Frankenheimer's television work included several plays for Playhouse 90 (including *Forbidden Area* in October 1956, and *Days of Wine and Roses* in October 1958) as well as *The Browning Version* for Dupont Show of the Month in April 1959. Pollack directed *The Contest of Aaron Gold* for *Alfred Hitchcock Presents* in May 1965. In 1957, Robert Altman also landed a job on *Alfred Hitchcock Presents*, directing several episodes, including *Young One*, which aired in December of that year. Peckinpah, perhaps unsurprisingly, considering his later focus on the Western in his feature films, also concentrated on that genre on television, making several episodes of the series *Gunsmoke* (*Legal Revenge*, November 1956; *Poor Pearl*, December 1956), *The Rifleman* (*Home Ranch* and *The Marshall*, both in October 1958, and for both of which he wrote the script as well as directing) and *The Westerner*. In addition, he directed many single Western dramas, including *End of a Gun* for Twentieth Century-Fox Hour in January 1957.

Bob Rafelson worked at Channel 13 on its *Play of the Week* show, before going to Hollywood and working at Revue Productions, the television arm of Universal. William Friedkin, director of *The Exorcist* (1973), began his working life at WGN-TV in Chicago and innumerable local television stations before also moving to Los Angeles in 1965, where he directed the last ever episode of *The Alfred Hitchcock Hour* – *Off Season* – in October 1965. Even Steven Spielberg, now so fundamentally identified with the movie business, began in television. He directed several episodes of *Night Gallery*, including his TV debut in 1969, *Eyes*, starring Joan Crawford, an episode of *Columbo* (*Murder By the Book*) in 1971 and several feature-length television movies (*Something Evil*, for CBS Friday Night Movie and *Savage*, for NBC World Premiere Movie, both in 1972). The most famous of his tele-films, *Duel* (1973), was deemed so accomplished that it was released in cinemas. This tradition has been maintained to the current day. Mimi Leder directed the feature films *The Peacemaker* (1997) and *Deep Impact* (1998), for example, after having worked as a script editor, cinematographer and, finally, director of episodes on the television series *LA Law* and *ER*, as well as numerous feature-length television movies. The link between her television work, mostly for Warner Bros., and her movie work, for Warner Bros.' film division, indicates a productive symbiosis between the film and television branches of modern conglomerates.

What values did these directors learn from working in television? As already indicated, live television called for quick preparation, improvisation, ability to handle pressure, and discipline both personally and in terms of cast and crew control. Even the shifts from live to recorded television (with the advent of videotape in the late 1950s and early 1960s) and from series production to made-for-TV features, did not alter the sense of pressure and speed about making product for television. 'Most *Cheyenne* [a popular western series of the mid-1950s] films were shot in five days, with many economy measures'

(Barnouw, 1990; p.194). Although the adoption of videotape did substantially alter the concept of 'the take' from a one-off unrepeatable thing to something that could be done again if required, it did not substantially change the amount of time a director was given to make the programme. Nor did made-for-television feature-length films, although they allowed directors to work on longer stories, give them significantly longer production schedules or larger crews. Steven Spielberg, for example, was given eight days to shoot his debut television film, *Eyes*, in 1972 (Baxter, 1996; p.58). Television has remained a medium demanding shorter production times, more speed, less luxury. Therefore, while the two media were in many ways exact opposites, these qualities required of television directors made them attractive to film studio executives wanting films produced as quickly and cheaply as possible.

Television demands a particular aesthetic to work with its reduced screen size: close shots, an emphasis on the human and physical and verbal interaction rather than on spectacular and expansive surroundings. When television directors began to filter into the film industry in the 1960s and 1970s, they brought with them this aesthetic sensibility and, even though part of the reason for their move into feature film direction was to replace speed and cheapness with the luxury or time and money to spend on a production, the films they made retained elements of the television training they had received. So we can see the gritty rawness of Friedkin's *The French Connection* (1971), for example, as stemming from his work in television, although the contribution to the look of the film made by its cinematographer Owen Roizman should not be undervalued. Spielberg's reputation as a fast worker, gained from television, helped secure his first feature film directing jobs on *Sugarland Express* (1974) and *Jaws* (1975) (it is especially ironic in this context that, because of the considerable technical difficulties involved in the latter, shooting on it was unbearably slow).

The relationship between television and film oscillates across the period. In the 1950s it was attractive to work in television because it was seen as the up-and-coming medium, and a more likely bet if one were looking for more career security than the cinema, which seemed to be in decline, could offer. Nowadays, it has become respectable again to work in television, even if only as a star guest director. David Lynch's weird and wonderful *Twin Peaks* (1990) was sold on the basis of his reputation, even though he directed only a few episodes; Quentin Tarantino's guest spot as director of an episode of *ER* was similarly hyped. Oliver Stone produced a fairly successful mini-series in the early 1990s – *Wild Palms* – about the then hot subject, virtual reality. In September 1999, Francis Ford Coppola announced that his American Zoetrope company had signed a deal with the Canadian company Alliance Atlantis and Viacom Productions to develop television shows: a police drama series for CBS, six mini-series and eight television movies.

The movement of personnel between film and television has been facilitated by the interesting relationship between studios, independent producers working in close association with a studio and the television arms of that studio. This triangular relationship began in the 1950s as studios went into television production and as more producers and directors began to go freelance, and has increased with the efforts of the big media conglomerates to own film and television concerns under the one umbrella. Material and personnel are thereby constantly able to flow between these three poles; freedom and flexibility which has opened up opportunity for movement between television and feature film-making for those, like Steven Spielberg or Mimi Leder, who have wanted to make the shift.

Growth of film schools (1960s–70s)

The late 1960s and 1970s saw the emergence and rapid expansion of film courses within the humanities departments of universities as well as dedicated practical film courses at specialist universities. Francis Ford Coppola attended the graduate film programme at UCLA; George Lucas took the animation programme at the University of Southern California (USC), the same university that John Milius attended. Martin Scorsese went to New York University (NYU), where he took courses on film history. 'In 1973 there were about 613 film courses running in American universities and colleges, 186 more than in 1971 . . . [serving] a 22,466-strong multitude of students prepar[ing] to take a university diploma or a degree on some aspect of film-making' (Toeplitz, 1975; p.94). Graduation from such institutions was not, by any stretch of the imagination, a guarantee of employment. The major studios remained as impenetrable as ever. The most graduates could expect was work producing short films or educational television or, if they were 'lucky', low-budget exploitation films.

By common agreement, the person who first achieved the breakthrough was Francis Ford Coppola. At UCLA, Coppola expressed an interest in the more esoteric elements of the film-making process such as writing, drama and performance rather than in sheer technical proficiency, an interest which set him up to be a true auteur rather than a *metteur-en-scène*. While still at UCLA, Coppola began work for Roger Corman, writing, editing, acting as dialogue director, before being allowed to make his own film, *Dementia 13* (1963) on a minuscule budget. He worked as a writer for Seven Arts for the whole of the 1960s, before scripting *Patton* (1970) and *The Great Gatsby* (1974). He financed his first real film, *You're a Big Boy Now* (1967), with his own money (although Seven Arts soon took over the costs). He started the way he meant to go on, outside studio control. But in a move that casts some doubt on his claim at that time to be an auteur director, he then made *Finian's*

Rainbow (1968), based on a traditional Broadway show from the 1940s. We might perhaps take this as an example of how the 'revolution' in Hollywood was not as immediate or one-way as has traditionally been thought. On the set of *Finian's Rainbow*, however, he met George Lucas, who had also gone to film school: they were the only two personnel on the production to have done so.

Coppola's next film, *The Rain People* (1969), had no finished script as the film went into production, and a production schedule that was at least partly improvised as it went along. One can see *The Rain People* as an example of the kind of low-budget, small film, studios were beginning to favour in the aftermath of the 1969–71 industry crisis. Seven Arts financed the film partly because it had an acceptable, if modest-sized, star in Shirley Knight, and only cost $750,000, a very low figure for that period. *The Godfather*, released in 1972, was a studio product, financed by Paramount for $6 million, packaged as an event movie with inflated seat prices and saturation release. It returned its negative cost within days, and went into profit within weeks (Pye and Myles, 1979; p.90) Following the massive, but rather impersonal, success of *The Godfather*, Coppola made *The Conversation* (1974), a personal project which became a critical achievement (it won the Best Film prize at Cannes). Opinion is divided as to exactly how auteurist it is; considering the importance of sound in the film, its editor, Walter Murch, is credited with at least as much input and influence on the finished film as Coppola.

> *Essentially, Francis left me on my own . . . In the whole last half of the film there are only about five lines of actual dialogue, other than the conversation itself. It's a matter of exclamation rather than dialogue. All the content of the film is being carried by the sound. The material wasn't paced out, it wasn't itemised in the script. Shots were shot, and I structured them*

> *(quoted in Pye and Myles, 1979; p.99)*

Five years later, at the other end of the production scale and after the massive financial success of the first two *Godfather* films, Coppola was making *Apocalypse Now* (1979): grandiose logistics, substantially over budget and over schedule. Finally, in an attempt to permanently remain truly independent, he set up Zoetrope Studios, a small studio complex in which he planned to develop a new way of making movies using cutting-edge electronic technology. The first result of this, however – *One From the Heart* (1982) – was a disaster and box-office flop, and left him substantially in debt and facing many years as a jobbing director.

Jon Lewis suggests that 'Coppola has always been a far more important and far better film-maker than businessman' (Lewis, 1995; p.164). But Coppola's considerable efforts to manipulate the financial and industrial conditions within which he made his films, to the point of sinking all his money into a small studio in an attempt to break free of the majors' control, together with his many artistic and commercial failures, makes one wonder if his auteurist credentials lay more in business matters rather than artistic vision. Certainly, he was intent on establishing something new, something anti-system, something alternative. But the degree to which he has succeeded in this is debatable, given that he has repeatedly had to agree to direct impersonal studio films – for example, *Peggy Sue Got Married* (1986), *The Godfather III* (1990) and *Bram Stoker's Dracula* (1992) – in order to bail himself out of his perennial financial crises. This oscillation, between film artist, jobbing director, and sometime independent studio head, gives Coppola an awkward, almost unique, position within the modern American film industry. Indeed, rather than an oscillation – first one kind of film-making, then the other – we should see Coppola's 'awkwardness' as emanating instead from a combination of art film and mainstream styles of film-making. From this perspective, we must view his films as displaying a tension between conventional narrative demands and the foregrounding of a signature style: the mark of the auteur (Lewis, 1995; pp.145–6). In this way, we can perhaps see the figure of Coppola as, if no longer a bestriding Colossus, then at least as a bridge across three decades of American film-making which has seen a constant play in the tension between art and mainstream cinema.

His friend George Lucas, with an interest in art, painting, and comic strips, entered the USC film course, initially focusing on animation, then cinematography, before finally settling on editing; thus demonstrating the all-tasks training of film school graduates that I mentioned earlier. At this time, Lucas was professing a serious interest in European directors (especially Godard, Truffaut and Fellini), and American avant-garde film-makers (such as Jordan Belson), both of which would indicate his auteurist credentials. While still a student, Lucas made the now-cult film *THX–1138:4EB* (1967), which he then remade with studio financing when Warner Bros. were persuaded, by Coppola, to back his new friend. The original film was much shorter and more enigmatically poetic, the longer version more conventionally structured. At Coppola's insistence, Lucas persevered with the screenplay, using it as a learning exercise in how to construct a feature-length film narrative. The latter film exhibits a tension between the almost abstract poetic visuals of the first, shorter, version, and the wider narrative demands of character and event development in the depiction of a sterile and authoritarian society of the future. Neither Lucas nor Warner Bros. was satisfied with the result.

His next film, *American Graffiti* (1973), was certainly personal. Lucas had difficulty getting the film green-lighted. By 1973 the executives' faith in the new auteurs had begun to dwindle in the face of continued box-office, if not failure, then at least lack of substantial success. Lucas had a similarly hard time getting *Star Wars* (1977) financed. The financiers had little belief that the film would do any more than adequate business, and forced a very tight budget on Lucas; which he then proceeded to exceed greatly in the effort to complete the complex and ground-breaking special effects on which the film depended for its impact.

It is Lucas' preoccupation with the films' merchandising tie-ins which is more interesting in the long term than any 'personal vision' which might be assigned to the visuals or content of his films, especially the *Star Wars* saga. The *Star Wars* films are more significant in terms of the way the possibilities of replicating images and characters from the film were built into their very creation. 'Normally you just sign a standard contract with a studio, but we wanted merchandising, sequels, all those things. I didn't ask for another $1 million, just the merchandising rights. And Fox thought that was a fair trade' (Pye and Myles, 1979; p.132). Lucas' vision in this sense was far ahead of that of the studio executives, who were virtually giving away the rights to the merchandising until Lucas stepped in and stopped them. Lucas' serious attitude towards the modern movie deal, in terms of the importance of merchandising, can be seen from his setting up of Lucasfilm Ltd in 1971 to handle all ancillary marketing matters. Later, in an attempt to capitalise on and control the growing importance of special effects in both his own films and those of the industry as a whole, Lucas set up a state-of-the-art special effects house, Industrial Light and Magic (ILM), in 1975.

As with Coppola, then, it is possible to argue that Lucas's originality lies as much, if not more so, in his business sense as in his artistic sensibility. For both men, business is as important as art. Coppola has run his own studio and maintained an intermittent independence, becoming jobbing director only when required to earn enough money to attempt to maintain his freedom from studio control. Lucas has built an industrial facility (ILM) and a merchandising empire as important support structures to his movie-making activities which are, on the whole, somewhat impersonal exercises. One feels, for example, that it was the technical challenge and financial implications of *Star Wars Episode I: The Phantom Menace* (1999) which engaged Lucas, rather than the drama or message contained within the narrative. The all-digital special effects environment would allow him to produce further prequels and sequels of the *Star Wars* saga for substantially less than conventional film-based methods would: between $60 and $70 million per film, as opposed to $120–140 million using conventional film technologies (Kelly and Parisi, 1997; p.74). Lucas is undoubtedly a major film-making figure, but his significance lies far more in what he has helped to change about the mechanics and financial set-up of the film-making process, than in the artistic quality of the films he has produced as a result.

Martin Scorsese is perhaps the film-maker who has retained his auteurist label more than the other film school graduates of his generation. Self-confessedly enamoured with cinema as a child and youth, he enrolled at NYU Film School in 1960, after studying, briefly, for the priesthood. There he was introduced to the auteur theory by his lecturers: an intellectual 'breath of fresh air' as he later put it. Certainly, his early influences, which included European directors such as Godard and Truffaut, confirm his interest and acceptance of the theory. 'What Godard was showing was new ways to use images to tell a story, new ways to shoot, to cut. In *Vivre Sa Vie*, when the guy comes into the record store where Anna Karina works, says "I want some Judy Garland," the camera tracks her all the way across the store as she goes and takes an album out of the top shelf and then goes all the way back. Little things like that suddenly open up your mind to other ways of doing things, not two people in a frame talking. There was a kind of joy that burst into me when I saw the movies by these guys' (Biskind, 1998; p.228). The British film-maker Michael Powell was another strong influence, leading to Scorsese's lengthy campaign to rehabilitate Powell within the industry:

> There was a programme on American television in the Fifties called 'Million Dollar Movie', which would show the same film twice in weekday evenings and three times on Saturday and Sunday. This was where I first saw The Tales of Hoffman: cut, with commercials and in black and white. I was mesmerised by the music and camera movements, and by the theatrical gestures of the actors. When we were doing Taxi Driver and the close-ups of De Niro's face, I shot these faster than usual, at 36 and 48 frames per second still under the influence of Robert Helpmann's reaction shot during the duel on the gondola.
>
> (forward by Scorsese in Christie, 1985; p.11)

He was also influenced by the still relatively new Direct Cinema movement of documentary film-making which had been pioneered in America by film-makers such as D.A. Pennebaker and Richard Leacock. The raw, unpolished filming of fly-on-the-wall, real slice-of-life material being practised by them would directly influence Scorsese, certainly in his first few films such as *Mean Streets* (1973) and *Taxi Driver* (1976).

Scorsese struggled to get going in the film business after graduating, largely because he insisted on sticking to his principles rather than compromising by, for example, taking jobs in television like some of his peers (although, as Biskind indicates [1998; p.57], he did show a slight interest in *The Monkees* television series, through his friendship with Bob Rafelson). Indicative of this determination was his four-year ordeal to make his first, self-financed feature (his father paid the lab fees), *Who's That Knocking at My Door?* between 1966 and 1970, produced by his NYU tutor, Haig Manoogian. *Mean Streets* (1973), a low-budget, raw and gritty feature about petty thieves in Little Italy, was his breakthrough film, and his reputation was established when he made *Taxi Driver* in 1976. His career to date has seen him mix conventionally mainstream films, such as *Color of Money* (1986) and *Cape Fear* (1991), with films more personal to him, such as *The Last Temptation of Christ* (1988), *Goodfellas* (1990) and *Kundun* (1997). But whether any one film is a mainstream or personal project, Scorsese always sees himself as a Hollywood director: Christie records him saying at a question and answer session in 1997, 'I am an American director, which means I am a Hollywood director' (Thompson and Christie, 1996; pp.xvii–xviii). What is most significant, perhaps, is the way in which this oscillation between mainstream and art cinema shows the flexible boundaries between the two and the difficulty of labelling a director as firmly and solely in one camp or the other.

Paul Schrader became involved in film writing via film courses at Columbia in the summer of 1966 and a job reviewing films in the *LA Free Press* (interestingly, he lost his job there for panning *Easy Rider*). In 1968, he then went to UCLA film school with the help of Pauline Kael, before writing *Taxi Driver*, which Martin Scorsese filmed in 1976. He has subsequently written/directed films including *Blue Collar* (1978), *American Gigolo* (1980) and *Mishima* (1985). Significantly, Schrader has also written *about* the cinema (as has Scorsese, with his 'Personal History of the Cinema' project): including a book on the 'transcendental' film style of the French film-maker Robert Bresson, the Danish film-maker Carl Dreyer, and the Japanese director Yasujiro Ozu.

Later generations of film school graduates include Oliver Stone, who was taught at NYU by Scorsese. Stone's career is perhaps the one which has mostly closely maintained its auteurist credentials. His almost obsessive working through of political and conspiracy theories – whether of US covert involvement in *Salvador* (1986), government involvement in John Kennedy's assassination in *JFK* (1991), or his attack on the invidious role played by the media in the construction of gun-happy hero-villains in *Natural Born Killers* (1994) – indicates a thematic and formal consistency of vision.

The importance of the film schools is that they helped educate the generation of film-makers coming into the business from the early 1970s, in the history and theory of cinema. They had an intellectual distance from it that was to have a major impact on what kinds of films were going to be made and their self-conscious sense of style. Lucas and Spielberg directly reference the sci-fi and action B-movies of the 1940s in the *Star Wars* and Indiana Jones series of films; in *New York, New York* (1977), Scorsese makes explicit references to the MGM musicals of the 1940s and 1950s. Brian De Palma makes an extended play on the Odessa Steps sequence from Eisenstein's

Battleship Potemkin (1925) in *The Untouchables* (1987). Indeed, De Palma is the figure who perhaps represents this tendency more than anyone else, because he has virtually founded his career on parodying the style and content of other directors. Alfred Hitchcock's voyeurism and misogyny are echoed in *Sisters* (1973) and *Body Double* (1984), both owing a debt to *Rear Window* (1954), *Obsession* (1976) was a film indebted to *Vertigo* (1958), and *Dressed to Kill* (1980), a film which married 'Hitchcockian suspense with 1980s-style sex and gore' (Cook, 1998; p.29). *Blow Out* (1981) contains allusions to the dark conspiracy elements in Welles' *Touch of Evil* (1958) and Antonioni's *Blow-up* (1966), as well as Coppola's *The Conversation* (1974). *Scarface* (1983) is a remake of Howard Hawks' 1932 original, but with more 1980s-style sex and gore added (the scene showing, off screen, the chainsaw killing of the main character's friend in a shower, is justifiably infamous). In the 1990s, De Palma eased off on such overt and often heavy-handed movie references. *Carlito's Way* (1993), for example, is a stylish and modern account of a gangster trying, but finding he is not to be allowed, to go straight; *Mission: Impossible* (1996) is a hi-tech, all-action blockbuster adapted from the cult TV series, and starring Tom Cruise. Perhaps this tailing off of the explicit referencing of film history indicates that it was to some degree a phenomenon of a certain time, when a generation of film-makers fresh out of film school were filled with the excitement of discovering the past classics of world cinema.

The growth of film courses provided a double influence on the way films were produced and received in America from the 1970s onwards. Practical film-making courses in universities trained a new kind of film-maker in all aspects of the craft, as well as framing that practical knowledge within a critical and historical understanding of their field. Secondly, film studies courses, in which cinema was *studied* rather than films actually made, helped produce a generally intellectually inclined and educated audience for films, ready to read the films in terms of their artistic pretensions and, because of the acceptance of auteurism, with an interest in their directors. Today, most young independent film-makers are graduates of America's film schools: Spike Lee, Jim Jarmusch and Tom DiCillo (*Living in Oblivion*, 1995; *Double Whammy*, 2001) went to NYU and James Gray (*Little Odessa*, 1994; *The Yards*, 2000) to USC.

Advertising and pop promos

A later generation of potential candidates for the job of film director came from the field of advertising. In the 1970s, for example, Ridley Scott, his brother Tony Scott, and Alan Parker, having established their reputations in television and film advertising, made the move into feature film production. The increase in the numbers of such candidates is directly linked to the increasing shift from print-based advertising to audio-visual-based advertising during the 1970s. The generation of high-gloss, high-production value advertisements, designed to make their products irresistible, trained a new generation of film-makers to focus on the seductive qualities of image in the service of a nominal narrative line. This focus, greatly expanded, would help to account for the 'triumph' of style and spectacle over story in the special-effects blockbusters which have come to dominate the industry since the mid-1980s. What this line of training has also produced in its 'graduates' is an interest in visual conceits: simple visual ideas that make a quick, clever, instantly understandable point.

The high-quality visuals so typical of the top adverts have, since the mid-1980s, increasingly been produced using computerised imaging technologies. It is easy to make the link from those film-makers working in advertising in the 1980s and the development of digital effects technology in advertising at the same time, to directors making high-concept, special-effects movies in the 1990s. By the time they had worked their way high enough up the ladder of importance, the computer technology had finally been developed fully enough to perform the task. Take, as an example, Ridley Scott, who, having made hundreds of commercials in the 1970s, moved into feature film direction by directly transporting the soft-focus, romantic look of his Hovis bread adverts into his first feature, *The Duellists* (1977). His advertisement for Apple Computers, a parody of George Orwell's *1984* which suggested that IBM and Big Brother were one and the same, had a sensational screening during the Superbowl, and helped instigate the Macintosh revolution. The high tech blue-sheen look of the commercial can be seen to have directly influenced the similar look of Scott's *Alien* (1979). In recent years, Spike Lee has made advertisements for Nike, and Martin Scorsese for Armani, but these film-makers are doing so not so much out of financial need as personal belief, whether political, as in Lee's focus on black American athletes like Michael Johnson, or simply style-statement, in Scorsese's case.

The influence of pop promos on the film industry is more recent but equally important to the look and style of many contemporary films. Pop promos are short, intense and, like advertisements, have an emphasis on high-gloss images. They also have a foregrounded sound layer. Images are edited to the beat of the music; music is used to motivate the visuals. Like advertisements, pop promos invariably have elementary storylines, depend for their success on immediate effects – a kind of impact aesthetics in which each new work has to top the spectacular visuals and effects of its predecessors. Moreover, pop promos are, obviously, targeted towards the young audience that is the primary purchaser of the products to which they make reference. The influx of pop promo makers into the film business might at least partly have been intensified as a result of ever younger executives coming to run the major film studios. Their natural frame of reference is a pop culture one, a context that must incline them towards pop promo-makers who relate more closely to their young audiences.

As with advertising, the look and feel of pop promo visual style have been absorbed into feature film production. Many of the big-budget films are becoming more collections of self-contained sequences rather than fully worked-out, coherent narratives. Further, many of these sequences have an overdetermined relationship between their audio and visual layers. A good example here would be the work of Russell Mulcahy, who made many music videos between 1979 and 1986, notably for Duran Duran (*Rio* and *Hungry Like a Wolf*, both 1982; *The Wild Boys*, 1984), Spandau Ballet (*Musclebound*, 1981; *True*, 1983) and Queen (*A Kind of Magic* and *Princes of the Universe*, both 1986). His work for Queen feeds directly, stylistically speaking, into his two Highlander films (*Highlander*, 1986 and *Highlander II – The Quickening*, 1990), both of which are notable for their set-piece action sequences, their use of Queen's music, and highly stylised images, to maximise emotional affect at strategic moments during their narratives.

A more recent exponent is Michael Bay, who spent his twenties working in both advertising and music videos, making advertisements for Nike, Reebok, Coca-Cola, Budweiser and Miller Lite, and picking up numerous awards for the visual quality of his work. His work in music videos includes those made for Tina Turner (*Nutbush City Limits*, 1991; *Love Thing*, 1992); Meatloaf (*I'd Do Anything For Love*, 1993; *Rock and Roll Dreams Come True*, 1994), and Lionel Richie (*Do It To Me*, 1992). Again, it is relatively easy to make the link from these high-profile, slickly imaged, edited-to-music works to his high-action, visceral, music-led, feature films such as *The Rock* (1996) and *Armageddon* (1999). Similarly, David Fincher directed a number of big-budget videos for the Rolling Stones (*Love Is Strong*), Madonna (*Express Yourself* and *Vogue*) and Aerosmith (*Jamie's Got a Gun*), before making his feature film debut with *Alien³* in 1992, a film which has been criticised for its lack of narrative coherence and overelaborated visual qualities.

It is also important to recognise that the direction of travel between directing advertisements, making pop promos and feature film direction is not only one-way. Film directors often make pop promos after having established themselves as feature film directors. A notable early example of this would be John Landis who, having made *American Werewolf in London* in 1982, was invited to make Michael Jackson's *Thriller* (1983) video. More recent notables include Joel Schumacher (*Letting the Cables Sleep* for Bush, 1999) and Abel Ferrara (*Don't Change Your Plans* for the Ben Folds Five, 1999). The back-catalogue of Spike Jonze is perhaps the most impressive, spanning the years 1992 to 2000, for artists such as the Beastie Boys (*Sabotage* and *Sure Shot*, both 1994; *Root Down*, 1998), REM (*Crush With Eyeliner*, 1995; *Electrolite*, 1997), the Notorious B.I.G. (*It's All About the Benjamins*, as part of Puff Daddy and the Family, and *Sky's the Limit*, both 1997) and Fatboy Slim (*The Rockafeller Skank* and *Praise You*, both 1998).

WOMEN DIRECTORS

It has probably not escaped the reader's notice that the vast majority of directors discussed in this chapter are male. The American film industry, even in these liberated days, is overwhelmingly controlled and operated by men. Such has always been the way, although the early years of cinema saw a greater number of women in important positions in the industry. Screenwriters such as Frances Marion and directors such as Lois Weber, Alice Guy-Blaché and Lillian Gish made important contributions to American cinema throughout the early period. During the studio era, a later generation of women directors, such as Dorothy Arzner (director: *Christopher Strong*, 1933; *Dance Girl Dance*, 1940) and Ida Lupino (actress and director: *Outrage*, 1950; *Hard, Fast and Beautiful*, 1951) did the same, carving out respectable careers within the patriarchal structure of Hollywood.

The case of Lupino highlights a favoured route into directing for women in Hollywood: that is, to move into it from acting. Into the contemporary period, a number of female stars have become directors after having established themselves as powerful figures in the industry through their star-status. Barbra Streisand led the way with *Yentl* (1983), which she also co-wrote and co-produced, and *The Prince of Tides* (1991). Penny Marshall, after an early career as a comedienne in TV shows such as *Happy Days* and *Laverne and Shirley* (she directed several episodes of the latter), has directed several notable features. *Big* (1988), became the first feature by a woman director to break the $100 million barrier at the American box office; *Awakenings* (1990) and *A League of Their Own* (1992) were also successful, making Marshall a solid and dependable director. Jodie Foster has mixed her acting career with occasional forays into directing; for example, *Little Man Tate* (1991), and *Home for the Holidays* (1995) both of which were more critical than box-office successes. Similarly, actress Diane Keaton has directed in both television and film; her television work including a guest spot directing an episode of *Twin Peaks* (1990) and *Pasadena*, a TV series made in 2001. Her films as director include *Heaven* (1987), and *Hanging Up* (2000), a bigger-budget production starring Keaton, Meg Ryan and Lisa Kudrow from the popular TV sitcom *Friends*.

A particularly interesting mainstream woman director is Nancy Meyers, who has scripted many of the more significant women-centred films of the last 20 years. *Private Benjamin* (1980) and *Protocol* (1984), both starred Goldie Hawn (a significant player in modern Hollywood) as a slightly eccentric woman operating in male-dominated arenas of the military and the diplomatic corps, respectively. *Baby Boom* (1987) and *Father of the Bride I* (1991) and *II* (1997) take a gentle look at women as mothers in the modern American family. Most significant, perhaps, is her latest film, *What Women Want* (2000), starring Mel Gibson and Helen Hunt, in which, as the title suggests, the issues surrounding what women really feel about, and want from, men are explored, again in terms of gentle comedy. The gentleness of the comedy, however, does not necessarily mean that these films do not offer pertinent observations about women in contemporary America.

Other women film-makers have been working in a similar vein. For example, Jocelyn Moorhouse began her directing career in Australia, with *Proof* (1991; distributed by Fine Line in the US), before coming to America to make *How To Make An American Quilt* (1995) and *A Thousand Acres* (1997). *American Quilt*, especially, shows how women directors can make mainstream films for a predominantly female audience (it was specifically made to be released during the American hosting of the World Cup, to give women something to go to while their partners were watching football). Starring Winona Ryder and financed by Amblin and Universal, the film focuses on a group of women who recount their past loves as they make the quilt of the title. The relative lack of action – there is a love-interest sub-plot, but it is of secondary importance except as a catalyst for the story-telling – throws attention fully onto the interrelations between the women.

However, it has to be borne in mind that, within mainstream American film-making, very few women directors are given the kinds of big-budget projects regularly entrusted to their male counterparts. Of contemporary directors, perhaps only Mimi Leder, with films like *The Peacemaker* (1997) and *Deep Impact* (1998) (the latter assigned to her only after Steven Spielberg, significantly, withdrew from the project in order to make *Saving Private Ryan*), has been given the kinds of budget that would habitually be given to directors such as Michael Bay (*The Rock*, 1996 and *Armageddon*, 1998), and Barry Sonnenfeld (*Men in Black*, 1997). No doubt this is largely due to a combination of paternalism and misogyny: the mistaken, but prevalent, feeling that the overwhelming pressures which accompany projects upon which hundreds of millions of dollars ride are too great for women to handle. As Hillier notes several prominent women directors observing, Hollywood is still a largely unreconstructed male stronghold:

> *Most women film-makers feel to some degree that they are participating in an activity whose terms and conditions seem predominantly male, particularly in the all-important process of setting movies up. Producer Gale Anne Hurd talks*

of 'the boys-only club' and Susan Seidelman of the industry being 'a bit of a boys' club', while Amy Jones talks of the 'game' being 'very male.'

(Hillier, 1992; p. 127)

The lack of women in top positions also undoubtedly militates against women being assigned to the biggest films of any year.

Nor is there any doubt that the continuing 'blockbuster mentality' of mainstream American film-making – with its fixation with explosion-ridden, all-action narratives featuring white male heroes – almost automatically favours male directors over their female counterparts. This is in spite of Kathryn Bigelow's spirited attempts to dismantle this particular presupposition:

Conventionally, hardware pictures, action-oriented, have been male-dominated, and more emotional kind of material has been women's domain. That's breaking down. This notion that there's a woman's aesthetic, a woman's eye, is really debilitating. It ghettoises women . . . [Women] should just be encouraged to work in as uncompromised form as possible, be that tougher or softer.

(quoted in Hillier, 1992; p.127)

To date, only Bigelow herself, in a limited way, and Mimi Leder, in a more substantial one, have made action narratives with male characters as their central guiding force. (See Chapter 6, on independent American cinema, for more on Kathryn Bigelow.)

Given the resistance of mainstream Hollywood to women film-makers making high-action, big-budget features, the main arena for female directors has become, almost by default, the independent sector. And here we encounter a seeming paradox. One might suppose that since young women directors are prevented from making 'action-oriented hardware pictures' by the patriarchal Hollywood machine, if the desire was sufficiently strong, they would make them on the fringes of that mainstream instead. But the reality is that independent women film-makers do not tend to make action movies; they tend to make character-based, observational movies instead. The specific study of those films will have to wait until Chapter 6. But, as a closing thought, it might be interesting to ponder whether Bigelow's agenda might be the exception rather than the rule. Even given the freedom, women film-makers might still prefer to explore human emotions and relationships rather than stage-managing mindless pyrotechnic displays and clichéd heroics.

Again, this situation has been given a new focus as a result of the terrorist attacks on American in September 2001. The greater desire, perhaps even need, of audiences for small intimate human dramas rather than action blockbusters might offer greater opportunities for women directors over their male counterparts. But again, a note of caution must be aired. It is by no means certain that this general desire for films based on real human values and issues will be maintained far into the future. When the immediate rawness of emotion being felt in response to the attacks passes, the big-action blockbuster, and its male-dominated directors, may well return to its former dominance.

CHAPTER FIVE

The Talent II

The actors

Actors, in many ways, are the most visible element of cinema, certainly in its American form. They are manifestly present up there on screen, dominating the framing and composition, controlling the camera's look and flow, organising the narrative. American cinema is one which foregrounds its actors, not just as ordinary human beings, but as fundamentally privileged and valorised entities: stars. Because of this focus, actors – and even more so stars – are also economic forces, marketable commodities who help create other marketable commodities: the (hopefully successful and popular) films in which they appear. Such is the wealth that can be gathered from a film finding popular favour that the actors/stars are given an important and powerful place within the industrial structure of the film industry. This has never been truer than it is at the time of writing, in the year 2002, when the leading stars, both male and, to a lesser extent, female can command both dominating control of the production process and massive payment for lending their talents to the creation of films. Mel Gibson, for example, can not only demand over $20 million and a percentage of profits for any film in which he appears, but has enough power within the industry to insist that his character in *Payback* (1999) be rewritten to tone down his sadistic qualities. This chapter will examine the historical process whereby this industrial power and financial reward have come about.

A NEW FREEDOM

The studio system, as noted in the introductory chapter, saw actors as employees of a film company. They were on the payroll, locked into contracts stretching forward several years, but which gave the studio the power to cancel that agreement if they thought the star was losing his/her popular appeal, and therefore their ability to earn the studio rich rewards at the box office. With the demise of the studio system, actors went freelance, selling their talents and popularity on the open market. Recognising the importance of the appeal to the mass audience that fundamentally made films so potentially profitable, actors came to want more of a say in how and why films were made in Hollywood. They became the foregrounded selling point in 'package deals' which were organised around them, usually also involving their agent, together with a small number of other major creative talents: director, writer, and co-stars.

> *The stars, aware that they were the real draw of the movies, had begun to chafe against the onerous contract system, which had made them little better than highly paid wage slaves throughout the 1930s. It was time for them to break free. With the help of a young agent, Lew Wasserman of MCA, they began to do so, ushering in a new era in the age of celebrity.*
>
> *(Puttnam with Watson, 2000; p.173)*

Actors/stars began to control the choice of material, the moulding of their screen image, the balance of power between themselves and the people who used to hold the reins of power in the film-making process: the producer, the director, the studio head. During the studio period, the process began when certain stars – Bette Davis, Olivia de Havilland – refused to accept certain film projects their studios told them to do, preferring instead to go on suspension. Although a move of passive resistance (refusing roles, rather than choosing them), it was a first step to recognizing that stars could have some say in the kind of role they played.

After the Paramount decrees, some of the major stars of the 1950s and 1960s formed independent production companies as a means of more closely controlling their screen personas. Burt Lancaster, together with, significantly, his agent Harold Hecht and an associate, Harold Hill formed Hecht-Hill-Lancaster in 1948, both to produce films in which Lancaster would star, and other features, such as *Marty* (1955). Similarly, Kirk Douglas formed his Bryna production company in 1955, for which he made *The Indian Fighter*, in association with UA, in 1955 and Stanley Kubrick's masterful *Paths of Glory* in 1957. Such actor-led productions demonstrated a potential within the industry that lasted until the 1969/70 film industry crisis. When the crisis hit, the major studios retrenched while simultaneously enlisting the aid of maverick actor-film-makers such as Dennis Hopper and Peter Fonda (who, along with Bert Schneider, co-produced *Easy Rider* through their production company Raybert).

The demise of the studio system also, importantly, shifted the means and logic whereby films were financed. Actors changed from being hired and salaried employees to solo operators who could demand individual fees for their work on any film. Moreover, they could, if they chose to, defer this fee. Essentially a one-off, often sizeable, payment, it was given to them all at once and was therefore liable to prohibitive taxation (amounting to some 90 per cent of the amount). In its place, they received a share of box-office profits. James Stewart, for example, struck a percentage deal with Universal in 1952, on just such terms, as will be outlined shortly. This arrangement allowed star actors to spread the income from any of their films in smaller payments across the life of that film in the cinemas (and later, into television broadcasts, videocassette, and cable and satellite screenings as well). In this way, they were allowed to keep a far greater percentage of their earnings by having each separate payment taxed at far lower levels.

Lew Wasserman was again at the centre of this important economic shift. In 1950, Wasserman and his agency, MCA, brokered a deal between Universal and one of its clients, James Stewart for his involvement in the western *Winchester '73* (1950) which gave Stewart a participating share in the film's profits. As McDonald notes, this kind of arrangement was not entirely new. 'Mary Pickford earned half the gross box-office receipts from her films. Similar terms were agreed in the 1930s by Mae West and the Marx Brothers' (McDonald, 2000; p.79). The difference lay in its formulation of a process which could be adopted as a template for future negotiations across the entire industry in the coming years. The Wasserman/MCA/Stewart deal involved a certain hedging of bets for the studio. In return for offering Stewart a profit-share arrangement, Universal received the rights to the stage success *Harvey*, a comedy about a drunk who sees and befriends an imaginary giant rabbit, in which Stewart was appearing at the time. Universal assumed that the material could be made into a similarly big success as a film. In such circumstances, the studio could afford to take a gamble on *Winchester '73*, which was seen simply as a standard genre film. Allowing the star to share potential profits instead of being given a large fee upfront, meant that the studio did not pay anything until the film was a success, at which time they would also make a great deal of money. As it happened, *Winchester '73* was a success, and made Stewart a rich man:

> By tying an actor's earnings to the actual value of the film, Wasserman created a mechanism that acknowledged the star as the real selling point of a movie. . . . The deal Wasserman engineered, and those that followed, had a momentous effect on the business, beginning to move the locus of power away from the studio to the star, and by natural extension, to the agent.
>
> (McDonald, 2000; p.80)

Over the next few years, Stewart's percentage demands would increase, as he felt himself to be in an increasingly powerful position within the film-making process. By 1953, he was demanding, and getting, 50 per cent of profits from a film like *The Glenn Miller Story* (1953), which made him over $1 million.

What this development also created was a top-level elite of actors/stars, who became the leading movers and shakers in the industry. As a result the main body of second- and third-string acting talent was left behind – actors such as Jack Carson and George Sanders, actresses such as Ann Sothern and Linda Darnell – who had no such leverage in the marketplace. With the loss of an in-house system of nurturing new talent and bringing it up through the system, fewer and fewer hopeful actors made it to the top. 'For the most successful stars, it became possible to rapidly increase the fees for their services. Star wages therefore grew more rapidly than they had in the studio era, further extending the hierarchical division between stars and other film performers, and making the employment of stars an even more expensive cost in the budgeting of productions' (McDonald, 2000; p.75). This imbalance, between first-tier stars who could command the big money and second-tier actors who could not, would grow across the coming three decades to produce the now alarming situation which will be examined shortly.

Recognition that this industrial structure was a dangerous development came much earlier than this, however. The crisis within the American film industry in the late 1960s and early 1970s was partly the result of overinflation and overdependence on certain 'stars' who were appearing in bloated, overproduced spectacles – such as *Dr Dolittle* (1967), *Star!* (1968), and *Hello Dolly!* (1969) – that were increasingly out of tune with changing audience profiles.

The recognition of a new, youth audience which older members of the industry felt they did not, and did not want to, understand, led to the emergence of a new generation of young actors, like Dennis Hopper, Jack Nicholson, Robert De Niro, Jane Fonda, Faye Dunaway and Ellen Burstyn. This new kind of performer was both unglamorous, in comparison to the glossy sheen of classical Hollywood, and manifestly anti-establishment. Instead of studio grooming, '[m]ost of these new faces had been trained in the "Method" [style of acting] by Lee Strasberg at the Actors Studio, or trained by the other celebrated New York teachers: Stella Adler, Sanford Meisner, or Uta Hagen. In fact, a lot of the energy that animated the New Hollywood came from New York . . .' (Biskind, 1998; p.16). And, of course, this transition had been in progress since the early 1950s, when young actors like Marlon Brando and James Dean had first challenged the orthodoxy of clean-cut image and clearly enunciated dialogue.

It would also be a mistake to treat the new generation of actors monolithically, and see them as all coming from the same background and having the same formative experiences. Dennis Hopper, for example, had been in films since 1955, with James Dean, albeit in a supporting role in *Rebel Without a Cause* (1955). Jack Nicholson entered the profession through the back door, having got a job in the mailroom of the MGM studio, before becoming involved with local theatre groups and then asking for, and being given, a screen test at MGM. Peter and Jane Fonda, obviously, had an automatic right of entry because of their father, Henry. But whatever their individual backgrounds, they did share a desire to shake up the establishment, to create new forms and styles. In so doing, they matched the *Zeitgeist* which artists in other fields – Elvis Presley in popular music, for example – were also expressing.

However, this new 'anti-star' trajectory lasted only a few years before fizzling out in an anticlimax of poor audience reception and modest box-office return. What followed was a kind of uneasy peace, in which some of the leading members of the older generation of actors continued to make popular and successful films, while the stronger of the newer generation adapted themselves to play in slightly more conventional films. There is no doubt that a new phase of American film-making was getting underway: one that tackled difficult social issues and sexual taboos head-on (and, in the case of the latter, full-frontally), using increasingly strong language. But at the same time, more traditional film entertainment was also being made. Paul Newman, for example, having played Butch Cassidy alongside a younger Robert Redford in *Butch Cassidy and the Sundance Kid* (1969), teamed up with him again for the similarly successful *The Sting* (1973), a solid entertainment film. Meanwhile, Jack Nicholson was receiving Academy Award nominations for his roles as a foul-mouthed US sailor in *The Last Detail* (1973) and a detective in *Chinatown* (1974), a film whose denouement revealed an incestuous relationship between father and daughter. Eventually, the anti-stars became stars themselves, replacing some of the older ones, and becoming absorbed into, and helping to redefine, a newer notion of stardom. The slightly grungy image of many current movie stars, such as Keanu Reeves, Brad Pitt, and Julia Roberts, might be seen to have originated during this period of anti-stardom.

But another aspect of this crisis period was to have a greater long-term effect. The new breed of young actors created a kind of norm of actors being allowed to assume other roles in the film-making process. Again, this is not totally new. Other actors had done so in the past: Charlie Chaplin and Buster Keaton during the silent period, and Orson Welles, Ida Lupino before the Paramount case, and Burt Lancaster and Kirk Douglas after the Paramount decree, as noted above. But such multi-role-playing was always relatively rare within the studio era, which functioned efficiently only by preserving strict role segregation. Indeed, the actors just cited almost all began directing from the 1950s onwards, when the dismantling of the studio system was already underway.

The tendency of young actors to also take on other roles in the production process can be seen to have started during the crisis of the late 1960s when Warren Beatty produced as well as starred in *Bonnie and Clyde* (1967). It is well documented that he was also active in the scriptwriting process and, no doubt, offered considerable advice to the film's director, Arthur Penn. Beatty was followed almost immediately by Peter Fonda and Dennis Hopper who, on *Easy Rider* (1969) took on the producing and directing roles respectively, and the screenwriting duties jointly (although Hopper has always vigorously claimed that Fonda's scriptwriting role was minimal).

Actors also began to acquire material for themselves to star in – for example, Robert Redford's purchase of the rights to *All the President's Men* in 1974. While such a manoeuvre can be seen as a continuation of processes already begun by acting colleagues in the previous decade or so, it also marks an escalation of such activity. Clint Eastwood, for instance, began directing himself in his films from 1971, with *Play Misty For Me*.

Sylvester Stallone's 'sudden' emergence as writer-star of *Rocky* (1976) can therefore be seen as part of this trend. But it represents more than this. Pre-*Rocky*, Stallone was a bit player whose biggest role was in the small-budget 1950s nostalgia film *The Lords of Flatbush* (1974). As has now gone down in movie legend, Stallone wrote the script of *Rocky* out of desperation at not getting the kind of serious acting assignments that he felt would make those who mattered notice him. His agent then hawked the script around for a couple of months before United Artists offered $75,000 for it. Stallone turned them down, until they agreed that he could play the lead character, Rocky Balboa.

The decision to go with an inexperienced actor and first-time writer such as Stallone confirmed the new model of industrial practice. This new model was marked by a lack of apprenticeship and a certain openness of possibility. What is even more significant about *Rocky* is that it was a huge success, earning $117.2 million ($341.2 in 2000 terms) at the box office, and making Stallone a star overnight. In an era which was witnessing fewer films being made and an uncertainty regarding what might make any of those films succeed with an increasingly unpredictable public, such unexpected and substantial box-office success established a precedent. It enabled actors to believe that they could both initiate their own material and take on multiple roles on the films made from that material, thereby being the principal creators of films which garnered massive box-office returns. Such a self-perception both continued and escalated the sense of actor-power that had begun in the 1950s with the demise of the studio system and the development of the actor-led package system.

In such ways, actors came increasingly to select their own material, to fashion that material into a workable script, and then to realise that scripted vision. In this context, we might argue that the actor began acting as the film's auteur, the central force that can change and mould a film's shape and narrative drive. This can be achieved on both a localised and a wide-ranging level. At the former end of the spectrum, Brad Pitt's involvement with the film *Seven* (1995) actually ensured the maintenance of the script's original vision in the face of pressures to change the ending. '"The ending *would* have changed if it weren't for Brad Pitt," Gavin Polone [United Talent Agency agent] contends. "He's the reason why it didn't change because once the movie's going, he's got a tremendous amount of control and he exercises it"' (Taylor, 1999; p.102).

At the other end of the spectrum, there are major stars with their own production companies, who are co-producing the whole film, and whose active control of the film's shape and direction can be substantial. For example, Tom Cruise has set up Cruise-Wagner Productions (co-producers of *Mission: Impossible*), while Mel Gibson's Icon Productions has been responsible for co-producing several of his biggest films, including *Braveheart* (1995), *Payback* (1999) and *What Women Want* (2000). Of course, involving themselves and their companies in a film's production does not only mean greater control over that production process and how they are positioned and used within it. It also means greater profits for themselves as heads and owners of those production companies when the films made by them and starring them then go on to make hundreds of millions of dollars at the box office.

This is auteurism almost by default, as a by-product of an actor's insistence that he/she have an input into the development of the film. In the increasing control that actors/stars exert over the production of the films in which they appear, we might argue that this relationship has become unbalanced in favour of the actor over the other creative personnel responsible for the film's narrative and aesthetic development:

> In a real sense, the 'stars' . . . are the ultimate buyers, not the studios. You can't make a buyer purchase a script, nor can you make an actor perform in a picture they do not like. To the studio, the script itself is never really commercial or noncommercial, that is, until a star enters the picture. But when a Mel Gibson or a Tom Cruise or a Julia Roberts says, 'I want to do this,' then the word 'noncommercial' would never, ever leave a studio executive's lips.
>
> (Taylor, 1999; p.119)

There is little doubt that the leading stars are now commanding a central position within the industry, not only in the influence they have over the material that is selected and developed for production into films, but also in their demands for large fees for doing so. The current 'market-leaders' in these terms are receiving upwards of $15–20 million per film. With such financial pressures placed on a film's budget, it becomes ever more necessary, and ever more difficult, for that film to return huge dividends at the box office. A vicious circle is thus created, in which escalating costs mean either massive rewards or equally massive losses, with stars' financial demands as a prime generator. Ironically, the growth of 'personal projects', such as films either scripted by leading actors such as Billy Bob Thornton and Matt Damon and Ben Affleck, or simply selected and supported by them, might result in a reduction in the high salaries such stars demand in the future. Star actors, with a vested interest in a project, tend to be more willing to work for reduced salaries because of their belief in the material and their desire to enact it. Between *Mission: Impossible* (1996), for which he earned about $70 million ($20 million fee plus, as the film's producer, 25 per cent of the gross) and *Mission: Impossible 2* (2000), for which he is set to earn even more, Tom Cruise worked for scale (a Screen Actors Guild-mandated $596-a-day minimum) on the film *Magnolia* (1999). On a slightly less dramatic reduction, Jim Carrey starred in *The Truman Show* (1998) for $12 million as opposed to the $20 million he usually earns to star in films such as *The Cable Guy* (1996). Similarly, George Clooney, although a more 'up-and-coming' star actor, received $10 million for his high-profile appearance in *Batman and Robin* (1997), and $5 million for *Three Kings* (1999; he asked for $10 million again, but his star standing had presumably been dented by the relative failure of the Batman film). In contrast, he asked only $1 million for *O Brother, Where Art Thou?* (2000) because he wanted to work with the Coen Brothers. For his next big-budget action picture, he went back to the high salary demands, asking for $8 million for *The Perfect Storm* (2000), although he is reported to have underbid Nicolas Cage for the role.

CHANGE AND CONTINUITY

The maintenance of a star actor's position within that top elite group mentioned earlier is an interesting, two-way process that is in continual tension. On the one hand, a distinctive star image, with its attendant set of mannerisms, gestures and stylistic flourishes (whether Marlon Brando's floor-staring and 'method-mumble' or George Clooney's 'head-on-a-tilt' quizzical look) needs to be established as an instantly recognisable and, more importantly, persistently desirable, entity. On the other hand, there does need to be variation and development, otherwise a star's audience can become bored and uninterested in seeing more of the same.

If we examine the career of Jack Nicholson, for example, we can see in action this tension between continuity and change. Nicholson's career has gone through several style shifts. In the 1960s, he was the young and eager actor, but also a fledgling screenwriter on psychedelic films such as *The Trip* (1967) and *Head* (1968). Following his breakthrough film *Easy Rider* (1969), throughout the 1970s he became the angry, disaffected, rebellious young(ish) man of *Five Easy Pieces* (1970) and *One Flew Over the Cuckoo's Nest* (1975). But even though he was now established as one of the leading actors of his generation, he continued to gain directorial experience, on films such as *Drive He Said* (1970) and *Goin' South* (1978). The first half of the 1980s saw him first playing sinister and increasingly deranged roles in *The Shining* (1980) and *The Postman Always Rings Twice* (1981), before changing tack again to begin appearing in increasingly comic roles in *Terms of Endearment* (1983) and *Prizzi's Honour* (1985).

By the end of the 1980s, Nicholson had taken this comic phase a step further to become the clown-with-menace, actor-for-hire, typified by *The Witches of Eastwick* (1987) and *Batman* (1989). Following on from this latter caricatured role, the early 1990s was his most troubled period, during which he veered from serious (*A Few Good Men*, 1992) to trivial (*Man Trouble*, 1992) and back to serious (*Hoffa*, 1992). Finally, he has undergone another reincarnation to become an actor who can bring echoes of his early 'troubled soul' persona to depictions of more mature, more worldly-wise characters in films such as *As Good As It Gets* (1997), for which, significantly, he won his second Oscar for Best Actor, The Pledge (2001) and About Schmidt (2002).

Nicholson's ability to survive relatively near the top of his elite grouping is a result of his ability to adapt to shifting tastes and market changes while maintaining enough of what is recognisably 'Nicholson'. These identifiable traits include a certain kind of easy charm masking a repressed sense of danger and violence, and a specific enunciatory style, often accompanied by extravagant hand movements, which shift his big speeches up through several gears to a level of hyper-expressivity. It is these mannerisms which are consciously played upon so successfully in his Oscar-winning performance in *As Good As It Gets*, in which he plays a neurotic-compulsive character prone to explosive loss of temper and foul-mouthed insulting of other characters.

On the other hand, many actors harbour desires to demonstrate their acting range, to prove their credentials as true actors. One means by which they do this, a phenomenon which ultimately lies outside the parameters of this book, is by returning to the 'legitimate' stage, or, increasingly, going onto it for the first time. The last few years have seen an increase in this kind of 'relegitimisation' process. Actually, it is not new; it has always been a factor in an actor's negotiation with the labelling and defining of themselves which come about as a result of their involvement with cinema. But in contemporary

American film-making, when each new film release becomes an (over)hyped event, the appearance of leading film stars in plays on Broadway or – perhaps an even more significant phenomenon – the London stage (England being seen as having a more respected and established tradition of theatrical acting) is foregrounded as a similar 'event'. So, over the past two decades, we have seen Al Pacino appear in *American Buffalo*, Dustin Hoffman play in *The Merchant of Venice*, Jessica Lange take on the role of Blanche in *A Streetcar Named Desire*, and Kevin Spacey appear in *The Iceman Cometh*. Significantly, each of these productions has been a sellout, the lure of a major Hollywood actor being sufficient to ensure massive interest in a production. The desired goal for the actor in such exercises – apart from, admittedly, in certain cases a true desire for a different acting experience – is to garner positive reviews about the actor's ability to pull off a coherent and believable performance, live – i.e. 'real' acting.

The other way an actor can demonstrate a wider acting range is consciously to take on non-typical roles. Again this is not new: archetypal good guy Henry Fonda achieved considerable effect by appearing as the sadistic villain Frank in *Once Upon a Time in the West* (1968). But this film, one of the best examples of the Italian spaghetti Westerns, was so to speak, a detour from Fonda's American career; after it, he returned to his established persona in American films and television productions. But similarly Clint Eastwood, having established his sardonic 'man-with-no-name' screen image in several spaghetti westerns (*A Fistful of Dollars*, 1964; *For a Few Dollars More*, 1965; *The Good, the Bad and the Ugly*, 1966), adapted that slightly sadistic character into American roles such as *Dirty Harry* (1971) and *The Enforcer* (1976): roles which appeared to have become definitively 'him' by the mid-1970s. But against these, he developed a softer, more slapstick comic persona, evidenced in films such as *Every Which Way But Loose* (1978), *Bronco Billy* (1980) and *City Heat* (1984). This dual persona has developed ever since, in films such as *The Rookie* (1990) and *Unforgiven* (1992). It seems that certain actors, having spent a number of years establishing a specific and identifiable screen persona, can now claim the right, have earned the right, to develop a second one, inverse to the first. Certainly, this is how we can read Jack Nicholson's career outlined above. This duality is one of the strategies by which long-term successful actors maintain their popularity and ensure that they remain a fresh screen presence.

In contemporary times, actors are trying to display their potential range from within American film-making. The leading stars tend to establish a fairly clear screen persona and then maintain it, with only minor diversions, across a number of performances. Tom Hanks tends to play the genial, bumbling guy next door (*Sleepless in Seattle*, 1993); Jim Carrey the slightly crazed fool (*Ace Ventura*, 1994; *Dumb and Dumber*, 1994); Harrison Ford the solid and

Julia Roberts on the case in *Erin Brockovich* (Steven Soderbergh, 2000)

dependable hero (the Indiana Jones trilogy, 1981, 1984, 1989; *Air Force One*, 1997); and Julia Roberts the mildly eccentric free spirit (*Pretty Woman*, 1990; *My Best Friend's Wedding*, 1997). Variations on these basic characterisations are then developed: Hanks can play a straighter hero role as Jim Lovell in *Apollo 13* (1995) or an embittered AIDS victim in *Philadelphia* (1993), but he is still the easy-going, regular, funny family man in the former, and loses his abrasive edge in the latter. Julia Roberts's role as a feisty working class woman in *Erin Brockovich* (2000) is not too far removed from her prostitute in *Pretty Woman* (1990). From this solid base, stars will then occasionally try out different roles. For example, in his next film, *The Road to Perdition* (2002), Tom Hanks is set to play a man driven to murderous revenge when his family is killed by a stranger.

These new roles might suggest that the stars of the new century are seeking further dimensions to their acting repertoires, and this is no doubt true, at least in part. But the room for manoeuvre is tight and invariably short-lived. Stars can play against type only if they have already firmly established that type in a number of similar roles, and ensure that they confirm it by returning to it in future performances. Tom Cruise, with his now ex-wife Nicole Kidman, therefore allows himself to undergo a physically and emotionally punishing experience in the making of Stanley Kubrick's last film *Eyes Wide Shut* (1999) in order to prove that he is capable of acting beyond his usual broad-grinning, awesomely handsome, action hero.

In attempting these counter-image roles, stars are attempting to win the critical kudos, and audience acceptance, which will confirm their eminence within the industry. But audiences can often prove resistant to such changes of image: they simply do not want to see their stars in other kinds of roles. Sylvester Stallone, though he may now express dislike of his action-hero persona, generally fails when he tries to play any other kind of character. His attempts at comedy in films such as *Stop, or My Mom Will Shoot!* (1992), or his stumbling cop in *Cop Land* (1997), although the latter gained some critical acclaim, were rejected by his fans. This pressure, together with the high-cost, high-risk reality of modern American mainstream film-making means that stars more often abide by the rules and limitations of their well-known screen personas.

VANITY PROJECTS

The scope for stars to perform roles outside their normal range is often provided by so-called 'vanity projects': personal films which stars, for a variety of reasons, want to star in, write, direct, produce – or, indeed, all four. Such projects can also demonstrate the power that leading actors and actresses have in contemporary American film-making. Thus, we see Michelle Pfeiffer buying the rights, producing and starring in *The Deep End of the Ocean* (1999) because she connected with its theme of losing a child at a time when motherhood was a dominant force in her own life. And we find Tom Hanks writing, producing, directing and co-starring in *That Thing You Do* (1996), partly because he is a fan of early 1960s pop music. The films almost always fail or break even at the box office – *The Deep End of the Ocean* took $13.4 million, *That Thing You Do*, $25.8 million. The studios which finance these personal projects indulge the actors in order to 'maintain a relationship' with them – that is, to ensure that they will be willing to consider lending their names, and talent, to new, big-budget film projects, if only at an unspecified time in the future. 'The reason they get made, never stated, but always unstated, is that having a relationship with Robert Redford or Tom Cruise is going to mean that down the line maybe that studio will have a project that they will be in, so we'll do the small project' (producer Jonathan Sanger, quoted in Base, 1994; p.119).

Such a phenomenon is further evidence of the megastar/big-budget block-buster teaming which is designed to see that the few big films that are made each year reap huge rewards at the box office. In order to help ensure this financial success, studios are willing, effectively, to lose a few million dollars, every now and then, on small films that are not expected to make a profit. These films keep their star creators happy, and help to secure the services of those stars for the movies which really matter – the big-budget blockbusters which return the $100–200 million which studios now require several times a year in order to continue in business. Hanks was given the chance to make *That Thing You Do*, part-financed by Twentieth Century-Fox, but it was his starring roles in *Saving Private Ryan* (1998), financed by Dreamworks and Paramount, with box office, to date, of $479.3 million worldwide, and *Castaway* (2000), financed by Twentieth Century-Fox, with worldwide box office of $229.2 million by May 2001, which *really* mattered to the studios.

INSECURITY OF STAR SUCCESS

Because they are now working freelance, actors/stars have become responsible for their own careers. The success or failure of each film stands alone, exposed, obvious to everyone in the industry. The adage of 'you're only as good as your last film' has, in some ways, never been truer. Certainly, it is possible, and perhaps inevitable, that the careers of even the most successful and dependable of stars can have greater ups and downs than in the studio period. The less successful films of the studio era were always cushioned by the longer-term investment in the star being made by the studio that had that star under long-term contract. The modern star, going it alone with each new film project, is altogether more exposed.

In the post-studio period, McDonald argues:

> *working freelance could only benefit the stars and only the most popular stars at that . . . [many retained contract terms with studios, making regular films] With stars making so many films, it was possible for a performer's career to survive a number of box office failures when supported by regular successes as well. This situation contrasts with the package-unit system in which a star's status is only as good as his or her last couple of movies. In such a system, it is possible to see examples of the rapid rise and fall of stars across only a few films.*

> (McDonald, 2000; p.109)

I have to disagree with this analysis. Arnold Schwarzenegger who had a string of disappointing movies across the 1990s, was still making major films in 1999 (*End of Days*) and in 2000 (*The Sixth Day*). Similarly, Sylvester Stallone was supposedly washed up after a string of poorly received films. *The Specialist* (1994), *Judge Dredd* (1995), *Assassins* (1995) and *Daylight* (1996), all took only about $30–60 million at the box office, culminating in *Cop Land* in 1997, which fared as badly at the box office. But in the past year or so,

Stallone has made several major movies, including a remake of *Get Carter* (2000) and *Driven* (2001), although neither has been a critical or box-office success (*Get Carter* has grossed only $15.4 million worldwide; *Driven*, to date, $25.5 million). In spite of this relative failure, however, in 2001/2 Stallone has had, and will have, four more films released: *D–Tox* (2001), *My Little Hollywood* (2001), *Avenging Angelo* (2001) and *Dolan's Cadillac* (2002). Although most of these are hardly mega-budget productions, it seems that the American film industry is still prepared to invest in him, in the hope that one of his films becomes a hit.

The most spectacular rise and fall is perhaps that of Kevin Costner. The actor/director/producer could do no wrong up to *The Bodyguard* (1992), thereafter suffering a string of critical and financial flops, none of which gathered more than $30 million box office, except *Waterworld* ($88 million, but with a huge budget wiping out this revenue) and *Tin Cup* (1996) (a modest, but reasonable $51 million). Industry buzz for the past few years has had it that Costner is indeed a spent force as a major power in modern American film-making. But even he has kept making movies, and the release of *13 Days* (2000), about the Cuban missile crisis of the early 1960s, has been critically well received, giving Costner much-needed kudos within the industry (although box office has been average, at $50.2 million worldwide).

One of the best examples of career fluctuations is Julia Roberts. If McDonald's theory held water, Roberts would have been history following the string of failures she suffered between *I Love Trouble* (1994; $30 million at the US box office) and *Michael Collins* (1996; $11 million at the US box office). But she carried on making films, and scored an impressive success with *My Best Friend's Wedding* in 1997, which gathered $126.8 million at the box office. Since then, she has had a string of box-office hits – *Notting Hill* (1999; $355 million worldwide), *Runaway Bride* (1999; $281.5 million worldwide) and *Erin Brockovich* ($125 million domestic to July 2000) – which have ensured her position as top female Hollywood star.

In reality, however, there is a perversely double-edged nature to this. If a star's latest expensive film bombs at the box office, it could be argued that they might lose ground in the power rankings of the industry. But, the very high-risk nature of the contemporary American film-making process means that the *possibility* that that star's next film might be huge tends to allow them still to be considered worth betting on again, even after they have had a series of failures (or non-successes).

In a quirky, and ultimately somewhat unnerving, way this small but elite stratum of stardom is seen as a stable, if slightly desperately desired, entity in the increasingly unpredictable arena of modern American film-making. The high-stakes, film-to-film, gambling on the possible huge financial returns of a box-office smash is becoming so nerve-wracking that the presence of a star who, even if they have not achieved massive box-office success in their last couple of films, has proved more than once in the past that they are *capable* of doing so, perversely becomes the calm centre of the maelstrom. It is not so much a case of 'you're only as good as your last film' but more a case of 'you're only as good as the one of your last several films which earned over $100 million'. There is no doubt that the increasingly high salaries demanded by the major stars, and the unpredictable response of audiences to the films they make, indicate that the over-dominance of stars in the film-making process is becoming something of a liability for those companies financing new big-budget features. However, in the absence of any other strategy or element capable of attracting the huge potential financial returns that come with a box-office hit, highly paid stars are the best option currently available.

The upper echelon of American film stardom is dominated by white males. The standard yardstick for a film actor's power-position in Hollywood is his ability to 'open' a film; that is, to ensure that a film will attract a huge audience on its opening weekend. Very few actor/stars are able to do this in the current financial climate, and almost all of these are white males – Tom Hanks, Mel Gibson, Jim Carrey, Bruce Willis, Harrison Ford, Brad Pitt. Female stars, with the exception of Julia Roberts, are seen to have far less chance of opening a film in which they are the leading star. Black actors, again with the exception of a few names – Will Smith (possibly), Samuel L. Jackson (just possibly) and Eddie Murphy (even less possibly) – are not perceived as strong enough to gather audiences in the sizes now required to make a successful opening weekend – i.e. one with takings of between $25 and $30 million. This may change as a result of the success of Black actors Denzel Washington, for Best Actor, and Halle Berry, for Best Actress, at the 2002 Academy Awards. But such a situation still indicates serious biases in the nature of the material being chosen for the 'star vehicles' and the consequent disenfranchisement of sections of the audience.

> Box office performance has meant that many stars have secured great economic and symbolic power in the film industry. Yet even the most cursory of glances at contemporary popular cinema will reveal that Hollywood stardom remains a system organised by gender and racial difference. Julia Roberts's performance at the box office stands out amongst rankings dominated by male stars. Will Smith's success in the 1990s was exceptional in a system defined by the overwhelming presence of white stars.
>
> (McDonald, 2000; pp.107–8)

A useful way of doing this, as I will discuss further in Chapter 7, on genre and sequels, is for an actor to establish a character in a series. Harrison Ford becomes identified as Indiana Jones or as Jack Ryan in the series of films, such as *Patriot Games* (1992), adapted from the novels of Tom Clancy. Tom Cruise establishes himself as Ethan Hunt in *Mission: Impossible* and its sequel in 2000. Julia Roberts, in *Pretty Woman* and *Runaway Bride*, does not, admittedly, play the same character, but maintains familiar parameters and an identical leading man (Richard Gere). Sigourney Weaver plays Ripley in all four parts of the *Alien* series. Such dependability and familiarity, not only of character type but also of lucrative work, provide the base from which stars can temporarily experiment with the boundary lines of their screen image.

An increasingly acceptable arena for this experimentation is the independent movie; small-scale, personal (often literally, as stars offer the benefit of their name and fan-base to friends or interesting new talent); films with more modest expectations and higher artistic pretensions. The shift from mainstream, big-budget, to independent, low-budget, production opens up a space in the public's collective psyche in which the star is allowed, albeit temporarily, to adopt an alternative persona and a more experimental performance. Failure in these ventures does not substantially impact upon their status as star; success will only add to their kudos.

> *Box office performance offers one economic indicator of popularity but can be misleading: stars may choose to take leading or supporting roles in film projects not intended for popular audiences but which offer prestige and increased artistic credibility.*

> *(McDonald, 2000; p.108)*

This is one way in which a star can appear in several films without major box-office success and still be regarded within the industry as a potential sure-fire hit for the next blockbuster production. A prime example of this is Bruce Willis who, throughout his career, has alternated between big mainstream and small independent productions. For example, he followed the surreal Terry Gilliam-directed *Twelve Monkeys* (1995) with *Die Hard With a Vengeance* (1995), the third instalment of his lucrative John McClane franchise, which was, in turn, followed by *Last Man Standing* (1996), a low-budget Walter Hill gangster movie. Willis's mega-success in the *Die Hard* series has meant that no matter how his other films perform (*Twelve Monkeys* made the relatively modest sum of $56.9 million at the US box office, *Last Man Standing* only $18.1 million), his agreement to star in another instalment of the extremely successful *Die Hard* series assures his continued status as a leading player in modern Hollywood. Recently he has initiated a new, potentially long-term and financially very rewarding franchise, albeit without strict continuity of character, by starring in the first two films by the new director M. Night

Shyamalan, *The Sixth Sense* (1999) and *Unbreakable* (2000). The critical and box-office success of both films, with the former earning $660.7 million and the latter, $244.5 million, worldwide, has extended Willis' list of characters who can be made to return in new projects. Following the terrorist attacks on New York and Washington, Willis has announced that he has dropped plans to make *Die Hard 4*. It is quite conceivable that, in the present climate, he will opt to make more low-key drama-based films rather than action blockbusters. If so, he will probably not be alone. The universal reaction to the attacks, and the reassessment of values that this has brought, will make many stars who have become identified with big-action films re-evaluate their positions.

Stars maintain their positions over time and despite the vagaries of unpredictable markets by keeping a balance between the familiar and the new. Movement back and forth between the two is partly the result of the freelance nature of the modern industry. Each actor is a free agent, able to move unhindered between projects of various kinds. If the experimental ventures do not work, it is always possible to star in a film that echoes previous successes. This oscillation is not universal; some stars aim for a wider range of performances and films than others, who select projects more carefully to maintain a consistent bankability.

The important thing to recognise is that the public has not tired of these screen personae. Stars do not need to display a staggering range of characterisations in order to retain their audience – quite the opposite. People come to their films precisely in order to 'revisit' familiar characterisations, favourite characters. This is by no means a modern phenomenon; indeed, it is as old as movie stardom itself. John Wayne never played anyone but himself, and remained a star for four decades. And again, it might be another reason why stars can appear in several movies without a major hit if they ensure that the characterisation with which their audience is most familiar and of which it is most fond, returns in future movies.

The definition of a contemporary movie star is a complex issue:

The formula that determines a star's value – i.e., the number of zeros in his or her paycheck – isn't quite so mathematically pure as you might think. Along with the tangible, measurable variables how many seats they can fill on opening weekend, how many they can fill on the second weekend, how many they can fill in overseas theatres – there are other more ephemeral elements. How, for instance, do you calculate a star's ability to generate buzz? To sell their films on the chat-show circuit? To make magazines want to put them on their covers? In a word, to excite?

(Ascher-Walsh et al., 2000; p.24)

The escalation in the profile of the film star is partly a result of the smaller number of films being made in the modern era, and the need for them to earn massive amounts of money at the box office. Each film star has to become more desirable to the public than his or her peers, in order to make his or her next film the true 'must-see' one. Defined more succinctly, major movie stars 'open films'. By this is meant that second-string movie stars make the public want to see a film *soon*, or *sometime*. The top stars make the public want to see their new film *immediately*.

An example will show this phenomenon in action. Alec Baldwin appeared in the first Jack Ryan movie, *The Hunt for Red October*, in 1990, setting up the possibility of a series of sequels featuring the character. When the second film project – *Patriot Games* – went into development two years later, Baldwin asked both for a pay rise and for the shooting schedule to be built around his appearance on Broadway in *A Streetcar Named Desire*. Paramount, the producing studio, refused him both requests, and replaced him with Harrison Ford. Ford had just dropped out of another Paramount project and the studio wanted to keep him attached to them. Harrison Ford starred in *Patriot Games*, which made $180 million worldwide; Baldwin's next film, *Prelude to a Kiss* (1992), failed at the box office, even though it co-starred Meg Ryan. The situation was repeated with *The Fugitive* (1993), when Baldwin was again considered but judged not to be weighty enough to carry the film; Ford was again chosen instead. 'The people who keep an eye on such matters could not help but notice that Harrison Ford had opened his movie[s] while Alec Baldwin, charged with the same function, had not' (Base, 1994; pp.263–5). Harrison Ford is an A-list movie star; Alec Baldwin is not, because the public want to see a Ford film as soon as it comes out, but can wait to see a Baldwin film.

FROM SMALL TO BIG SCREEN

One way in which actors can help to offset the high risk involved in modern mainstream big-budget film-making is to bring with them from their success in television a potential audience for their work in cinema. There are numerous examples of this. Most recently, perhaps, George Clooney has moved from an acclaimed success as Dr Doug Ross in the hit television drama series *ER* to a number of hit movies, such as *One Fine Day* (1996), *The Peacemaker* (1997), *Out of Sight* (1998), *Three Kings* (1999), and *O Brother, Where Art Thou?* (2000). Clooney's impact on possible audience figures in each case is variable. *One Fine Day* also features Michele Pfeiffer, who could be assumed to bring to the film her own fan-following. *O Brother, Where Art Thou?* was written and directed by the Coen Brothers, who could certainly be assumed to be capable of making the film an attractive package, with or without Clooney in the starring role. Nevertheless, an actor moving from a hugely popular television series in which he has, because of its longevity and regularity, built up a loyal and devoted audience base, can be seen to bring with him to his early big-screen roles at least a portion of that television audience.

The use of the word 'early' in that last sentence is deliberate. The legacy from television roles, and the loyalty of their audiences, remains in play only so long before the actor must have established a 'stand-alone' big-screen presence and persona. Hence Clooney's early big-screen roles explicitly draw upon his character in *ER*: Doug Ross, the charming womaniser capable of heroic actions, as witnessed in one of the series' most popular episodes, *Hell and High Water*, in which he dramatically rescues a boy trapped in a water drainage tunnel. Both characteristics are drawn upon in his first big-screen roles, in which he portrays the iconoclastic journalist capable of turning on an almost overwhelming charm and sexual charisma in *One Fine Day* and is also capable of playing the overtly macho action hero in *The Peacemaker*.

STARS AND SPECIAL EFFECTS

It should not be assumed, however, that the massive box-office success for which the industry is continually striving is automatically due to the stars appearing in those films. The films that reap the major rewards are now quite capable of not featuring any of the major stars at all. *Jurassic Park* (1993) featured Jeff Goldblum, Sam Neill and Laura Dern, all of whom are second-division players in American film industry terms.

> *Stars are therefore certainly not a pre-condition at the box office. Equally, box office success does not immediately make a performer a star. During the 1990s, Jeff Goldblum appeared in some of the largest-grossing films of the decade, including [Jurassic Park and* The Lost World: Jurassic Park II*] and* Independence Day. *While a well-known actor, it is open to question whether Goldblum himself has the box office appeal to give him the status of a star.*
>
> (McDonald, 2000; p.103)

It is important to register, however, that *Jurassic Park*'s eclectic and second-string cast list also betrays director Steven Spielberg's B-movie tastes, while also ensuring that he remains the star of the show: it is his name above the title, not that of a star actor or actress. Even *Titanic* (1997), though it starred Leonardo DiCaprio (who only gained a star name in a coincidental way during the actual production period), had a cast – Kate Winslet, Billy Zane,

Kathy Bates – who could hardly be called major box-office draws. The audiences flocked to *Titanic* because of the much-hyped special effects and the film's by-then scandalous reputation as an 'event movie'.

This brings us to a serious issue in modern film-making – the relationship between the special effects that are an increasingly prominent feature of certain kinds of film, and the humans – actors, stars – who appear alongside them. It is now certainly being argued that the special effects are coming to dominate, even overwhelm, the human element involved in some contemporary films. The *reductio ad absurdum* of this might be seen to be the 'avatars' – digitally created, virtual actors – which James Cameron is reported to be trying to perfect in a move which will, it is hyperbolically feared, spell the end of flesh-and blood actors. Mystery and confusion shroud the status of the production, with wild and unsupported reports appearing on the Internet of successful tests of believable 'CGI humans', astronomical budgets ($300–350 million), and Cameron's withdrawal from the project.

Even if it becomes possible to create such artificial characters, a credible counter-argument would offer the view that the 'human actor' will become ever more vital as insubstantial worlds are created by computer. They will become a means of maintaining a link, amidst all the virtuality, to the reality we know and to which we will still need to feel connected. Actors, not only in their physical presence, but in the nuances of their speech and gesture, will represent the real and the believable, and will thus offer a grounding for the virtual worlds surrounding them.

The other effect of this development will be to lend added value to those films which will still be created which will not feature digital environments as their major selling point: the intimate, emotion-based films which are about 'real' people and their lives. Such films will still be desired, even needed, in the future. Not all films will show futuristic digitally created landscapes and battle-cruisers; that would be ridiculous. Audiences will still want other kinds of film, showing the world as they actually know it. In these films, the actor's more traditional talents will still have currency.

THE BODY BEAUTIFUL

Actors in contemporary American film-making are being asked to offer themselves as increasingly overt physical entities. I am certainly not suggesting that this is purely a direct response/reaction to the surrendering of the real involved in acting against special effects in modern film-making. However, there is a strange way in which the exposing of more and more of the physical body of the star does effect a confirmation of their corporeal reality. Indeed, it is possible to trace the increased contemporary emphasis on the hyper-perfect body of the star, typified in the pumped-up biceps and pectorals of a Stallone or a Schwarzenegger, from the advent and development of digital processing techniques during the 1980s. From this perspective, the two trends are perhaps not wholly unconnected.

Also evident is the increasing sexualising of the actor's body. Of course, the actor's body has always been a sexualised thing: the face of Garbo; Gable's torso (which, when bared in *It Happened One Night* (1934), caused sales of vests to slump); Betty Grable's legs, insured for $250,000 with Lloyds of London. But since the relaxation of censorship towards the depiction of sex and nudity on-screen, from the brief but controversial baring of a female character's breasts in *The Pawnbroker* (1965) onwards, the fuller and franker depiction of sex and nudity has become a central issue in American film-making generally, and in the definition and profile of its actors in particular.

Hence we are now not only allowed the conventional privilege of seeing our favourite stars displayed in beautiful and desirable costumes, doing enviable things. We are also being given the additional, and perhaps dubious 'privilege' of seeing everything of our favourite stars that was previously hidden by those very costumes: whether the buttocks of Mel Gibson or Kevin Costner, or Sharon Stone's genitalia. Nudity, in this context, almost perversely acts as a confirmation of the star's status: that revealing an intimate part of their bodies on screen has such a powerful effect *because* it is *their* intimate body-part. Ironically, perhaps, it is often not their body-part at all, as many such shots actually show the body of a stand-in rather than the star him/herself. But, ultimately, this does not matter – it is enough that the construction of such sequences sets up the expectation and belief that it is the star's body.

This also means that the full terms of an actor's status within the industry are at least partly determined by what that actor is physically prepared to do, rather than what they are capable of emotionally and psychologically acting. Sharon Stone may, in *Basic Instinct* (1992), be able to create a believable, psychologically complex, sexually dark, character through gesture, delivery of line, and so forth. The full effect of that character creation comes, however, through her agreeing to physically perform a number of sexually explicit, full-frontal love-scenes with co-star Michael Douglas (who has similarly agreed to do so, in order to bring out the full terms of *his* own character).

This emphasis on the physical and sexual perfection of stars is also augmented and extended in contemporary America through the burgeoning, almost overwhelming media coverage each star continually has to endure. Whether on television or in the countless celebrity and gossip magazines, the elite stars are perpetually delivered to their publics in all their glamorous and, sometimes, increasingly, their not-so-glamorous, glory. Images of them appearing in stunning outfits at the latest 'showbiz' function jostle uncomfortably with exposé shots of them dressed in jeans and sweatshirts collecting kids from school or shopping with their latest flames. The endless fascination with the physical reality of favourite stars accompanies the desire to see them perfectly perform physically on screen.

Actors are therefore the central focus and organising principle around which mainstream American film-making is constructed. They are the main attraction for audiences deciding which film to see, the lead element in the package which now determines whether a film project will be green-lighted. In a character- and narrative-driven film system, they will always command centre stage. Even the advent and threat of digital special effects will not change this; eventually, those special effects currently so much in the foreground will become absorbed into the fabric of their film texts, providing context and background for actors to create their characters. Humans want to see humans up on screen, want to empathise with them and use them to understand more about their own humanity. That desire is a large part of the reason why and how the American film industry continues. Under such conditions, a price tag of $20 million per movie for a leading actor still looks like a bargain.

CHAPTER SIX

Going it alone

Independent American Cinema

In 1985, some 50 independently produced films were released in America. In 1998, that figure was in excess of 1,000. This chapter will explore the reasons behind this exponential growth and investigate the implications for the current state of both studio and independent film-making in America in the early years of the twenty-first century.

The first issue is one of definition. What, exactly, is an independent American film? What categorises it; what are its essential elements? In trying to reach a definition, we must be careful not to treat independent cinema in monolithic terms; as, simply, one style of film-making, with one unified intent. Independent film production in America over the past three decades has covered a wide range of different types of film text. At one end of the scale are small, personal, and personally financed films, such as Kevin Smith's *Clerks* (1994), whose $27,575 budget came from his alternative use of film school tuition fees and money earned by working at a grocery store. At the other end are larger-budget productions, such as Alan Rudolph's *Afterglow* (1997), with second-level stars such as Nick Nolte and Julie Christie, which are intended for distribution by the major studios (Sony Pictures Classics, in the case of *Afterglow*). There are certainly various aspects of film production that could be considered in order to begin developing a definition of independent cinema: methods of financing (size of budget, or lack of it; sources of funding); identification of a 'personal vision', a voice describing a particular way of looking at the world; aesthetic questions such as narrative structure, *mise en scène*, and visual gloss (or lack of it); the presence or absence of well-known names, actors and stars. Perhaps Emanuel Levy sums up best the 'traditional' idea of an independent film when he says that '[i]deally, an indie is a fresh, low-budget movie with a gritty style and off-beat subject matter that expresses the film-maker's personal vision' (Levy, 1999; p.2). But as I hope to show during the course of this chapter, independent film-making in America is much more than this.

Changes in mainstream film production philosophy; new methods of financing productions; the opening up and redefinition of channels of reception; expanded education possibilities for potential film-makers and the emergence of a range of organisations designed to support independent film-making have all contributed to changing the landscape of the American film industry over the past two or three decades. Each of these will be examined in turn.

CHANGES IN MAINSTREAM FILM-MAKING

Independent film-making is often framed in terms of a David facing the Goliath of Hollywood. An anti-Hollywood stance has certainly been an distinct, foregrounded, element in independent cinema's identity over the past few decades. That 'independence' must now be questioned. It has certainly been the case that the style of film-making practised by the Hollywood majors – big-budget, star-focused films which tell undemanding and uncontroversial stories – has been held up as a model of what *not* to do by independent film-makers in America in the last 20 years. The perception that Hollywood had abdicated its responsibility for making socially relevant films was a strong one.

This abdication had begun with the dismantling of the studio system during the 1950s and into the 1960s and the resultant loss of the steady production of modestly sized features. It became entrenched with the re-establishment, from the late 1970s, of a philosophy arguing that it was wiser to make fewer, larger films, such as *Jaws* (1975), *Superman* (1978), and *Raiders of the Lost Ark* (1981), which promised substantial box-office profits, rather than more, lower-budgeted films. That double-bind – the production of fewer films that did not seriously address what might be termed the social and emotional reality of America – opened up an oppositional space and aided the emergence of what we can now identify as modern independent American cinema.

An additional factor that has aided the growth of the independent sector in America has been the gradual withering of the foreign film market there. By the late 1990s, as has been demonstrated in an earlier chapter, foreign-language films shown on American screens accounted for only 2 per cent of the market. The values associated with foreign film-making – serious treatment of adult issues, self-conscious cinematic style, film seen as art – were taken over by American independent film-makers.

FINANCING INDEPENDENT PRODUCTION

Independent film-makers have raised finance for their films in several ways. Self-financing of their own work by budding (and not so budding) film-makers has been the stuff of legend in independent film-making. Occasionally, this has been true. Robert Townsend used money made from acting jobs to finance *Hollywood Shuffle* (1987). Matty Rich raised the $12,000 of the budget needed for his debut feature, *Straight Out of Brooklyn* (1991) by using the credit cards of his friends and family (the rest came from investors shown early footage he had shot). We might call this the 'flexible-friend' school of movie-making, in which film-makers bypass funding bodies altogether and become self-dependent, with all the potential drawbacks that entails – namely, financially ruining your loved ones if your film fails to cover its costs.

Private investment is a far less risky route to take. Individuals are persuaded, by the film-maker's 'pitch' or by hard evidence of actual footage from the film, to meet part of the film's budget, often for the promise of a share in profits. It took the Coen brothers a year to raise the finance for their first feature, *Blood Simple* (1984); they finally managed it partly through family and friends and partly by making a three-minute trailer designed to convince potential private investors that they were capable of making a feature film. Spike Lee made *Get On the Bus* (1996) through investment by a number of African-American businessmen, who formed a company – 15 Black Men – in the process. Again, failure means the loss of personal money, but at least private investors are allowed to make the choice themselves without the emotional coercion that persuading friends and family almost inevitably involves.

As the prominence of the independent sector of American movie-making has grown over the past decade or two, so has the number of organisations able to offer grant subsidies. Examples would be the Independent Feature Project, Association of Video and Film-makers; Black Film-makers Foundation; and the Association of Independent Video and Film-makers. Spike Lee received $18,000 from the New York State Council on the Arts to part fund *She's Gotta Have It* (1986).

Increasingly, independent film-makers are raising capital for their films by pre-selling the rights, especially to European parties, to cinema release and to domestic and/or foreign video distribution, and cable and satellite transmission. The budget for Boaz Yakin's *Fresh* (1994), for example, came from the Paris-based Lumière company. Jim Jarmusch's last two features were funded by JVC. Similarly, home video has financed many independent productions, including Neal Jimenez's *The Waterdance* (1991), by RCA/Columbia Home Video and Quentin Tarantino's *Reservoir Dogs* (1992) part funded by Live Entertainment.

INFLUENCES AND MENTORS

The experience of certain film-makers from the beginning of the period covered by this book – most notably, John Cassavetes and Robert Altman – offers a blueprint for the problematic relationship between independent film-makers and an increasingly depersonalised Hollywood film industry. If I concentrate only on these two, it is because their careers perfectly illustrate the range of issues involved in the subject as a whole.

Throughout John Cassavetes's acting and film-making career, he sought to negotiate a position between the two camps of mainstream and independent cinema. As so many independent film-makers were to do after him, he used the money he was able to earn acting in conventional films (*The Killers*, 1964; *The Dirty Dozen*, 1967; *Rosemary's Baby*, 1968) and television series (*Johnny Staccato*, 1959) to fund his more experimental and personal film-making efforts. His first feature, *Shadows* (1959) was made after a radio audience collectively donated $20,000 to him following his revelation during an interview that he would like to film an improvisatory project. It tells the story of the troubled lives of three black siblings, two of whom pass themselves off as white in order to gain greater social acceptance – a courageous examination, given the date, of racial tension and attitudes. More significant, perhaps, is the fate of the film itself, which was passed over by American distributors until Cassavetes won the Critics' Award at the Venice Film Festival.

The film's later success in the US led to Cassavetes being wooed by the studios to make further films; an offer he accepted for a short while (*Too Late Blues*, 1961 for Paramount, and *A Child is Waiting*, 1963 for United Artists, and starring Burt Lancaster and Judy Garland). The subjects of the two films might be said to be prophetic of Cassavetes' relationship with studio film-making. *Too Late Blues* describes a jazz musician's fears of selling out by going commercial. *A Child Is Waiting* concerns a confused spinster joining the staff of a school for mentally handicapped children. Both are therefore about the relationship of the individual to 'the system', and about how integrity can be maintained in the face of pressures to conform. Significantly, studio interference on these two films made Cassavetes disillusioned with mainstream film-making and he went independent again, continuing to establish his position as a founding father of modern independent American cinema with such films as *Faces* (1968), *Husbands* (1970), *The Killing of a Chinese Bookie* (1978), and *Gloria* (1980). However, he continued this on/off relationship with the studios in terms of distribution, by organising the release of some of his films himself while using major studio networks for others. For example he released *Woman Under the Influence* (1974) and *The Killing of a Chinese Bookie* under his own distribution initiatives, Faces International and Faces

Distributing Corporation, respectively, while using Universal and Columbia, respectively, to release *Minnie and Moskowitz* (1971) and *Gloria*.

Cassavetes' films take an unremitting look at human relationships and the failure of people to communicate. *Faces* ends with the couple, their relationship having irreparably broken down but unable to finally leave one another, sitting blankly on the stairs of their home. *Husbands* shows a group of men exploring their innermost emotions when one of their friends unexpectedly dies. These emotional and psychological examinations are figured formally. Lengthy takes with hand-held camera, multiple-camera shooting, and harsh lighting give the films the look of cinéma vérité, putting the characters under scrutiny and refusing to allow them, or the audience, to look away. Improvisation in the acting continually pushes the exploration of emotion further, to the outer boundaries of bearability. Technical faults are left in, if the emotional content of the scene is right. Elliptical editing often throws the spectator into the middle or end of a scene, giving the feeling that the action is actually occurring and we have suddenly happened upon it. All of this is the complete opposite of Hollywood film-making, with its emphasis on polished images and smooth continuity. Cassavetes' total independence – he largely financed his films himself – gave him the luxury of open filming schedules. He could take as long as he wanted over each film. Although, or perhaps even because, he stuck rigidly to his artistic principles, Cassavetes never really made a financial success of any of his films. Nevertheless he has become a beacon for the new generation of independent film-makers who will be discussed throughout this chapter.

After 15 years of intermittent directing work, Robert Altman had a significant success with *M*A*S*H*, in 1970. With $36.7 million in rentals, the film became the third highest-grossing motion picture of 1970, behind *Love Story* and *Airport* (Biskind, 1998; p.97). Moreover, as a full-fledged 'Altman' film, it announced him as both an auteur, and as a major player in the changing Hollywood landscape. He maintained this identity with his next few films. *McCabe and Mrs Miller* (1971) reinterpreted the romantic myth of the West by filtering it through Altman's cynicism regarding contemporary politics. *The Long Goodbye* (1973) performed a similar refiguring by taking the assured detective character from the classic 1940s film noir and placing him in a dark and confusing contemporary setting, filmed, as Robert Kolker argues, with a disorientating style which 'uproot[s] perceptual stability, preventing a secure, centred observation of the characters in their surroundings' (Kolker, 2000; p.344). Finally, in *Nashville* (1975), Altman employs a distancing cinematic style in which scenes are cut off before emotional connection can be made between characters and spectator, and the multi-thread narrative ensures that no one character is kept on screen for long enough at any one time to establish audience empathy.

At a time when the studios were looking to irreverent new talent to help save the industry from the crisis in which it found itself by the late 1960s, Altman, nearly 50 years old in 1970, was both a little too old to be one of the new kids on the block, and, with his maverick, anti-establishment manner, perfectly suited to the iconoclasm of the times. 'Throughout the seventies, he had been able to use the economic and emotional system of Hollywood film-making to the advantage of his work and the benefit of exceptional film-making' (Kolker, 2000; p.330). By the late 1970s, however, Altman had a multi-film deal with Twentieth Century-Fox cancelled after a string of failures. His last big-budget production, *Popeye* (1980), made for Paramount and Disney in 1981, was also a box-office failure. Thereafter, he went into independent production throughout the 1980s, making a series of films based on contemporary American plays – for example, *Come Back to the Five and Dime, Jimmy Dean, Jimmy Dean* (1982) and *Fool For Love* (1985), both with scripts by the original playwrights, Ed Graczyk and Sam Shepard respectively. These plays-into-films allowed Altman to take material being written by writers who were the most incisive of thinkers about modern relationships and the state of the American Dream and add his own twist to their observations. The restricted physical spaces of these films, dictated by their stage origins, also allowed the production budgets for the films to be kept at a reasonable level. The 1990s saw Altman's 'comeback', first with *The Player* (1992) and then *Short Cuts* (1993), both films made by Avenue Picture Productions and Spelling Entertainment, with Guild contributing to the former and First Line Features to the latter, and distributed by First Line Features and the Spanish company Lauren Film.

Altman's iconoclastic position and style of film-making was representative of Hollywood's bright new future after the failure of bloated big-budget films of the mid-1960s. It is a marker of the shift of values that occurred during the 1970s that this style could so soon fall out of fashion as Hollywood regrouped and returned to making expensive mass-appeal films again by the end of the decade. A film like *Superman* (1978), for example, featured the same kind of massive sets and expensive stars (Marlon Brando received $3 million for a few days' work on it) as a film such as *Dr Dolittle* (1967). The difference, of course, is that the latter flopped and the former went on to make hundreds of millions of dollars at the box office.

In some ways Altman's career, constantly oscillating between working within Hollywood and outside it as an independent, neatly represents the troubled but interconnected relationship between the mainstream and independent strands of the American film industry. It would be a great mistake to see the two arenas as fundamentally and irrevocably separate: each needs to identify the other as 'Other' and needs that other for what it can bring them. For Hollywood that means fresh talent and new creative blood. For the independent film-maker, it means the tools and money by which to get their film made and, more frequently, seen by the largest possible audience.

Together, Cassavetes and Altman illustrate the various dynamics operating to define the relationship between the independent and mainstream sectors of the American film industry. They demonstrate the need for Hollywood to use original and creative film-makers to rejuvenate its periodically stagnant industry, as well as its habitual difficulty in controlling, and then finding unacceptable, the films those maverick talents create. Ultimately, they high-light Hollywood's inherently conservative nature coupled with a willingness to absorb, and make use of, a talent it does not really understand. Most importantly, perhaps, they illustrate that 'what goes around, comes around'. The situation at the end of the 1990s was in many ways similar to the one at the end of the 1960s, in that idealistic and personally motivated young film-makers are entering into relationships with the Hollywood majors which will inevitably compromise their artistic aspirations. In an on-line interview James Gray, for example, commented that 'if you keep making films, things like distribution will follow, because quality always wins. Don't let anyone tell you anything else' (America On-line Transcript, 1995; p.2). Gray has also expressed admiration for Coppola and Scorsese, as well as non-American directors such as Kurosawa and Fellini; indeed, in the online interview he cites Visconti's *Rocco and His Brothers* (1960) and Coppola's *The Godfather* (1972) as direct influences for the project he was then just beginning to develop: his second feature *The Yards* (2000). But the reception of his two films to date – *Little Odessa* (1996) and *The Yards* – indicates the qualitative difference between the two films, with the first being seen as a film with clear personal vision, the second a more conventional crime narrative with star actors. The first was financed by the independent company New Line and its independent subsidiary Fine Line Features, the second by the mini-major (and Disney partner) Miramax.

THE SUNDANCE INSTITUTE

It is perhaps ironic that the most significant element in the expansion and legitimacy of the American independent film sector has come about due to the efforts of one of the American mainstream cinema's most enduring and iconic stars: Robert Redford. In 1980, Redford established the Sundance Film Institute at Park City in the mountains of Utah, which offered screenwriting and film-making labs for new film-makers wanting help to get their first projects underway. It was soon realised that, while such facilities were important to new film-makers, an exhibition arm was also required in order to ensure that the films that were being made would actually be seen.

Therefore, in 1985, Redford took over the moribund USA Film Festival, turning it into a premiere exhibition platform for independent films. For the next three or four years, the number of films made and exhibited at the Institute and its festival steadily grew. Its importance for independent film-making during the early 1990s is summed up by Jon Pierson, when, writing about the 1992 festival, he observes that:

> *From here on in, Sundance would be bursting at the seams . . . While everyone is looking for the next Quentin, they should think about all the other notable film-makers that emerged from or were boosted by the Sundance between Soderbergh in 1989 and Tarantino in 1992: Reggie Hudlin, Maggie Greenwald, Norman Rene, Whit Stillman, Hal Hartley, Julie Dash, Todd Haynes, Richard Linklater, Matty Rich, Jennie Livingston, Joe Berlinger, Allison Anders, Alexandre Rockwell, Tom DiCillo, Gregg Araki, Tom Kalin, Neal Jimenez, Anthony Drazen.*

(Pierson, 1995; p.211)

The film-event which put Sundance firmly on the map, as indicated by Pierson's use of Steven Soderbergh as his first temporal bookend in the above quote, was the screening of Soderbergh's *sex, lies and videotape* at the 1989 festival. The buzz around the film, and its subsequent box-office success, both foregrounded the importance of Sundance as an outlet for independent cinema, and illustrated the potential profitability of at least some of the films being made within the independent sector. Hollywood had been forced to sit up and take notice.

But equally significant in the above quote is Pierson's comment that 'from here on in, Sundance would be bursting at the seams'. Many independent practitioners – such as directors John Fitzgerald, Shane Kuhn and Dan Mirvish, whose films *Self Portrait* (1994), *Redneck* (1995) and *Omaha: The Movie* (1994), respectively, were snubbed by Sundance in 1995, causing them to found the Slamdance Festival in response – are expressing concern at the direction that the Sundance festival has taken in recent years (Levy, 1999; p.44). Because of its importance as a site for exposing new films and new talent, and because Hollywood has now become very interested in acquiring both those films and their talented creators, it has been accused of selling out and becoming a mere middleman for the mainstream industry's efforts to buy into, and buy up, the independent sector. This effort is operating on a far wider scale than simply once a year in the hills of Utah, as the final section of this chapter will show. But as a symbol of the way in which the independence of the independent sector is becoming compromised, the increasing numbers of studio executives to be found negotiating deals with independent film-makers during each Sundance festival is a potent image. 'When the main-

Andie MacDowell behind the camera in *sex, lies and videotape* (Steven Soderbergh, 1989)

stream industry realised there was financial profit possible here, that started the ball rolling . . . Hollywood comes here for a very clear reason – to discover talent they think will be profitable, or to buy films they think will be profitable' (Robert Redford, quoted in Levy, 1999; p.43).

So much for the context within which independent films have been made in America over the past two decades. But what about the individual film-makers and their works; is there a way of organising a diverse and frenetic production field into some clear thematic lines? As has been noted at the beginning of this chapter, one of independent cinema's strongest claims is that it offers a mouthpiece to those segments of American society which are habitually refused a voice of their own. One of the ways in which the field can be organised, therefore, is in terms of its minority groups. Several main groupings can be identified, aligned along both racial and sexual axes: Black film-making, Asian-American cinema, Native American cinema, Hispanic cinema, gay and lesbian cinema, feminist cinema. We must be careful here, however. Most, if not all, independent film-makers would be keen to avoid such simple pigeonholing, which amounts to a stereotyping of a different kind. Many of the films under discussion throughout this chapter do not offer such easy definitions or neat boundaries. White directors make films about Black characters and issues; gay directors describe heterosexual relationships;

Asian directors explore white American family life. Nevertheless, it is still necessary to carry out some kind of organisational grouping, if only nominally to offer a route, or series of routes, through the mass of independent films that have been made in America over the past 20 years.

SEXUAL IDENTITY AND GENDER IN INDEPENDENT CINEMA

This section examines two main areas of 'sexual politics' cinema which are not wholly separate and distinct from one another: feminist film-making and gay/lesbian, or 'queer' cinema.

Female writers, directors, producers have been present in the American film industry since its inception. The screenwriter Francis Marion, director Lois Weber, and star/producer/directors Lillian Gish and Ida Lupino are only a few of the names that could be mentioned. Women have been especially active in the experimental and avant-garde arena. In the 1930s, Mary Ellen Bute, with films such as *Rhythm in Light* (1934), *Synchromy No. 2* (1935) and *Dada* (1936), explored abstract formal constructions. Maya Deren in the 1940s played with notion of temporal and personal identity in films such as *Meshes of the Afternoon* (1943) and *Ritual in Transfigured Time* (1946). And in the 1950s and 1960s, Shirley Clarke made films such as *The Connection* (1961), *The Cool World* (1963) and *A Portrait of Jason* (1967) which used film to explore the worlds of the outcast and downtrodden. It is perhaps this greater degree of activity which gives us a lead in to understanding the importance of the relationship between the independent sector of American film-making and its female creative personnel.

Even in supposedly enlightened times, there is continued industry resistance to women reaching the top creative and managerial positions in the American mainstream film industry. 'As Martha Coolidge put it, "if I were a man, I would have been directing major features long before this, but what's the point of dwelling on it?"' (Hillier, 1992; p.127). In the face of this frustration, independent film-making becomes an important arena where women film-makers can get a start and where they can articulate a specific female-oriented agenda.

Many independent films made by female directors directly address subjects which are either denied or underrepresented in a mainstream cinema largely made and controlled by white males. These might include the oppression and violence suffered by women across their history, or more positive images such as their perseverance and endurance, winning over the odds, and maintaining their integrity. Further, independent films allow a space in which the specifics of women's relations with other women and the taboo subject of female desire, whether hetero- or homo-sexual, can be discussed.

Allison Anders often explores the theme of working-class women persevering under exhaustingly difficult circumstances. In her *Gas Food Lodging* (1991), she tells the story of the difficulties experienced by a single working mother bringing up two teenage daughters in a New Mexico town. Unsentimental but not heavy-handed, Anders uses humour to depict the reality of disadvantaged women's lives. *Mi Vida Loca* (1993), although it succeeds at the level of acting, largely through the mixing of professional with real-life female gang members, has a weak narrative. Levy is heavily critical of *Grace of My Heart* (1996), for what he sees as its overly schematic structure and cliché-ridden dialogue; an opinion backed up by Richard Corliss (Levy, 1999; p.382). *Sugar Town* (1999) repeated Anders' awkward tendency to reduce the effect of strongly realised characterisation by surrounding it with a convoluted and muddled narrative line. Her latest film, *Things Behind the Sun* (2001), a film about the traumatic effects of sexual abuse set amongst rock music and journalism, maintains some of the same flaws, although the balance between characters and their story is more even. Indeed, when it was shown at Sundance, it received a five-minute standing ovation. Perhaps her stint as a director on the TV series *Sex and the City* in 1998 instilled in her a clearer grasp of story-telling.

Susan Seidelman began her career by examining similar subject-matter to Anders. In the low-budget *Smithereens* (1982), she shows the lead female character (Wren) as someone whose dreams of becoming famous can never be backed up by the necessary talent. Seidelman continues this theme in her next film, *Desperately Seeking Susan* (1985), in which Rosanna Arquette plays a bored housewife fantasising about the exotic life of people whose names she reads in the personal ads in her local paper. One of the exotic people was played by Madonna, who had her big break in the music industry as the film was moving from production to release. The semi-independent film was financed with $5 million from Orion.

Seidelman soon moved more fully into the studio-financed mainstream with films such as *Making Mr Right* (1987), *Cookie* (1989) and *She-Devil* (1989). The first and last of these only nominally purported to explore feminist issues; the middle one was a misjudged attempt at comedy, being about the relationship between a mobster and his wild daughter. After this string of failures, Seidelman moved into television, directing episodes of several series, including *Tales of Erotica* (1996), *Early Edition* (1996), *Sex and the City* (1998) and *Now and Again* (1999). However, in the last couple of years, she has returned to feature production, with *A Cooler Climate* (1999), starring Sally Field and Judy Davis, and *Gaudi Afternoon* (2001).

Kathryn Bigelow adopted a different tack in order to forge a career for herself in the male-dominated world of film-making, by taking on the values of that industry on her own terms. During the 1980s and early 1990s she made a series of action-based films which reworked a number of the major genres: horror in *Near Dark* (1987), the cop movie in *Blue Steel* (1990), the male-buddy action-thriller in *Point Break* (1991), and science-fiction in *Strange Days* (1995). In many of these films, she was able to engage with certain gender-specific issues concerning the ability of her women characters to be proactive rather than passive. The Black female lead played by Angela Bassett in *Strange Days*, for example, effectively becomes the saviour of the leading male character, played by Ralph Fiennes. In *Blue Steel*, the police-woman stalked by a psychopath turns aggressor in order to find and capture him.

But Bigelow frames these active female characters within her own career trajectory. As Levy says of her, she 'was determined to shatter gender stereotypes, to push the envelope of women's film-making. In an age when women directors were still expected to make "women's films" – small, modest, sensitive – she proceeded with flamboyant pictures' (Levy, 1999; p.368). *The Weight of Water* (2000) interweaves two stories – one modern, the other period – in an attempt to draw comparisons between past and contemporary characters. The concept is flawed and clumsily executed. Visually, however, as with all of Bigelow's films, it is very striking. At the time of writing (2002) she has directed another big-budget action blockbuster, *K19: The Widowmaker*, starring Harrison Ford as the commander of Russia's first nuclear ballistic submarine, which suffered a malfunction in its reactor on its maiden voyage in 1961.

Other women directors have chosen to explore the terrain of female desire. Joyce Chopra's *Smooth Talk* (1985) tells the story of a young woman coming under the spell of a male stranger who seduces her, at first verbally through his overtures to her, and then, ambiguously, physically in a long, dreamily photographed scene in which she gets into his car. The sexually charged atmosphere, which represents the female character's own sexual awakening, is subtly created. Through the formal style of her film, with its soft focus, its pastel colour palette, and its floating, dreamy camerawork, Chopra shows that, for a young woman, attraction is as much – if not more – to do with sensuality, seduction and fantasy as it is about sex. The lack of an explicit sex-scene as a climax to the narrative line is significant in this respect. A male director might well have felt the need to use nudity and simulated intercourse to represent the final seduction. In so doing, he would have made concrete what works far better as abstraction. Having made such a distinctive debut, however, Chopra made only one more feature, *The Lemon Sisters* (1990), before moving into television for the whole of the 1990s; her latest produc-tion there has been *Blonde* (2001), a mini-series about Marilyn Monroe.

A number of issues arise from these short biographies. Firstly, they demonstrate the difficulty experienced by women directors in sustaining consistent careers in the American film industry. Seidelman, Anders and Chopra have all, for greater or shorter periods, given up on trying to make films and have become jobbing directors for television, where their hopes of making personal works are inevitably severely compromised by the impersonal formats of the television series, and the time pressures of television production. Significantly, the only one of the group to have maintained a film career is Kathryn Bigelow, largely by making the kind of male-oriented action films that have a greater chance of succeeding at the box office.

This fact brings into focus a particularity about many of the films just cited: namely, that, with the exception of Bigelow's films, they tend to display a preference for character over narrative. This indicates, perhaps, a certain female film-making sensibility which is more interested in exploring emotion and states of mind than in describing events. And the relative failure of many of them in box-office terms suggests that the public, while possibly indicating that it would like films which more directly relate to real life and the human condition, is as dependent upon escapist fiction narrative as ever.

These are only a few film-makers and a few of their films. I have chosen them because they seem to offer a number of different strategies used by women directors to claim a stake in the contemporary American film industry, as well as a number of perspectives on the female-centred subject matter being chosen. None is unproblematic, not merely because of the specific professional pressures felt by women film-makers operating in a predominantly male industry, but also because of the particular difficulties of expressing a sensibility which has long been forced into silence by that industry.

QUEER CINEMA

As with the expression of a true female sensibility (as opposed to a male-imagined female sensibility), the issues involved in the gay lifestyle are another area which has been steadfastly underrepresented by mainstream Hollywood. Again, as with the reluctance to address female-centred concerns, this has been the result of an industry dominated (at least purportedly) by white heterosexual males. The independent sector has therefore provided a vital outlet for explorations and depictions of that alternative lifestyle.

The rise of contemporary gay and lesbian independent cinema over the past two decades was kick-started by a series of important and influential documentaries. In 1971, Ken Robinson made the cinéma-vérité influenced *Some of Your Best Friends*, in which he interviewed some of the members of the Gay Liberation movement about its history and that of their own oppression. *Word Is Out: Stories of Some of Our Lives* (1978), privately financed after two years spent trying to get funding, was produced by Peter Adair and directed by

Lucy Massie Phoenix and Robert Epstein. The film is split into three sections: 'The Early Years', 'Growing Up' and 'From Now On' and shows a diverse range (in terms of age, social class, sexual orientation) of participant interviewees, who are asked to talk about their experiences and perceptions of being gay. Neither does the film shy away from difficult representations, including the question of stereotyping and how the gay community both uses it and resists it.

Gay USA (1977), made by Artists United for Gay Rights and directed by Arthur Bressan, takes a different approach. Filmed in one day (June 26 1977) by six crews in six different cities, and focusing on a series of gay marches and parades, the film flips continually between them to show the common threads running through the experiences of gays living in modern America. As such, the film is about community rather than individual experience, setting this in a wider social frame: the marches are compared, for example, with similar civil rights marches.

The Times of Harvey Milk (1984), in contrast, focuses on one man, the openly gay Harvey Milk, who won an official position as City Supervisor in San Francisco in 1978, before being murdered by fellow Supervisor Dan White. The murder, and subsequent sensational court case, provoked Robert Epstein to make the documentary film about Milk's life and death. Poignant and uplifting, rather than proclamatory and depressing, the film was a tribute to a significant member of the gay rights community, and a clarion call for the movement.

It is perhaps not surprising that documentary was such an important format for exploring gay issues in the 1970s and 1980s. Hollywood resistance and the cumbersome nature of feature film production (expensive, lengthy, fraught with institutional problems like actors, scripts, etc.) meant that the documentary format – cheaper, showing real people who could be quickly interviewed, observing self-defined events – became the form which initially most empowered disenfranchised gay film-makers.

Of course, from the early 1980s onwards, the emergence of the AIDS epidemic galvanised and focused attention on a crisis that threatened to overwhelm the gay community. The exploration of the issues involved in the AIDS crisis began in a relatively softly-softly manner, offering treatments which only partly improved upon such studio-produced pre-AIDS films as *Making Love* (1982) and *Personal Best* (1982). The independently produced, Donna Deitch-directed, *Desert Hearts* (1985), although it showed a sensitivity to the emotional truth of its characters, echoed this soft-focus, beautifully photographed, view of gay sex. *Parting Glances* (1986) tackled AIDS head-on, although its final agenda was more an attempt to describe honestly the reality of life in the New York gay community than it was an examination of, or reaction to, the epidemic itself. Indeed, the characters are all represented as flawed to varying degrees, rather than as paragons of virtue. In spite of the threat of AIDS within the narrative, the film's final message is upbeat and positive. Perhaps it had to be, given the fear that AIDS was beginning to strike into gay (and heterosexual) communities everywhere by the mid-1980s. This positive spirit was certainly tested as the epidemic continued to expand through the second half of the decade. Norman Rene's *Longtime Companion* (1990) is a more pessimistic film, showing the invidious effects of AIDS on a group of white middle-class men. A few years later, mainstream American film-making caught up with gay subject matter as the basis of feature film narratives – most famously in *Philadelphia* (1993), starring Tom Hanks, who won an Oscar for his role in the film. The film's treatment of gay issues and the AIDS crisis is regarded as too 'broad and clinical', but 'the commercial success of *Philadelphia* in Middle America made it easier for adventurous gay films to thrive in the marketplace' (Levy, 1999; p.463).

What strikes one about these fictional accounts of gay life and AIDS is that the protagonists all come from a certain stratum of society. They are all fairly affluent, leading comfortable, stylish lives. This choice of social milieu has a specific agenda. It suggested to audiences, who might not be immediately attracted to the idea of seeing them, that not only would the films look good, but that they would be peopled by characters to whom the general audience, both homo- and hetero-sexual, could relate. Moreover, it suggested that AIDS was not simply a gay disease, but could easily have struck at other sections of the public, people 'just like themselves'. The other thing one realises is that, as with its decade long denial of the Vietnam war, Hollywood needed a considerable temporal distance before it could even begin to address adequately the issues involved in the decimation of the gay community by the AIDS virus.

One film-maker who did explore gay social groups other than white middle-class professionals, and put them in wider contexts than just their sexuality, was Gus Van Sant. In *Mala Noche* (1985), a self-financed film about a doomed affair between an American and a Mexican immigrant, Van Sant established his penchant for exploring the lives of young 'grunge-culture' characters. His second feature, *Drugstore Cowboy* (1989), however, explored the world of the young, drug-addicted, petty criminal, and only concerns itself tangentially with homosexuality. Finally, in *My Own Private Idaho* (1991), a film which depicts a homoerotic liaison between two male hustlers, his narrative concerns were focused on the two main characters' search for father figures rather than their sexual liaison. In recent years, in films such as *To Die For* (1995), *Good Will Hunting* (1997) and the remake of *Psycho* (1998), Van Sant has left the gay milieu behind and gone more mainstream.

Lesbians have suffered as much as homosexuals from stereotyping in mainstream American film-making – perhaps even more so. Indeed, they have rarely featured at all in Hollywood productions. When they have, their sexuality has generally either been airbrushed in order to minimise potential offence to mainstream audiences (for example, in the toning down of the lesbian material in Spielberg's *The Color Purple* [1985]), or represented by dangerous and psychotic characters (such as Sharon Stone's ice-pick wielding bisexual in *Basic Instinct* [1992]). Given the continuing resistances (social, psychological, emotional) to women film-makers even in independent cinema, it is perhaps not surprising that films about lesbians are even thinner on the ground than films about gays. Even those that have appeared in recent years show signs of their difficult development. Nicole Conn's *Claire of the Moon* (1992), for example, is overly schematic in its attempt to orchestrate polar characters so that interesting interactions can be manufactured in order to allow the film-maker to explore her themes. The most fully realised lesbian film of the early 1990s is perhaps Rose Troche's *Go Fish* (1994), a comedy with a real sense of lesbian sensibilities and a unerring eye for how women interact when by themselves. Its quirky, off-centre style and tenor allow it to avoid the slightly straight-faced approach to the subject suffered by some of its stable-mates, such as *Claire of the Moon* and, earlier, *Desert Hearts*.

Another strand of gay American film-making has a harder, more uncomfortable edge to it, designed to challenge more forcefully preconceived notions about gay culture and society. Less concerned about neatness and form, these films directly question the audience's reaction to their depiction of deviant characters and transgressive acts. Todd Haynes' first feature, *Poison* (1990) is composed of three interwoven stories – labelled 'Horror', 'Homo' and 'Hero' – in which themes and relationships are juxtaposed in order to bring up the full terms of the subject. Haynes takes a far more brutal and unremitting look at the real issues involved in homosexual love, by imaging those issues in terms of decaying bodies and exaggerated visuals. Even the title, as Levy observes, 'refers to society's practice of penalising deviants by stigmatising them' (Levy, 1999; p.465).

The films of Gregg Araki – *The Living End* (1992), *Totally F***ed Up* (1993), *The Doom Generation* (1995), and *Nowhere* (1997) – are even more angry, outrageous, violent, and uncomfortable, in their attempts to depict young lives torn between desire and apathy in the face of the increasing inevitability of death brought by AIDS. Araki's agenda is to aggressively resist homophobia in all its guises, even if, perhaps expressly because, this will court controversy. In *The Living End*, for example, homophobic characters are beaten up and a policeman has his head blown off. Araki's films are very low-budget: at $20,000, *The Living End* is his most expensive to date. This means that the films do not really have to earn very much at the box office in order to make their money back; a strategy which continues to allow Araki to say what he wants to say in exactly the way he wants to say it. Interestingly, even the abrasive style of Araki can be tamed: in 2000 he moved into television to make *This Is How the World Ends*.

A marker of the significance and potential of the new queer cinema was the establishment of specialist distributors, such as Frameline and Strand Releasing, who were specifically interested in handling gay material. Strand markets its films like exploitation horror films, spending nothing on publicity, but using word of mouth to spread awareness of new feature releases. Such small distributors can do things this way because of the clearly defined nature of the community they service and the efficient communications network it has set up. But alternative film-making communities have also had to develop different methods of distribution in the face of the mainstream's endemic strategy of blanket marketing and saturation release. Small independent gay film-makers, with specialist agendas and little hope of getting the majors to finance production or handle expensive marketing campaigns, truly had to 'go it alone'.

RACE AND MINORITY CINEMAS

Non-White cinema – an awkward umbrella term for a vibrant and productive range of film-making practices – is a major arena for the independent sector. There is space here to consider only two of these: African-American and Asian-American. Each will be dealt with in turn, beginning with perhaps the largest and most dominant one: Black film making.

Black independent cinema has been concerned to create and promote a specifically Black form of American culture. It draws upon distinctively Black art forms – such as gospel and spiritual, hip-hop and rap, as well as an acute sense of the history of oppression suffered by African-Americans over the past two centuries. Spike Lee's naming of his film company – 40 Acres and a Mule – is an obvious reference to this.

An examination of African-American film-making over the last two or three decades must begin by considering the blaxploitation cycles of films made in the 1970s. Although Ossie Davis had made *Cotton Comes to Harlem* (1970) for the Goldwyn company in 1970, the cycle is generally acknowledged to have started with Melvin Van Peebles' *Sweet Sweetback's Baadasssss Song* (1971). The blaxploitation movies revealed the presence of a potentially huge Black audience who were not being given films specific or relevant to their lives and concerns. *Sweet Sweetback's Baadasssss Song* was independently financed by donations from the African-American community, when the studios refused to back such a potentially controversial film. The main character, played by the film's writer/producer/director Melvin Van Peebles, works as a sexual performer in a brothel, kills three policemen and has sex with several women during the course of the film. The film, an angry denunciation of White American attitudes and treatment of Blacks, born out of the political and social upheavals of 1960s – the civil rights and women's movements, race riots, and political assassinations including that of Martin Luther King – established many of the elements that would be developed across the whole canon of blaxploitation films.

Almost immediately, once *Sweet Sweetback* had proved the existence of a new, Black, audience, the studios moved in to commandeer the blaxploitation film, with MGM and Warner Bros., for example, financing *Shaft* (1971), and *Superfly* (1972), respectively. More cheaply made, Black-themed action films, of generally decreasing quality, followed, including *Detroit 9000* (1973) and *The Black Godfather* (1974), in an effort to maximise profits before the seam ran dry and the bubble burst. A secondary strand of films featured female characters in an attempt to expand the market by appealing to female members of the audience. Most notable examples were *Coffy* (1973) and *Black Girl* (1972), the latter offering the standard wish-fulfilment narrative of a young women who wants to escape the ghetto by becoming a dancer.

It is debatable whether the blaxploitation films, with their exaggerated sexual stereotypes such as the 'jive-talking, sex-machine' male, ever fully represented Black reality. However, the presence of so many Black characters commanding the foreground in a long series of films was instrumental in shifting the base-level perception of Blacks in American cinema. Black actors, henceforth, could be seen to carry a film's narrative, and capture a fan base that would ensure a returning audience for future films in which those actors might appear.

The success of some of the early blaxploitation films inevitably roused the interest of the major studios, which then financed the rest of the blaxploitation film cycle. Studio control drew the strength out of the cycle, resulting in a 'law of diminishing returns' as it went on. But it also, negatively and positively, galvanised future Black film-makers to determine not to have those social and sexual stereotypes maintained. Later generations of Black film-makers would use the forms and distortions of the blaxploitation films as a starting point for more truthful and honest depictions of Black characters. Those efforts would largely be played out within the independent film-making sector.

An unavoidable presence in contemporary Black American film-making, against which the efforts and activities of many other Black film-makers are inevitably compared, is that of Spike Lee. Lee has been the cause of considerable debate regarding his talents and political position. He has been criticised, for example by Amiri Bakara, for being ahistorical, for creating cartoon-like characters, and for being an upwardly mobile, petit bourgeois professional film-maker who has left his roots behind (Bakara, 1993; p.146). Others, such as Houston A. Baker, Jr., disagree:

> [a]lways [going] beneath the covering sentimentality, and forever breaking the quiet silences of Black, middle class respectability, Lee unmasks those truths that Black people know to be self-evident, but seldom have the courage to speak of . . . Lee's first films are low-budget, minor masterpieces of cultural undercover work. They find the sleeping or silenced subject and deftly awaken him or her to consciousness of currents that run deep and signify expansively in Black America.
>
> (Baker, 1993; pp.164, 166)

She's Gotta Have It (1986), Lee's debut feature, was made in 12 days on an $80,000 budget. The Los Angeles Times, on 21 August 1986, thought that 'There's something genuinely different here, a perspective we don't see enough – the joy and liveliness of an often neglected present. The movie's breeziness is tonic, refreshing [sic]' (quoted in Merritt, 2000; p.334). The refreshing thing about the film was its sexual frankness. It not only depicted Black men as ridiculous in their sexual vanity, but also gave a sexually confident and at-ease female character centre stage; an almost unique thing in the history of Black movies.

From this promising start, it is perhaps regrettable that Lee should so soon have become amenable to the idea of making studio-financed films, such as School Daze (1988), distributed by Columbia, Do the Right Thing (1989), released by Universal, and Malcolm X (1992), distributed, amongst others, by Warner Bros. Perhaps this is an unduly harsh comment. Certainly, Do the Right Thing has an emotional rawness and evident artistic integrity which would belie accusations of Lee's capitulation to mainstream studio pressures. Lee's saving grace has been that, while he has indeed made a number of larger-budget studio features, he has continued to make small independent films such as Get On the Bus (1996). Lee's career overall is marked by his constant oscillations between the two sectors of American film-making.

But, of course, there is much more to Black American film-making than blaxploitation movies and Spike Lee. As a sector of society that has, perhaps, justifiably more to protest about in the suppression of its identity, the film-making potential of African-Americans has been copious and forceful over the past three decades. In the early 1970s, for example, the Los Angeles Black Independent Film-making Movement emerged, founded at the University of California by African and African-American students under the aegis of Charles Burnett. It sought to question all aspects of the representation of Black people in film. Screenings and seminars interrogated the conventions of dominant cinema, and students dismantled the curriculum and instituted their own, more politically focused, one. 'A declaration of independence had been written in the overturning of the film school curriculum and in the formation of student-generated alternatives' (Bambara, 1993; p.119). Important works emerging from the movement included Haile Gerima's *Bush Mama* (1976) and Charles Burnett's *Killer of Sheep* (1977). Burnett's *To Sleep With Anger* (1990) is perhaps the most important of all. In its presentation of what appears to be a perfectly respectable Black middle-class household in the manner, as Levy notes (1990; p.408) of TV's *Cosby Show*, it marks the degree to which the depiction of Black families and characters has become normalised in American cinema. Having done this, however, Burnett places in tension with the conventional respectability of the Black family a character, Harry, played by Danny Glover, who, in his manner, amorality and belief in superstition and spells, represents a different, older order of Black man. This opposition of Black identities is resolved when it is revealed that Harry is a demon, 'the soul of the Southern sharecropper, who comes to haunt gentle folks who fondly remember the past in terms of food, music, and farming' (Levy, 1999; p.408). Burnett seems to be saying that Blacks, even when they have acquired the trappings of White Western living, should never distort their own history or forget their past oppression.

Robert Townsend has been a presence in Black American film-making for the last 20 years. After a period spent acting in films such as *A Soldier's Story* (1984), he used the money he had earned to finance his own film, *Hollywood Shuffle* (1987), about the struggles of a Black actor to make it in Hollywood. Ultimately unfocused in its attempt to lampoon while still saying serious things, the film is a reputable example of the determination of Black film-makers to have their frustrations and opinions heard.

The efforts of these early Black American film-makers opened the way for a new generation of Black film-makers, many of whom were coming out of film school. The new, young directors brought with them the values and sensibilities of 1990s Black American culture and strongly announced themes and issues – inner-city violence, drug-culture, the need on the part of young Black males for strong father-figures (echoed in many of the songs by Black artists hitting the charts at the same time). John Singleton's *Boyz 'N' the Hood* (1991) is perhaps the most significant in a crop of films by Black directors appearing that year, including Matty Rich's *Straight Out of Brooklyn* and Spike Lee's *Jungle Fever*. Its tale of warring gangs and young men desperate for older males to act as role models fitted the *Zeitgeist*. It was the first all-Black film to be financed by a major studio: Columbia. *Boyz 'N' the Hood* generated a series of films detailing Black gang culture, including the Hughes brothers' *Menace II Society* (1993) and, within a more specific gangster milieu, Van Peebles' *New Jack City* (1991).

But contemporary Black cinema has been too often identified solely with guns, gangs, sex and violence. There are other, less explored, strands, such as the comedies of Charles Lane – *Sidewalk Stories* (1989) and *True Identity* (1991) – which explore racial bigotry and homelessness in gentler ways, and the Hudlin brothers' *House Party* (1990) which shows a gentler Black culture with positive values, and which spawned a number of sequels.

As important as the films of Black male film-makers, though less fore-grounded, are the activities of a number of Black women directors. Julie Dash's *Daughters of the Dust* (1991) began the decade in which several important Black women film-makers would emerge. *Daughters of the Dust* explores the insecure sense of identity experienced by Black American women. 'A celebra-tion of a now forgotten culture [Sea Island woman off the coasts of South Carolina and Georgia], the film conveys Dash's version of history through the personal journeys of half a dozen women' (Levy, 1999; p.387). Other films take on more contemporary subject matter. Leslie Harris, in *Just Another Girl on the IRT* (1992) explores the pressures being suffered by young Black women in today's America by showing a central character who demonstrates irreconcilably contradictory reactions and emotions to the events she experi-ences during the film. Finally Darnell Martin, with *I Like It Like That* (1994), the first studio-produced film by a Black American woman director, explores the problems of an interracial marriage between a Black woman and a Latino; a touchy subject even in the mid-1990s when each section of minority America was seeking to identify and address its own identity.

Clearly these films, by both male and female Black film-makers, show a race which is painfully exploring the truth of its own social, political and cultural identity. The rawness – emotional, aesthetic, narrative – of many of the works in trying to achieve this definition is something that the major studios would never have accepted. Achieving such honest depictions of Black realities required the freer environment of the independent sector.

ASIAN-AMERICAN CINEMA

The explorations performed by Asian-American film-makers have more to do with feelings about their home countries, and the different set of spiritual and emotional values experienced there, than they do about defiantly defining an American consciousness, as Black film-makers are striving to do. Asian-Americans seem to want to leave their old countries behind, while simultaneously feeling compelled to refer to them. In this tension, the focus almost inevitably falls on the family.

Wayne Wang's debut film, *Chan is Missing* (1981), is an examination of Asian stereotypes, which explores issues of assimilation and identity as well as the political schism between Taiwan and China (Levy, 1999; p.328). Immediately we see an agenda in which clashes of social values and references from multiple cultures are consciously being played out. Wang uses irony and a comic playfulness to bring out a serious central core. These issues are continued in *Dim Sum: A Little Bit of Heart* (1985), in its examination of family relations and the erosion of traditional values, and *Eat a Bowl of Tea* (1989) and *The Joy Luck Club* (1993), Wang's only studio film, in which similar themes are dealt with in a glossier, bigger-budget production. *Smoke* and *Blue in the Face* (both 1995) see Wang moving away from Asian issues to explore specifically American ones, in the story, centred on a tobacconist's store, of a group of misfits who revolve around one another. Wang's ability to explore freely the cultural values of both Taiwan and America stems from his rootlessness: 'Because of the complete avoidance of talking about China, and having grown up in a British colony, and my parents being very pro-American, I grew up with no sense of identification with a country' (Thomson, 1985; p.24).

Ang Lee began his film-making career in Taiwan before moving to America. He had therefore established his major thematic and formal concerns before entering the American film industry. In *The Wedding Banquet* (1993), a gay couple set up a marriage of convenience to fool the Taiwanese partner's parents into thinking him straight. Both in the criticism of parental oppression and in the breaking of sexual taboo – it was the first Chinese film to show a gay couple kissing – Lee can be seen to be using the sexual situation to politically satirise China–Taiwan relations.

Lee soon shifted to making films about non-Asian subjects: *Sense and Sensibility* (1995) and *The Ice Storm* (1997). Such a move shows that he feels he has assimilated Western values, although it could be argued that he remains a detached observer of them. Central to Lee's development as a filmmaker, especially his integration into the American film industry, is the figure of James Schamus, who has acted as writer and producer on almost all of Lee's films: *The Wedding Banquet, Eat Drink Man Woman* (1994), *Sense and Sensibility* (co-producer only), *The Ice Storm*, and *Ride With the Devil* (1999). Recently, Lee and Schamus have returned to Asia to make *Crouching Tiger, Hidden Dragon* (2000) in China. However, Lee is adamant that his sensibility is American; indeed, specifically New York:

I'm a New York film-maker. Whether I'm doing an American or a Chinese film, whether I shoot in Taiwan or China, I will always have a New York point of view. I was very conscious of whether I was Chinese or American for a while, but then, what the hell, I'm myself. Let me be an individual film-maker and try to do the best I can.

(Blaine, 1993)

Perhaps this pairing of Lee and Schamus contributes to the mixing of agendas in their films together – Asian-American relations; sexual taboos and homosexual love; a male director making female-centred dramas. In creating these complex, multi-influence texts, Lee and Schamus demonstrate the difficulty in sharply defining areas of minority independent film-making.

EXPLOITATION MOVIES

Exploitation movies are an area of American film-making with which the studios have been reluctant to get too involved because of their associations with the unsavoury, distasteful and, depending upon the cultural climate, illegal. 'As usual, the Hollywood factories shied away from gratuitous gore and raw terror, so it was up to maverick moviemakers to give the teenagers what they wanted' (Merritt, 2000; p.285).

In the modern period, Roger Corman is acknowledged as the father of the exploitation film. Beginning in 1954, he has directed over 50 films and produced hundreds more. He has been responsible for launching the acting and directing careers of many of the most significant figures in the contemporary American film industry, including Francis Ford Coppola, Martin Scorsese, Jack Nicholson, and James Cameron. Corman's philosophy has always been to make films as fast as humanly possible on extremely low budgets, on the assumption that most of them would earn their money back and go into modest profit. He recognised that the exploitation arena was not one which expected its films to achieve the heights of artistic excellence. What was wanted were films which delivered cheap escapist thrills.

In recognising this, Corman contributed an overriding philosophy to both the 'movie brat' generation who moved into Hollywood in the early 1970s (to most of whom he had given their start), and the independent sector, which has thrived ever since. That is to say: investing millions of dollars in huge productions that have to play safe and conventional in order to gain a big enough audience to become profitable, results all too often in bloated and lifeless works with nothing to say. Better to take a novel idea and turn it as quickly as possible into a finished film, then move on to the next. That way, freshness and energy can be maintained and retained. Perhaps this, rather than his own film output, is Corman's abiding contribution to the American cinema of the past 30 years.

From this inspiration, many of the seminal horror films of the 1970s were made by film-makers operating independently. John Carpenter's *Halloween* (1978), made with a budget raised from foreign investors, George Romero's *Dawn of the Dead* (1979) and *Friday the 13th*, directed in 1980 by Sean S. Cunningham, were all independently produced, and were all big hits. *Halloween*

THE BLAIR WITCH PROJECT

A teaser image for *The Blair Witch Project* (Daniel Myrick and Eduardo Sánchez, 1999)

grossed $50 million domestically, *Friday the 13th*, $45 million. Once again, a sector of film-making ignored or rebuffed by the studios had proved itself to have massive financial potential. And as with other areas of film-making, the studios were not slow to realise this and move in. Subsequent sequels in the main horror cycles were studio-produced, usually by anonymous directors, and were invariably inferior.

A truly independent strain of horror films has continued, however, especially the so-called 'video nasties', starting with *The Texas Chainsaw Massacre* (1974), and moving through *Snuff* (1976), *I Spit On Your Grave* (1978), and *The Driller Killer* (1979). Hollywood has clearly differentiated between those horror films which are acceptable and those which are not. Those which are have been absorbed into its system and remade as sequels; those which are not have been, until recently, banned and shunned.

Independent horror film-making does, however, remain to the present date, most notably in *The Blair Witch Project* (1999), a micro-budget horror film which is self-referential in its independent status. As one of its writer/directors, Eduardo Sánchez has admitted: 'It used all the weaknesses of independent film – used them in its favour – like shaky camera work, no lighting, no-name talent' (Timberg, 1999; p.20). The significant difference with *The Blair Witch Project*, though, is that it imaginatively employed other aspects of modern media – namely, the Internet and the World Wide Web – to build up a public expectation about itself which converted the small film into a media event. Most significantly, this operation was conducted partly to circumvent the problem of interesting a studio in distributing and publicising it.

Similarly, the porn film has always offered a huge potential market. Even more unacceptable to conservative tastes than horror films, the porn film industry is the great 'unsaid' of the contemporary cinema. The early 1970s saw, not so much an explosion in the number and popularity of porn films (they already existed in quantity), but a public acknowledgement of them. Sexual mores had been changing for a decade or more, censorship had been relaxing generally, and the industry was still in disarray following the crisis of the late 1960s. Many small cinemas, unable to survive on dwindling mainstream audiences, turned to showing X-rated films to make ends meet. Porn became public, rather than private, big business. A number of seminal porn films – such as *The Devil in Miss Jones* and *Deep Throat*, both released in 1972, made millions at the box office. Particularly successful throughout this period (mid-1960s to mid-1970s) was Russ Meyer, who made a long series of trashy erotic films featuring big-breasted heroines and much tongue-in-cheek humour. Most notable amongst his output are *Faster, Pussycat! Kill! Kill!* (1965), *Vixen* (1968) and *Beyond the Valley of the Dolls* (1970). Although his films delivered exactly what the porn audiences wanted – nudity and lascivious action – Meyer was, at least, able to deliver these qualities with a degree of style and humour.

With the advent of new, portable equipment – lighter film, then video, cameras, and readily available digital editing equipment – the porn industry has moved into overdrive. Literally anyone can now become a porn-film maker. The potential of the porn market has been increased by new distribution media: videocassettes from the late 1970s and the World Wide Web from the mid-1990s. The ethos of independent film-making – minimal financial outlay, quick filming schedules, alternative distribution channels – is central to the porn film industry. Today, it makes more money for its operators than Hollywood.

DOCUMENTARY

There has been a rich vein of documentary film-making in America since the days of Robert Flaherty from the 1920s to the 1940s (*Nanook of the North*, 1921; *Louisiana Story*, 1948). At the beginning of the 1960s, a group of aspirant documentary film-makers – D.A. Pennebaker, Richard Leacock, the Maysles brothers – emerged under the aegis of *Time* magazine to develop the Direct Cinema or cinéma vérité style of documentary film-making. Aided by advances in equipment, especially lightweight 16mm cameras able to be synchronised to portable tape-recording machines, their style was marked by unsteady hand-held camera work, unmodified direct sound, and a reluctance to edit (although this latter element varied according to each individual's attitude to representing truth). Together they transformed modern American documentary film-making. In *Primary* (1960), Richard Leacock and Robert Drew covered the Wisconsin primary election campaign contest between

J.F. Kennedy and Hubert Humphrey. In *Don't Look Back*, Pennebaker recorded Bob Dylan's trip to England in 1967, while the Maysles filmed the infamous *Gimme Shelter* (1970), the Rolling Stones' 1969 tour of America, which culminated in the murder of a member of the audience by Hell's Angels. Together, these films announced a significant new American film-making movement, and enabled documentary films to reach a wider audience.

Moreover, the Direct Cinema style of documentary film-making seeped into fictional feature film production. Its influence can be seen throughout the 1970s in some of the most significant narrative films made by the leading directors. William Friedkin's *The French Connection* (1971) and Martin Scorsese's *Mean Streets* (1973), to take only two examples, exhibit some of the same techniques: unstable camera; edgy framing that threatens continually to lose the character it is trying to hold in vision; grainy texture to the film stock and natural lighting conditions. As Biskind notes: 'He [Friedkin] was comfortable with the documentary idiom and used it, giving the film a loose, handheld feel that anticipated *Hill Street Blues* by a decade . . . Scorsese gave us one [a coming-of-age story] as the Maysles brothers might have done it' (Biskind, 1998; pp.205, 250). It is no surprise to us that American documentary film-making should strongly influence the feature film directors emerging in the 1970s. Just as the documentarists rejected the glossy, professional look of mainstream cinema, the avowed aim of many of the new 'movie brats' was to shake up stale, traditional structures and film-making methods in Hollywood. The match was one waiting to be made in heaven.

Later documentaries, such as Errol Morris' *The Thin Blue Line* (1988), or the 'confession' documentary represented by Ross McElwee's *Sherman's March* (1986), and Michael Moore's *Roger and Me* (1989), ushered in a more personal style of documentary, in which the voice and presence of the film-maker, previously studiously omitted from the films of the Direct Cinema film-makers, were far more evident. *Roger and Me* was particularly influential. A personal vendetta against General Motors after they closed the car plant in his home town, throwing many of his friends and family out of work, Moore's funny and passionate film established him as a major presence in the documentary sector of the industry. Most significantly, the film was bought for $3 million by Warner Bros., which then spent $6 million promoting it. The $7 million it grossed domestically was disappointing for the studio, but counted as a major success for a documentary film. Warner Bros. eventually recouped its costs through a successful video release (85,000 units). Jon Pierson's estimate of *Roger and Me*'s final revenue total is around $13 million (Pierson, 1995; p.174). Moore's most recent, and equally crusading film, *Bowling for Columbine* (2002) won the 55th Anniversary Prize at Cannes.

The visual and aural qualities of Direct Cinema and its more modern incarnation, fly-on-the-wall, have also influenced the latest generation of independent film-makers. Films such as Kevin Smith's *Clerks* (1994) and Larry Clark's *Kids* (1995), for example, display the same unsteady camerawork and long takes in observing a group of individuals as they interact both with one another and their environment. *Clerks'* grainy black and white photography is a direct reference back to the early-1960s documentaries of Pennebaker and the Maysles brothers. And, as Levy has commented, Clark 'uses a restlessly mobile camera to give the picture an improvisational feel; the cinéma vérité style is uncompromising. *Kids* achieves a remarkable feat. It is a polished film that feels like a documentary' (Levy, 1999; p.289).

The influence of Direct Cinema also lies in the desire to explore unknown or neglected pockets of American society, to allow previously ignored individuals and social groups to gain a voice, or at least have their stories told. In this we see a direct line from Morris' *Gates of Heaven* (1978), a report on pet cemeteries in California, and *Vernon, Florida* (1981), which forms a loosely connected set of tales about a small southern town as recounted by some of its more eccentric inhabitants. It is possible to make the connection between the latter film and a film like Harmony Korine's *Gummo* (1997), not so much in its visual style or address (*Gummo* does not have straight-to-camera interviews, for instance), but in its quirky semi-humorous and slightly unsettling view of oddball, small-town American life.

WHITE GUYS CAN JUMP

Although it is too sharp a division, it is possible to discern a twin phase of 'White male' independent American film-making in the past two decades. The first phase consists of mature figures – Jim Jarmusch, John Sayles, and David Lynch – who have consistently tackled serious political and emotional issues in their films. They have investigated the difficult and sometimes unpalatable aspects of human life, relationships, and personal feelings. Theirs is a philosophical approach to their subjects, even though they are often explored using a comedic tone. Jarmusch's *Stranger Than Paradise* (1984), although nominally a comedy, uses an austere black-and-white aesthetic to depict a group of characters who find it difficult to relate meaningfully with the world. Its relatively small budget ($110,000) and international success (although it only grossed $3 million domestically, it was hailed as a masterpiece at several film festivals, including Cannes and New York) made it the beacon for all aspiring independent film-makers. *Down By Law* (1986) and *Mystery Train* (1989) form, together with *Stranger Than Paradise*, a trio of films which show America as viewed by the outsider. As Jarmusch himself has commented: 'America's a kind of throwaway culture that's a mixture of different cultures. To make a film about America, it seems to me logical to have at least one perspective that's transplanted because ours is a collection of transplanted influences' (quoted in Merritt, 2000; p.325).

In a different vein, John Sayles has repeatedly tackled serious social and political issues in his films, whether lesbianism in *Lianna* (1983), interracial love in *Baby, It's You* (1983) or striking coal miners in *Matewan* (1987). 'Sayles's diverse output is unified by a distinctly American dilemma: the tension between personal life and social responsibility, or·self-interest versus collective interest' (Levy, 1999; p.82). Although he can sometimes seem a little overearnest, there is no denying that Sayles has maintained his independent credentials for almost two decades now. Indeed, much of his later work is as formally accomplished and as politically contentious as his earlier films. *City of Hope* (1991) and *Lone Star* (1996), for example, both explore official corruption by using plots organised around family relations. The first explores corruption in the building industry by depicting a father under pressure to raze properties to the ground in order to make way for new building work, and a son caught up in the resultant power politics. The second uses a murder mystery plot, in which a law-enforcer son discovers the secret truth about his famous sheriff father, to explore interpersonal and interracial tensions in a small town in Texas. In *Men With Guns* (1997), a doctor takes a trip to visit former students now working in impoverished villages, and becomes politically awakened when he finds out that one of his students has been killed by guerrillas. Finally, in *Sunshine State* (2002), two woman return to their hometown roots in Florida, to deal with family, business, and the threat of encroaching real estate development. Taken together, Sayles's body of work reveals a consistently and passionately committed independent film-maker who has rarely compromised his integrity.

David Lynch has become something of a cult figure within independent and, indeed, mainstream American cinema over the past two decades or so. Since he made his notorious 'calling-card' film, *Eraserhead* (1977), he has been noted for his surreal, controversial and highly stylised work. As with other figures in the independent field, Lynch has made a career out of treading the fine line between independence and mainstream production. *The Elephant Man* (1980), for example, was a lavish, traditionally plotted film, albeit with a slightly sensational subject matter (a hideously deformed man in Victorian times). *Blue Velvet* (1986) displayed more of Lynch's particularly off-centre take on small-town American values, containing much that was extreme in both plot and characterisation (especially a deranged performance from Dennis Hopper), while exhibiting an ambiguity of meaning and tone which left many aspects of the film uncertain. This combination of playfulness and darkness was repeated in Lynch's television series *Twin Peaks* (1990), which he generally oversaw as well as directing several episodes. Indeed, it is interesting that Lynch spent so much of the early 1990s in television: as well as *Twin Peaks*, he was involved in writing and/or directing episodes of *American Chronicles* (1990), *On the Air* (1992) and *Hotel Room* (1993). Perhaps he felt that his quirky, small-scale observational style worked better on the small screen than in larger-budget, big-screen feature films. Certainly, the failure of the film spin-off of the *Twin Peaks* series – *Twin Peaks: Fire Walk With Me* (1992) – would seem to indicate this.

Lynch's recent work has received a more positive reaction. *Lost Highway* (1997), deeply ambiguous and intentionally difficult to follow, displays a great sense of the cinematic, especially in its subtle use of lighting and camerawork. *The Straight Story* (1999), a true story of an old man driving a lawn-mower thousands of miles across America to visit his ill brother, is a return to the eccentric and off-beat territory of *Twin Peaks* but without the sinister edge. *Mulholland Drive* (2001) won Lynch the Best Director award at Cannes 2001. Although Lynch's career has taken a number of unexpected twists and turns, he remains a very significant player in the American independent film arena.

The second phase involves a new generation of film-makers, often film school graduates, whose youth and particular take on life framed a whole section of American society in the 1990s: Generation X, disaffected and goalless, disenchanted with the possibilities and opportunities life has to offer. They have a juvenile obsession with the excesses of modern life, whether drugs, alcohol or sex.

The archetypal movie of this kind is perhaps *Slacker* (1991), made by Richard Linklater. In it, a group of characters talk about life in an aimless and unfocused way, the camera following each of them for a while before moving on to the next. The casual appearance of *Slacker* belies a carefully arranged structure. Linklater's next film, *Dazed and Confused* (1993) is similar, although set in 1976, and concerns another group of characters who lack personal beliefs and ambition, and for whom nothing significant ever happens. This theme is continued in *Before Sunrise* (1995), in which two young people, an American male (Ethan Hawke) and a French female (Julie Delpy), meet and begin talking on a long train journey through Austria. The film essentially consists of them getting to know one another in the course of one night, their long conversations and emotional sparring partly improvised by the actors. Linklater then went mainstream, with the expensive ($27 million), and poorly performing, Western *The Newton Boys* (1998).

Kevin Smith's *Clerks* (1994) depicts one day in the lives of a convenience store assistant and his friend, who runs the video shop next door. The mundane conversation, black humour, and relentless profanity are all elements of the Generation X film. Such an emphasis on 'youth issues' is perhaps not surprising in a generation of film-makers, many fresh from film

Philip Seymour Hoffman and Lara Flynn Boyle sitting uncomfortably in *Happiness*
(Todd Solondz, 1998)

school, who are themselves the same age as the late-teen/early-twenties
audiences who see their films.

There are film-makers who take a more mature approach to similar subject
matter. One such is Hal Hartley, whose episodic style, languid humour,
carefully composed *mise-en-scène* and emotionless acting are all in the service of a series of films – from *The Unbelievable Truth* (1990) through to *Henry
Fool* (1998) – which explore characters painfully moving towards a state of
self-awareness. Levy refers to Hartley's style as cruelly impersonal, employing
precise editing rhythms and stylised visuals. Style echoes content for a film-
maker interested in creating more than passing effect and instant sensation.

But there is another aspect to many of these films which deepens their
seriousness. While often appearing to be simply flirting with the outrageous
for effect, they address real social taboos: incest, paedophilia. David O.
Russell's *Spanking the Monkey* (1994) deals with the subject of masturbation
while delivering the shock of the lead character's incestuous relationship with
his mother. Todd Solondz's *Happiness* (1998) describes the emotional and
sexual repression of the members of the film's central family before revealing
that one of them is attracted to young children. The taboo-breaking nature of
the material in *Happiness* is reflected in the fact that the film had to be self-
released by Good Machine, when October, pressurised by its parent company
Universal, refused to distribute it because of its paedophilic material.

ACTORS/WRITERS/DIRECTORS

Several of the leading independent films of the past decade have been written, and often directed, by actors frustrated at their lack of success in the business, or by the kind of material being offered to them. This strategy has an illustrious ancestry, most notably in John Cassavetes and John Sayles, both of whom have been covered earlier in this chapter. John Turturro's *Mac* (1992) and *Illuminata* (1998); Steve Buscemi's *Trees Lounge* (1996); Billy Bob Thornton's *Sling Blade* (1996); *Swingers* (1996), written by John Favreau; Stanley Tucci and Campbell Scott's *Big Night* (1996) and Robert Duvall's *The Apostle* (1997) are just some of the many independent films whose lead actors are also their creators. As Greg Merritt notes in reference to *The Apostle*: 'Like his friend Billy Bob Thornton (who returns the *Sling Blade* favour [Duvall played a small part] and plays a small part in *The Apostle*) Duvall cast himself in the plum sort of role that almost never comes around in Hollywood' (Merritt, 2000; p.408).

We must also acknowledge Sylvester Stallone as a forerunner of these later actor/writers. His creation of *Rocky* (1976) gave him his first substantial star role (and two Oscar nominations as actor and writer). It is perhaps not surprising that actors want this kind of control over the roles they play on screen. But it is again true that the independent sector offers more freedom for them to be able to do so than the studio-produced mainstream, where the sums of money involved are so high that risks must be minimised by giving film projects to established directors.

STRANGE BEDFELLOWS

I want, finally, to investigate the current relationship between independent and studio-based film production. Independent film-making has habitually seen itself and gained a sense of identity as being in direct opposition to Hollywood, with its traditionally monolithic production processes which continually threaten to quash any kind of personal style or creativity. Of course, this was never true, and in some ways the opposite can be argued: that the studio system offered a stability within which the best artists could create their best work. Nevertheless, the very notion of independent cinema relies on the positioning of Hollywood as the 'evil Other'.

However, beginning in the mid-1980s, independent companies began establishing working relationships with Hollywood studios. For example, Hemdale, in 1986, released some of its films – notably *Platoon* and *Hoosiers* – through Orion. 'Hemdale certainly wasn't a major studio, but it's difficult to view its movies as "independent" . . . The distinction grew even murkier as major companies began to produce films specifically for cinematheques.

Hemdale released *River's Edge* through Island, an art-house distributor. In the smaller-stakes indie world, it was a success' (Merritt, 2000; pp.347–8).

There are mutual advantages to collaboration between independent film-maker or company and major studio. The independent gets substantial financial backing for its productions, as well as the opportunity to take advantage of the studio's well-oiled publicity and marketing machines, which increase the chances of any film achieving far wider exposure and potentially far larger box office, than could be hoped for by going it alone: 'Studio distribution of indie pics carries another kicker . . . since it often increases TV and cable rights for each release from roughly $750,000 to the estimated $2 million packages the majors can squeeze from the two ancillary markets' (Frook, 1992; p.106). The studio, in return, gets new product more cheaply made, and access to the latest creative talent. Although David slew Goliath, their filmic counterparts see more advantage in partnership than in opposition. To demonstrate this, and to more fully investigate the positive and negative implications, we must look now at a specific case history: that of Miramax Films.

The case of Miramax Films

Since its inception in the late 1980s, Miramax has moved from an avowedly anti-studio position to one of intimate partnerships with several major Hollywood studios. In its earliest days, it was an aggressive operator that prided itself upon snapping up the most difficult movies; often foreign or controversial because of their content. Its breakthrough came in 1989 when it won the distribution rights for Soderbergh's *sex, lies and videotape*. In the following few years it gained a reputation as the most committed of independent distributors, with films such as Hal Hartley's *The Unbelievable Truth* (1990), Bill Duke's *A Rage in Harlem* (1991) and Tarantino's *Reservoir Dogs* (1992).

By the early 1990s, Miramax faced the problem of expansion; it could not increase its scale of operation without substantial additional financial re-sources. Miramax began considering partnerships with mainstream studios, and struck one with Rank which gave it $5 million. This was the beginning of loss of true independence for Miramax, although the Weinsteins continued to insist upon their independent status for several years to come.

In 1993, the company struck a deal with perhaps the bastion of the mainstream, Disney:

The independent filmmaking world changed dramatically [on] Friday when brothers Harvey and Bob Weinstein sold their 12-year-old, fiercely non-conformist Miramax Film Corp. to thoroughly mainstream Walt Disney Co.

The move marks the latest swell of a sea change in Hollywood, as studios and
independents increasingly align to battle booming marketing and production
costs, capture fragmented audiences and scramble for bigger market shares.

(Eller and Frook, 1993; p.1)

For many observers, the writing was already on the wall. The overemphasis on
Miramax's autonomy, and the rather chilling final comment that Disney had
the right to remake any of the 200 films in Miramax's back catalogue, was too
much for some. As Raymond Katz, a Lehman Brothers entertainment analyst,
commented in the same article, 'Of course, one of the questions is seeing the
Weinsteins fit into the Disney Corporate structure. It's difficult to see them
fitting in easily' (Weintraub, 1993; p.39). The danger could be seen manifest-
ing itself when, in an article in the *New York Times* in June 1996, it was said of
Harvey Weinstein that:

although he was entirely independent of Disney, which bought the company
three years ago, he had set some self-imposed creative limits. 'I'm not looking
to make an NC–17 movie anymore,' Mr Weinstein said. 'In the old days, it
wouldn't have mattered that much.' . . . Last year, Miramax was forced to
briefly set up a new distribution outlet to release Kids, *about a group of*
promiscuous pre-teenagers which had an NC–17 rating. The mantra at Disney
is to keep the ratings 'R', and I'm happy to do so . . . I don't want to cause
Disney any problems. Why ruin a perfect relationship?

(New York Times, 24/6/96; p.C11)

By April 1999, with the release of *Dogma*, the *New York Times* was reporting:

an embarrassment for Miramax Films [when] its owner, the Walt Disney
Company, has termed a new Miramax movie inappropriate because of content
involving Roman Catholics and said the film should not be released under a
Disney label . . . Harvey Weinstein said in a telephone interview tonight that
Disney did not directly ask him to shelve the film. 'What they said is, "We have
a problem" . . .'

(Weintraub, 1999; p.C4)

The consequence of this was that Miramax had to acquire all rights to the film
and sell it to another distributor.

By July 1999, after the Catholic Church had urged Disney to dump
Miramax over the *Dogma* controversy, Miramax was being referred to as

merely 'a unit of Disney', and was reported to be entering into agreement with another of the majors, MGM, to make up to eight films together. According to MGM's chief operating officer, Chris McGurk, 'We look to this as a great opportunity to almost borrow Miramax's development, production and marketing capability' and apply that against our library' (*New York Times*, 7 July 1999). One of the proposed Miramax remakes of classics from the hallowed MGM vaults was reported to be the James Stewart comedy *Harvey* (1950). Miramax did indeed seem to have strayed very far away from their original independent agenda. 'Miramax's deal with MGM confirms that the New York-based company is no longer an upstart – it is operating from within the heart of Hollywood' (*Variety*, 12 July 1999). In honour of its victory, the term 'nouveau major' was applied to it.

This pattern, though perhaps not as foregrounded and hyped as the Miramax situation, was repeated throughout the industry during the late 1990s. In 1990, New Line Cinema launched its Fine Line Features branch to handle lower-budget films. In 1994 both New Line and Fine Line were bought up by Ted Turner and absorbed into the Time-Warner conglomerate. Sony created Sony Classics in 1992; Fox, Fox Searchlight in 1995. In 1997, MGM bought up the Samuel Goldwyn Company and Universal acquired October Films. Finally, in 1998, Paramount created Paramount Classics. Merritt comments that 'There were another dozen or so truly independent companies that occasionally made noise, but, backed with the deepest pockets, the art-house arms of major studios were the most active indie companies of the nineties. They bid for the hottest properties on the festival circuit each year' (Merritt, 2000; p.354).

Writing in an on-line *Newsday* article posted 30 March 1998, Jack Mathews analysed the rationale behind the creation of Sony Pictures Classic:

> *The arrangement with Sony gives the team tremendous advantage over most of their rivals. Though they operate autonomously, they have the resources of a major studio to back them up. They have access to Sony's accounting and legal services, and they get the studio's rates when they buy advertising.*

Lindsay Law, president of Fox Searchlight, which is owned by Rupert Murdoch's News Corporation, told the *New York Times* that he had been given complete autonomy and had been told by executives at Twentieth Century-Fox, the parent company, to tackle any subject. '"The instructions are not to be afraid," Mr Law said' (*New York Times*, 24 June 1996; p.C11).

Conversely, and we must note the potential desire to construct a negative narrative for such developments in his comments, James Schamus, president of Good Machine, the independent producer of *The Wedding Banquet* (1993), commented in the same article that:

John Travolta and Bruce Willis relax between takes in *Pulp Fiction* (Quentin Tarantino, 1994)

> *Independent films will probably kill themselves off by virtue of their own success . . . With a cross-over hit like* Pulp Fiction, *the criteria by which art house movies are produced and marketed and exploited have changed. With studio money and overheads and budgets and deal-making machinery, a certain kind of narrative structure and popcorn-type pay-off start to infuse themselves. The real question is whether old audiences for art-house films will revolt or whether larger audiences will show up for more thoughtful and independent-spirited films.*
>
> (New York Times, *24 June 1996; p.C11*)

The positive thing to note in this comment is the last part of the final point. It does appear as if larger and larger audiences are expressing a preference for going to the smaller independently made films rather than the huge-budget blockbusters: to the *Something About Mary*s rather than the *Godzilla*s. Peter Bart has judged that the failure of certain big-budget films to perform during the summer of 1998 has led the industry to rethink its production strategy, cutting back on pricey event movies, and stepping up the output of relatively inexpensive comedies and genre pictures (Bart, 1999; pp.277–8). This shift in audience tastes will inevitably be intensified following the terrorist attacks on the World Trade Centre and the Pentagon, causing Hollywood to significantly reassess the balance between its high-budget action films and its low-budget dramas. Again, whether this adjustment is short or long-term remains uncertain. But at the very least it will show how Hollywood's production processes are perpetually subject to influence and change, and how good it is at reacting to such influence and change in order to maintain its dominant position.

In all of these manoeuvrings we can see a strategy that has been constantly at work throughout American film history. Whenever the major powers have perceived a new development that threatens their hegemony in the marketplace, they counter it by absorbing it. Whether the threat came from foreign national cinemas in the 1920s and 1930s or independent films in the 1990s, Hollywood's policy has always been to buy up the threatening talent (individual or company) and turn its virtues to work for itself, rather than enter into direct combat.

Steven Soderbergh

One figure who clearly illustrates the current two-way relationship between the independent and mainstream sectors of American cinema is Steven Soderbergh. As mentioned earlier, the success of Soderbergh's *sex, lies and videotape* at the 1989 Sundance Festival ushered in, or rather announced the arrival of, the modern independent cinema. As Levy says, 'The film forever changed the public perception of independent movies – and of the Sundance Film Festival, where it premiered' (Levy, 1999; p.94). The film, financed to the tune of $1.2 million by RCA/Columbia Home Video, was thought by Soderbergh himself to be 'too internal, too self-absorbed' (Levy, 1999; p.95). But this is the very reason for its significance: it showed that there was a substantial audience for quirky, off-beat and personal films. For the $1.2 million investment, the film returned over $100 million worldwide at the box office. As Merritt puts it, 'Art-house screens couldn't contain it. Soderbergh's and Sundance's and Miramax's movie entered America's consciousness. And so did independent film' (Merritt, 2000; p.351).

Soderbergh's subsequent career has, when judged by both financial and aesthetic criteria, oscillated between success and failure. *Kafka* (1991) was visually striking but lacked coherence or warmth on either mental or emotional levels. *King of the Hill* (1993) was a sensitive study of a child's coming of age in the Depression, but did not get an audience. *The Underneath* (1995), a remake of the 1949 film noir classic *Criss Cross*, came across as an empty exercise in cinematic style and self-reference.

Soderbergh's next two films: *Gray's Anatomy* (1996), a Spalding Gray monologue which was co-financed by the BBC and the Independent Film Channel, and *Schizopolis* (1996), financed by pre-selling domestic video rights to Universal, both failed disastrously at the box office. Although, as he says, Soderbergh is a tight, economical film-maker, there is still a bottom line for any film to make back its money. His following film, however, was the relatively big-budget *Out of Sight* (1998), financed by Universal. It starred Jennifer Lopez and George Clooney, the latter then still trying to break away from his image as TV's Dr Ross in the medical drama series *ER*, and establish himself as a bona fide movie star. *Out of Sight*, despite its convoluted narrative structure and quirky elements, is a manifestly mainstream movie, especially when compared to Soderbergh's previous few films: 'Cited as the best film of 1998 by the National Society of Film Critics, *Out of Sight* was a terrific studio movie, made without selling out. "It doesn't seem greedy to make a movie once every nine years that people show up to go see"' (Levy, 1999; p.101). *The Limey* (1999) combines mainstream (a murder case) and art movie (subtle examination of a father coming to terms with his failure towards his murdered daughter) in one film. This double formal and subject agenda indicates that Soderbergh, even while seeming to be moving firmly into mainstream film-making, still retains an interest in less conventional subject matter or, at least, in forging an alliance between the two.

Soderbergh has waited considerably less than nine years to make his next films that 'people show up to go see'. *Erin Brockovich* (2000), starring Julia Roberts, and *Traffic* (2000), starring Michael Douglas, Catherine Zeta Jones and Dennis Quaid, are two big-budget productions designed for wide release and major box office. *Erin Brockovich* earned $125 million at the American box office, *Traffic* $123 million. Although both were independently produced (*Erin Brockovich* by Jersey Films and *Traffic* by several companies, including Bedford Falls and the Initial Entertainment Group), their distribution has been handled by the major studios, *Erin Brockovich* by Twentieth Century-Fox of Germany, and *Traffic* by Columbia Tri-Star, Sony Pictures Entertainment Inc. and Universal Pictures [MCA/Universal Pictures]. Such commercial set-ups not only show that Soderbergh, the 'indies poster child' as Levy puts it (Levy, 1999; p.94) has definitely gone mainstream but, more significantly, that independent films are now, as a matter of course, big-budget, star-laden and expected to have both wide release and great financial success. Soderbergh's latest film is a remake of the Rat Pack movie *Ocean's Eleven* (2001), with an all-star cast including George Clooney, Brad Pitt and Julia Roberts as well as Matt Damon and Andy Garcia.

CONCLUSION

There is an inherent difficulty in identifying a sector of American film-making as large and diverse as independent cinema, that includes the smallest, no-budget short films at one end and relatively large-budget studio-financed feature films at the other, as any kind of unified movement. No such singularity exists. Instead, there is a loosely configured network of operators, all of whom share a certain interest in making films which offer a personal view of the world and which are made with as much freedom as the film-maker feels that film-statement requires.

Many independent film-makers are uncomfortable with being seen as the spokespeople for independent American film-making, or even being identified with a particular area with its attendant expectations, limitations and boundaries. Merritt comments, for example, that 'The most successful lesbian-themed movies [*Go Fish* (1994); *The Incredibly True Adventures of Two Girls in Love* (1995)] avoided the controversy of the New Queer Cinema' (Merritt, 2000; p.392). Stephen Soderbergh, 'indies poster child' though he is, when speaking of *sex, lies and videotape* as a marker of indie success said ruefully that: 'I think it's time for me to get a new middle name.'

The period under consideration in this book has seen a movement from truly independent micro-budget movies to large-budget semi-independent or studio movies. The independent sector has been, and will continue to be, constantly under threat of losing its most talented people to mainstream movie-making. What is noticeable is that some film-makers *want* to shift from independent production to studio-based film-making when the opportunity allows. This indicates not so much that the independent sector is ultimately meaningless or devalued, so much as the recognition that certain mechanisms of the American film industry hinder true independent films from reaching a sufficiently large marketplace. It is a problem of distribution and exhibition rather than production. This situation may change as new technologies open up different, more personally controlled, means of distribution and exhibition; this will be examined in Chapter 9. But in general, film-makers would prefer to accept the concessions required to make a film about which they feel strongly, than to make a small film on the same subject that does not get distributed, or gets distributed on such a small scale that it still does not reach the right audience.

CHAPTER SEVEN

Genre, Sequels and Remakes

Griffin Mill: *What's the pitch?*
Alan Rudolph: *Does political scare you?*
GM: *Political doesn't scare me. Radical political scares me. Political political scares me.*
AR: *This is politely politically radical.*
GM: *Is it funny?*
AR: *It's funny.*
GM: *It's a funny, political film.*
AR: *It's a funny . . . it's a thriller, too.*
GM: *It's a thriller . . .*
AR: *And it's all at once.*
GM: *So . . . what's the story?*
AR: *Well, I want Bruce Willis. I think I can talk to him. It's a story about a senator. A bad guy senator at first, likes travelling around the country on the country's dime . . . like that Zanunu guy used to.*
GM: *I see, sort of a cynical political thriller comedy.*
AR: *Yeah, but it's got a heart . . . er . . . in the right spot. Anyway, he has an accident.*
GM: *An accident?*
AR: *Yeah. He becomes clairvoyant, like a psychic.*
GM: *Oh, I see. So it's like a psychic political thriller comedy with a heart.*
AR: *With a heart. And not unlike* Ghost *meets* The Manchurian Candidate.
GM: *Go on, I'm listening.*

(Extract from Scene 1 of The Player, *Robert Altman, 1992)*

This dialogue sequence, a small part of a long, complex, continuous take which opens *The Player*, Robert Altman's hilarious satire on the phoniness of

Hollywood, is obviously designed to make fun of the processes which drive modern American film-making practice. But it contains a number of significant points within its humour: an accusation that contemporary American film avoids serious social and political issues; the patchwork, bricolage style of story-assembly which results in a hybrid, mildly ludicrous, mixed-genre plot (in this case, a combination of *Ghost* and *The Manchurian Candidate*); and the desire to name the superstar actor (Bruce Willis) before the story. This chapter examines the validity of these satirical views, to see if they are accurate.

THE PURPOSES OF GENRE

There have always been genres in cinema. Or almost always. The earliest period of film-making in America, in the last years of the nineteenth century, was strangely open, with all things possible, and all films undefined. They were just films, more often than not simply a means of demonstrating a piece of hardware; a camera or a projector. Only when the entertainment value of these strips of celluloid was recognised, when it was realised that people would actually pay money to watch them, did there develop a need to categorise the subject matter of films. This was done, not so much for the audiences themselves, as for the exhibitors, who needed some idea of the kind of films they were buying (at this time, films were bought outright, rather than being hired, as they were to be later). Films at this time, such as *What Demoralised the Barbershop* (Edison Manufacturing Co., 1897) and *The Burglar-Proof Bed* (Biograph, 1900), were short, under five minutes long, and were grouped together into shows for exhibition. All studios – Edison, Biograph, Vitagraph – made all kinds of film. Indeed, they had to, if they were to compete in the developing marketplace.

But, of course, this categorisation eventually found its way through to the audiences themselves, who began to use the categories to assess whether a particular film would be of interest to them. Audiences began to discern, to choose the kind of film they preferred to see. Film-makers began to specialise, to become identified with a certain kind of film, while still ensuring that they made films across all types of subject.

Such practices have remained a staple part of the American film-making practice ever since. The classic studio period of American film-making saw the culmination of this process. The kind of industrial efficiency practised by Hollywood during this period (1920–1960) lent itself to such clear definition. Studios became identified with particular kinds of subject matter: Warner Bros. with gangster and grittily realistic social problem films; MGM with glossy musicals; Universal with horror, and so on. Stars similarly developed associations with particular kinds of film – John Wayne and Henry Fonda with westerns; James Cagney and Edward G. Robinson with gangster films; Fred Astaire and Gene Kelly with musicals – even though they might make many other kinds of film during their careers. This is an explicit example of Hollywood's production efficiency: slotting easily identifiable elements together in as smooth and efficient a manner as possible, to ensure the regular generation of product which an audience can easily identify and assimilate into its existing knowledge base about the movies.

Certainties began to shift with the ending of the studio system with the Paramount decrees in 1948. Studios became less identifiable as the creators of regularly appearing films; stars broke their associations with those studios, and with the kinds of films generally associated with them. This did not mean that all films produced thereafter suddenly became uncategorisable; far from it. There were still westerns (*High Noon*, 1952; *Butch Cassidy and the Sundance Kid*, 1969) and musicals (*Seven Brides For Seven Brothers*, 1954; *Finian's Rainbow*, 1968). It is rather that the production of these genre films, while maintaining the tradition of American genre film-making, no longer had the stable industrial system of classical Hollywood studios behind it. At the same time, however, in many ways it still had an audience requiring the clear identification and familiar categorisation of each film within a recognisable generic schema.

In all of this, there is a paradoxical desire for the simultaneously safe and familiar and the novel and different. Studios had to ensure the maintenance of product identification and output, while also ensuring that product was not simply a stale replica of what had gone before. Audiences wanted more of what they had already enjoyed, yet did not want exactly the same film experience, which would simply be boring. Film genre is perpetually held within this tension between product standardisation and differentiation, between the established (what currently defines the genre) and what is new (what attempts to redefine it), and, as such, is never static.

So far we have simply taken an overview of the part genre has played in American cinema to the modern period. We will now examine in greater detail how the notion of genre is, and has been, negotiated in American film-making since 1970.

GENRE AND THE PRODUCTION PROCESS

The notion of genre has always been intimately tied up with the production process of cinema. Genre aids production efficiency by establishing predictability. A shorthand is established in terms of story subject matter (the lone gunfighter; the maverick cop), visual look (sepia tones of the Western; white and blue surfaces of science fiction), props (guns, horses) and costumes (ten-gallon hats; spacesuits, overcoats) and settings (spaceship and cratered planet; saloon; speakeasy). Together, these can allow the creative personnel working on a film project to produce the material for that production more quickly, more coherently, and with more co-ordination, than if everyone felt they were starting from scratch, with a totally free hand to invent everything that was to go into that film.

In more pragmatic and prosaic terms, the idea of genre has allowed studios to recycle their material – whether stories or sets, props or costumes – in order to extract the maximum economic value out of them. So, to take an obvious and classic example, Dracula's castle might reappear in another of Universal's vampire films, or perhaps as Frankenstein's laboratory. Film footage can also be re-used. At the low-budget end of production, Peter Bogdanovich's *Targets* (1968), for example, opens with a film clip from Roger Corman's 1963 film *The Terror*, starring Boris Karloff. Such a conception of reworking and repurposing has been maintained to the present day, although in a far more technologically advanced form at the opposite end of the production scale. Some of the computer-designed sets for George Lucas' *Star Wars Episode I: The Phantom Menace* (1999) were reused in the next episode, *Star Wars Episode II: Attack of the Clones* (2002), but were retrieved not from the set-store of the studio backlot, but from the server of a massive computer system at ILM.

In a sense, it becomes a question of emphasis and intensity. The process of repeating elements of previous successes in new works is endemic to American film-making, whether reusing songs from previous musicals in new musicals (the title song of *Singin' In the Rain* [1952] was first used in *Hollywood Revue* of 1929), or a particularly effective combination of guns, cars and fedora hats in gangster movies. The difference with contemporary films lies in the emphasis and weight placed on these elements. In films of previous eras of American cinema, the audience understanding of 'generic shorthand', of the use of specific and familiar iconographies, narrative trajectories and thematic concerns created a 'softer' generic text, a text which was always part of a larger whole. The 'larger whole' was also created by the regularity of product rolling off the studio conveyor-belt and into cinemas. In the contemporary period each individual film must capture its own audience anew. In this cut-throat environment, new films 'try too hard', foregrounding their generic elements and references, their list of attractions. More space – industrial, exhibition, economic – is opened up around each film, and each film must now stand alone in terms of its ability to attract an audience – a factor which is referred to in the hype and advertising surrounding each new release, framing audience reception of that film. *Scream* (1996) explicitly begets not only *Scream 2* (1997) and *Scream 3* (2000) but *I Know What You Did Last Summer* (1997) and *I Still Know What You Did Last Summer* (1998).

Hollywood's practice of attempting to copy the thing(s) which have proved successful in previous films – specific elements, character types, plot trajectories – creates a progressively more dangerous kind of cinematic in-breeding. The original integrity of the generic 'genes' gradually corrupts, becoming played out and overschematic. But this is not to say that the strand cannot be rejuvenated by an injection of originality. *Wes Craven's New Nightmare* (1994), for example, put an imaginative spin on a virtually played-out franchise by turning the generic elements inside out and building a complex, self-conscious play of references out of the 'straight' original horror elements. Indeed, a genre or sub-genre in some ways has to become routinised and stale before such a transformation can take place.

GENRE AND AUDIENCE

But genre does not merely provide a set of recognisable markers for the internal workers on a film project. It also provides what Neale calls the 'narrative image' of a film. An idea of what the film will be like is circulated and used by the critical media (press, television, radio, etc.) to identify the film within the larger industrial and aesthetic context. In turn, the public uses that idea in order to assess whether the film will be of interest to them, and to frame their understanding when they actually watch it. As Neale notes, '[g]enres are partly specific systems of expectation and hypothesis which spectators bring with them to the cinema and which interact with films themselves during the course of the viewing process' (Neale, 2000; p.31).

In terms of the audience demographic and genre, it has been widely observed that the most significant change in the make-up of the modern audience for American films (indeed, for cinema as a whole) has been a lowering of the age range making up the majority of cinema audiences. This emergence of the youth audience, as noted in the introductory chapter, began during the mid- to late 1960s, and has remained a significant factor ever since. The dominance of the 16- to 25-year-old age group in modern cinema-going almost inevitably puts pressure on film-makers to produce films specifically targeted at that age-range and its attendant set of concerns. In this way, subjects like high-school peer pressure; sex; drinking; irresponsibility become privileged over the preoccupations of other age bands: mature responsibility; intimate and subtly drawn emotional depth; middle-age crisis; and so on. Certainly, the critics of the superficiality of modern-day effects-laden blockbusters like *Armageddon* (1998) and *Pearl Harbor* (2001) lay the blame largely at the door of film-makers dumbing down to cater for immature cinema-goers looking for mindless, visceral escapism:

In the late 1990s, films aimed at a younger teenage audience, ages thirteen to nineteen, exploded on theatrical motion picture screens . . . in the late 1990s, 'teen presence' is essential in the enterprise of selling a motion picture, and so no matter what genre these individual films might belong to, their overriding audience appeal is to contemporary teenage filmgoers.

(Dixon, 2000; pp.125–6)

But this phenomenon needs to be looked at more closely. Certainly, there are modern genres which are obviously, though not exclusively, designed to appeal predominantly to the teenage and early-twenties age bracket. Although it has a much longer history, in the contemporary period the slasher movie (the *Scream* trilogy; *I Know What You Did Last Summer*) typically shows a group of teenage college students being systematically murdered in grisly and explicit ways. Other films aimed at the young – the younger, pre- and early-teen audience, for example – often contain a double address that is designed to appeal to a wider range of ages. A good example of this is *The Grinch* (2000), that contains both a child-oriented Toytown *mise-en-scène* and juvenile thematic concerns as well as many jokes and references aimed at the adult section of the audience. At one point, for example, the Grinch, having had a taxi speed past him and refuse to stop to pick him up, shouts 'It's because I'm green, isn't it?' Such a reference to issues of racism it not aimed at the young members of the audience, but at its older members (the parents, nominally, although also older members, generally).

CONGLOMERATION

Such audience shifts are set in the context of industrial changes taking place across the same period. The issue of conglomeration in terms of genre is a tricky one. One might argue, for example, that the takeover of the major film studios by multinational conglomerates from the mid-1960s onwards has produced an economic atmosphere in which safety, predictability, and security of investment are the paramount concerns, overwhelming any possibility of creative integrity or novelty. Certainly, this is a popular notion and is held to be the major cause of the exceptionally expensive but anodyne, 'movies by numbers' modern blockbuster.

However, other writers offer alternative perspectives. Thomas Simonet, for instance, explicitly argues that the conglomerate takeover of Hollywood has not increased the number of remakes, sequels and series being made, although the 1970s saw a slight increase in recycled scripts relative to the 1960s. Indeed, the studio period, Simonet argues, had a greater tendency to reuse script ideas because of the incessant need to make new product. As he goes on to note:

> *In the early 1980s, recycled scripts remained 'relatively few in number' Variety reported . . . However, a small number of high-visibility sequels received a disproportionate share of the box office.* Return of the Jedi *alone collected 9 percent of all domestic rentals in 1983. Bonanzas like that, accompanied by merchandising and ancillary versions in other media, brought the 'sequel trend' to journalistic attention but obscured the fact that Hollywood has recycled scripts throughout history.*
>
> (Simonet, 1987; p.161)

Of course, this analysis was written in 1987 and therefore, while perhaps holding true for the first two decades of the conglomerate era (roughly 1966–87), is not representative of the situation in the decade or so since. In those intervening years the industry has changed substantially. Costs have risen exponentially, not least due to the massive pay cheques demanded by the major stars (Mel Gibson's $25 million plus percentage of the gross on *The Patriot* [2000], for example). In such a climate, it is essential that risk be minimised, and one way in which this can be achieved is to fall back on tried and trusted formulas. Generic conventions are just such formulas, and give a strong lead to film-makers wanting to guarantee the success of their product. But it is more than this. It is not simply that films are now being made which can be strongly identified with particular genres. It is more that the films that are being made are either actually straight remakes of previously successful versions, or are assemblages of previously successful elements whether character types, plot situations or visual effects. While this might sound like the old identifiable elements of genre film-making, there is a difference in the explicit and almost naked calculation involved in piecing together the marketable combination of elements which will hopefully prove successful at the box office. Take as an example *Event Horizon* (1997), a science-fiction film that fuses together, none too smoothly, strands and elements from numerous other genres of film. The 'ruthless alien creature on the loose' motif is lifted from the *Alien* series. The patrol film format is imported from war films such as *Apocalypse Now* (1979) and *Platoon* (1986) into the science fiction genre by way of *Aliens* (1986) and *Starship Troopers* (1997). Other elements, such as the dimensional gateway, through which the malevolent force, which will come to threaten the characters, must pass, can be found in *2001: A Space Odyssey* (1968) and *Stargate* (1994) (Sanjek, 2000; pp.120–1).

Such 'film making by numbers' is a simple matter of laziness and economics, as Wheeler Winston Dixon notes:

The day of the modestly budgeted genre film is a memory: genre films are now beholden more to banks and stockholders than to any other entity, and even the slightest deviation from preconceived design is a matter of grave concern to a film's production entity. It has always been thus, but today, the stakes are considerably higher. Several poor marketing decisions may well put a studio in serious financial peril; why take risks when you can play it safe, recycle the past, and reap pre-sold rewards in the present-day marketplace?

(Dixon, 2000; pp.7–8)

A more significant factor concerning conglomerate influence on the recycling of stories and the particular formulation of genres comes from conglomerate ownership of talent and material across a range of media: film and television, music, newspapers (with syndicated comic strips) and others. It is an obvious move for the conglomerates to maximise the productivity of that talent and material across all of these media. So, a popular singer – for instance, Madonna – does not just perform in her chosen medium: recorded music and live concerts. She appears on television shows, gives interviews in magazines and newspapers owned by the conglomerate, and develops an acting career too. Similarly with story material: *The Mask*, for example, began life as a comic strip before becoming a film, starring Jim Carrey, in 1994, and finally ending up as an animated cartoon series on television. It is quite possible that certain stories are chosen because of their ability to be converted into various media forms, a process which possibly favours escapist, cartoon-like subjects over realist, human ones. *Inspector Gadget* (1999), starring Matthew Broderick, originated as a television cartoon character, as did *Scooby-Doo* (2002), produced by Atlas Entertainment for distribution by Warner Bros., and starring Freddie Prinze Jr and Sarah Michelle Gellar (television's Buffy, the Vampire Slayer).

The new configuration of elements in a remake, especially if it is made some time after the original, is interesting specifically because of the way the original is reformulated and given a radically new spin. 'The remake summons up both the internal and the external history of film in its relation to past films and past audiences: a film was made and now it is to be remade, revised, or even extended' (Braudy, 2000; p.327). We can see this tension operating between the original *Shaft*, made in 1971, and its remake/sequel (the boundary lines are blurred) *Shaft 2000*. The remaking of the original, which was itself made within the specific socio-political context of early 1970s American racial tensions and a rising awareness of Black Power, offered its creators the opportunity to use the same framework to explore the question of race in America in the year 2000. *Shaft 2000*'s emphasis on style and image, even more explicit than its predecessor, as well as its toning down of the sexual excess of its central character, speaks volumes about the racial discourse of early twenty-first century American society.

The modern conglomerate ownership of material in a variety of formats and media aids a process whereby selection of pre-known stories – whether originating from comics, novels, or television shows – acts as a shorthand for audiences in their response to a genre film. Familiarity with the story or subject of the story enables the audience to know, or at least anticipate, what it is going to see. In one sense, this repeats a process common in the earliest days of cinema. Well-known stories and events were used, whether fairy tales (*Jack and the Beanstalk* [1902]), current events such as political assassinations (*McKinley's Funeral Entering Westlawn Cemetery, Canton* [1901] or battles (*Charge of the Boer Cavalry* [1900]). Audiences were expected to fill in the narrative gaps with their own knowledge of the subject. Genre convention melds with narrative familiarity to produce a safe and comfortable end product. The result, then as now, is a certain thinness of characterisation and sketchiness of context.

But conversely, the self-reflexivity of modern films, especially those consciously playing on the idea of their own genre, has come to require a degree of cine-literacy on the part of their audience. Take, for example, the scene in *The Matrix* (1999), when Keanu Reeves and Carrie-Anne Moss decide to storm the building in which Laurence Fishburne is being held captive. When Keanu Reeves's character says 'We need guns,' and huge shelving stacks of countless arms of all sizes immediately sweep into view either side of him, he, the film, and we as viewers are all in on the self-reflexive joke. A high-tech, all-action science fiction film like *The Matrix* will inevitably have scenes of gun-toting mayhem. Or again, we can only fully enjoy the gag of Mike Myers's eponymous character having bad teeth in *Austin Powers, International Man of Mystery* (1997), if we catch the reference to the television character on whom he is based: Jason King. So, on the one hand there is, arguably, a dumbing-down of the audience, a tendency for genre films to play out simplistic stories commandeered from other media forms. On the other, there is a requirement and expectation that they have a body of reference that they bring to the supposedly passive viewing experience and use to understand the intertextual film work.

GENRE AND DIRECTORS

Given that the early 1970s were the great period of American auteurism, it is perhaps appropriate that our first area of concern should be how the notion of genre interacts with the role of the director in American film-making. Not only could studios and stars be closely associated with certain genres of film;

so could directors. John Ford, though he made war films (*They Were Expendable*, 1945) and quaint comedies (*The Quiet Man*, 1952), is forever linked with westerns. George Cukor is primarily known for romance and women's films, while Vincente Minnelli is associated with musicals (*An American in Paris*, 1951; *The Band Wagon*, 1953), even though he made many melodramas: *The Cobweb* (1955); *Lust for Life* (1956) and comedies, such as *Father of the Bride* (1950). As with stars, the studio period allowed directors to be permanently employed by one studio. Under such stable circumstances, each director would be regularly given those film projects for which they were deemed most suitable, largely on the basis of the success of past work. Over time, this process almost automatically ensures that a director would be identified with a particular 'brand' of film story; a self-generated predictability takes place.

As with so many other aspects of American cinema, all this potentially changed with the dismantling of the big studios during the 1950s. Within the newly emergent package system, an ability to identify themselves as experts in the making of a particular kind of film added clarity and strength to a bid for financing from a cautious studio. Studios would be more likely to green-light a project – say, a Western – if a director and star who were known already to have made several successful Westerns were the major talent involved.

The importation of auteurism from France into America during the late 1950s brought it into direct conflict with genre criticism. The auteur theory had originally been articulated directly in relation to the generic specificity of the American cinema. Its agenda was explicitly to foreground the ability of certain directors to rise above the generic midden of formula film-making, to put a personal stamp on the standard product while still operating within the confines of genre film-making, to create individual works of art in spite of generic constraint.

The young directors of the early 1970s, anxious to avoid being seen to be making standard Hollywood product in which generic predictability was paramount, took this conflict to heart. In this, theirs was an explicit reaction to the studio fare of previous decades – the overblown musicals and staple thrillers that had failed ever more spectacularly at the box office.

This rebellion was facilitated by the fact that the new generation of film-makers had been educated in the history of cinema, genre, and so on in the film schools they had attended during the late 1960s. This double agenda – a desire not to slavishly follow prescribed generic forms, and a simultaneous desire to display their knowledge of American cinema history – created a particularly knowing, self-referential style/period of film-making. The young film-makers of the early 1970s saw it as a confirmation of their knowledge to create a juggling act of the influences and the generic elements involved in the subjects they chose for their projects. They also saw it as a confirmation of their talent that they could successfully pull off the combination of various, potentially contradictory, elements in any one film. And again, we witness here the paradox of a group of directors raised on Classical Hollywood and auteur theory still working within generic boundaries while consistently and avowedly breaking their rules.

Such a sleight of hand also required a cine-literate audience which was capable of recognising the blend and manipulation of generic references, and able to react to, absorb and order the various trajectories into an understandable text. In some ways, therefore, many of the films of the early 1970s became a game played between audience and film-maker against the old-fashioned, passé, establishment. The opening scene of Sam Peckinpah's *The Wild Bunch* (1969), with its temperance league procession singing the hymn 'Shall We Gather By the River', explicitly references John Ford's Westerns, such as *My Darling Clementine* (1946), in which the same hymn is sung. In *Raiders of the Lost Ark* (1981) Steven Spielberg references adventure films of the 1950s, such as *Journey to the Center of the Earth* (1959) and *King Solomon's Mines* (1950). There is also something of the battle-of-the-sexes comedy-romances of Spencer Tracy and Katherine Hepburn in the love scenes between Harrison Ford and Karen Allen (Baxter, 1996; p.194). As Noel Carroll has argued, 'the reworking evokes a historical genre and its associated myths, commonplaces, and meanings in order to generate expression through the friction between the old and the new' (Carroll, 1982; p.57).

What is interesting is that, while the notion of generic rules was discarded by the new directors of the early 1970s, the eventual failure of the rebellion by the mid-1970s saw a reappearance of genre as a foregrounded force. The short-lived but massively popular disco movie – *Saturday Night Fever* (1977), *Car Wash* (1976); political thrillers – *The Parallax View* (1974), and *All the President's Men* (1976); slasher films – *Halloween* (1978 onwards), *Friday the 13th* (1980 onwards), and so on. But something had changed – genre was never to be the naturalised, taken-for-granted, thing it had been to the industry and its audience in previous periods of American film-making. The play of forms, the questioning of formal rules and boundaries between genres meant that those rules and boundaries could not be made to carry the same weight as before. The long-term effect of this shift will be explored in the next section.

SERIALS/SERIES/SEQUELS/REMAKES

Modern American cinema is characterised by four categories of generic production: serials, series, sequels and remakes. Each category has a combination of unique and overlapping features, which makes the four together, in the manner in which they intertwine, diverge, and reunite, a fascinating feature of modern generic film-making.

Serials are perhaps the oldest of the four, developing in the 1910s – most famously in such serials as *The Perils of Pauline* and the *Buck Rogers* space saga. These were made up of several episodes that, together, relate a long, exciting event-packed narrative. They were designed to make audiences return to the cinema week after week to catch the latest instalment of the yarn, much in the same way as the serialisation of Charles Dickens' novels in newspapers during the nineteenth century would ensure regular subscriptions for the newspaper's owners. Serials are not a common form in modern American cinema, although the Indiana Jones trilogy is a reference back to the old adventure serials. A peculiar instance has been in progress for the last 20 years in the shape of the *Star Wars* saga. This particular example is unusual because there are substantial time gaps between individual episodes: 15 years between the third production (*Return of the Jedi* in 1983, episode six of the saga) and the fourth (*Star Wars Episode I: The Phantom Menace*, 1999, the saga's first episode) and a further three between that latter production and the latest (*Attack of the Clones*, 2002, the second episode of the saga).

It is hard, not to say impossible, for modern cinema audiences to develop the same kind of interest in moving regularly and speedily from episode to episode of a breathless serial narrative. The demise of the full programme of double feature, serial episode, cartoons, newsreel which was the staple exhibition format of cinema until the 1960s has removed the specific viewing context which allowed those old serials to work in the way they did. Today the natural home of the serial form is television, which has largely taken over the role of providing them, although this has a return-in-kind aspect to it that will be addressed shortly.

Film series have also been a frequent form in cinema over the decades, from the popular *Thin Man* series in the 1930s, starring William Powell and Myrna Loy, and the Andy Hardy films starring Mickey Rooney in the 1940s. Cheaply produced and extremely popular, their regular, often impressive, income worked to offset the unpredictable success/failure of higher-budget features from the same studios.

Series are still an occasional feature of contemporary cinema. The most famous example, perhaps, is the British series of James Bond films, which have been in production since the early 1960s, surviving several changes of actor. Each of these stories is essentially discrete from the others, although they can and do share ongoing elements – comedic interaction between Bond and Q, for example, or references to past events, romances, and so forth. American series tend to be a little more interlinked, so that these cross-references are more explicitly stated and used to build a sense of continuity.

A frequent generic site for the series in American cinema is the horror genre. The 1970s and 1980s saw the proliferation of such series – *The Omen*, from 1976 onwards; *Halloween*, from 1978 onwards; *Friday the 13th*, from 1980 onwards, and *A Nightmare on Elm Street*, from 1984 onwards all produced long series of films, of variable, and usually decreasing, quality, which have nevertheless commanded reasonably regular and respectable audience figures. Made in 1978 for under $0.5 million and earning $47 million at the box office, the original *Halloween* spawned a series of sequels, each of which made an average of around $15 million from the early 1980s to the mid-1990s. *Halloween H20* (1998) starring the original's heroine, played by Jamie Lee Curtis, recorded $75 million worldwide. *Friday the 13th*, on the other hand, having made $37 million with the original in 1980, made progressively less with its sequels ($36.2 million for its third instalment, in 3-D, through to $14.3 for part eight in 1989). The *Nightmare on Elm Street* franchise has fared best of all, moving from $25.5 million for the first in 1984 through to $49 million for the fourth instalment, before the series finally petered out with the sixth, which only earned $34.9 million in 1991. However, the franchise was reprised for a final time (to date) in 1994, when *Wes Craven's New Nightmare* earned a modest $17.17 million after five weeks, before falling off *Screen International*'s box-office chart. The low budgets and lack of expensive stars in these films have meant that even these relatively low figures represent a profit for the films' makers.

In recent years, another horror cycle series has appeared to continue the tradition. *Scream* first appeared in 1996, *Scream 2* in 1997 and *Scream 3* in 2000. The makers – Dimension Films, Woods Entertainment and director Wes Craven – however, have indicated that three is enough and they plan to quit while they are still (relatively) ahead. And this 'short series' throws up an essential question – at what point does a sequel sequence become a series? Is the second film made on the same subject, using some or all of the same characters, a sequel (i.e., a sequel can only mean *Scream 2*), whereas any further productions automatically turn the original–sequel relationship into a series configuration (i.e., *Scream 1–3*: the *Scream series*)?

This question has something to do with expectation on the part of the film-makers. In the past, when an original film has been made, it has usually been conceived and executed to stand alone. Its laying out of the context and elements for its narrative, and the movement towards the climax of that narrative, assume a self-containedness, a resolution in terms of itself which results in closure of the narrative trajectory by the film's end. This narrative assumption is echoed on the industrial level, each film being separately produced with no assumption that further versions will be produced in the future. The success of the original, in this account, then takes the producers by surprise, prompting them to consider a sequel, a 'further adventures of . . .'. This sequel will then allow its makers to explore their story and characters further, while giving the audience, which made the original a success, a chance to repeat the pleasure it experienced when viewing the first film. The *Scream* trilogy is a good example of this, in the way in which each successive instalment has taken the same characters – Sidney Prescott (Neve Campbell), Gale Weathers (Courteney Cox) and Deputy Dwight 'Dewey' Riley (David Arquette) – through a series of similarly premised plots: serial killer appears/returns to terrorise a closed community.

The *Alien* quartet of films is a variation on this phenomenon. The four films were made by the same studio, Twentieth Century-Fox, but had different directors: Ridley Scott, James Cameron, David Fincher and Jean-Pierre Jeunet. The same character – Ripley, played by Sigourney Weaver – is taken through several phases of character development. She begins as an increasingly resourceful crew-member (*Alien*, 1979), becomes an all-action heroine and surrogate mother (*Aliens*, 1986), proto-medieval religious figure (*Alien³*, 1992), to finish as a part-human, part-alien clone in *Alien Resurrection* (1997). Part of the enjoyment of this particular series is seeing what will be done next with the Ripley character. In this context, familiarity and surprise are held in a carefully calculated balance.

The potential problem with the continual generation of sequels is that at some point in the process, it becomes apparent to the film-makers that the films they are making are consistently becoming successful and profitable. At this point, self-consciousness takes over, and further films in the cycle are made *on the assumption* that they will also succeed as their predecessors have done. The process thereby acquires a pre-meditatedness, a danger of becoming 'film-making by numbers', which threatens to flatten the freshness and vitality of the films' original material. Certainly, such an accusation can be levelled against examples such as the *Rocky* or *Rambo* series.

The originals in both series – *Rocky* (1976) and *First Blood* (1982) – were unexpected box-office successes; the latter even though it starred *Rocky*'s writer-star Sylvester Stallone and might therefore be argued to have a relatively strong box-office potential:

> *The $18 million film had been shot without a distributor. The prevailing feeling was that Stallone without* Rocky *equalled box office poison. There was little enthusiasm among the majors for a non-*Rocky *movie; certainly an 18-minute reel failed to impress Twentieth Century Fox or, curiously enough, Warner Bros., the studio that had set the project into motion in the first place.*

(Base, 1994; p.219)

But having established this success, the subsequent regular sequels, soon forming a series, acquire an air of predictability, an assumption that each new version of the story will find the old faithful audience, created by the first film, waiting for it. This success is bound up in the audience attitude to the star of the franchise – in this case Sylvester Stallone. As the above quote indicates, the worry at the time of the making of *First Blood* was that the public would only accept Stallone in the *Rocky* series. By the time of *First Blood* in 1982, Stallone had made three *Rocky* films (1976, 1979, 1982), each of which, self-evidently, had produced respectable box-office returns (if they had not, the franchise would have been cancelled). In between these, Stallone made a number of resounding failures. *F.I.S.T.* (1978), which he also wrote, and *Paradise Alley* (1978, for which he was also writer and director) were made between the first and second *Rocky*s. *Nighthawks* (1981) and *Escape to Victory* (1981, in which he appeared as, of all things, an American goalkeeper in a football match between Second World War POWs and their Nazi camp guards!) were made between the second and third *Rocky* films. Such a roller coaster failure/success economic trajectory indicates both the unpredictability of modern movie-making, and the importance, within this uncertain industrial terrain, of a relatively dependable series franchise. No matter what failures might occur, the massive box-office returns that can be generated by the next episode of a popular series will always redress the loss, and more.

Today we are seeing the extension of this phenomenon to the production process of the original film. A good example of this is *X-Men* (2000), a big budget, effects-laden comic book adaptation released by Twentieth Century-Fox. In an interview for *Empire On-line* in July 2000, Tom De Santo, the 'creative partner' of the film's director Bryan Singer, is quoted as saying that 'we actually planted the seeds in this for the next two' (Anon, 2000b; p 1) Such a comment reveals the degree of premeditation in today's sequel marketplace. No longer is the success of a film a surprise to the film-makers, prompting them to capitalise on it by making a second film based on the material of the first. Now, that second (or third, according to De Santo) is planned at the same time as the first.

This tendency is most clearly represented, perhaps, in the relatively recent phenomenon of back-to-back filming, where two films are made at the same time, saving on the massive costs involved in setting up the second produc-tion, raising sets, clearing the crowded diaries of the stars, and so forth. This method of 'economic bulk film-making' (two for the price – almost – of one) began with *Back to the Future II* and *III* (1989 and 1990, respectively), and is currently being used to make *The Matrix II* and *III*, as well as the latest two episodes in the *Star Wars* saga (*Attack of the Clones* and the currently untitled third episode). Again, this is not an entirely new phenomenon. Francis Ford Coppola made *The Outsiders* (1983) and *Rumble Fish* (1983) back-to-back, having begun planning the latter in the later stages of filming the former. 'While I was filming *The Outsiders*, I decided to make another movie, in a different spirit' (Lewis, 1995; p.103).

Note here that, unlike the older Coppola films, with the newer back-to-back sequels it is never a matter of making numbers *one* and *two* back-to-back. The industry invariably needs the proof of the success of the first before making a commitment to produce the next two together. The success of the first demonstrates the expectation that the popularity of a series/sequel franchise will survive in the marketplace long enough to allow the second feature to succeed as well as the first. It also displays a certain arrogance on the part of the producers and the studio; essentially that the public will continue to be satisfied with whatever is given to them, forcing their choices along predetermined routes.

The effect of this on the films themselves is to extend the narrative line beyond the boundaries of a single film, out through two, or more, films made across a number of years. The full understanding of that narrative requires the audience to return to each new 'edition' of the larger storyline, creating an automatic audience for each new film. This has significant consequences for the narrative content of the individual film. *X-Men* is a good example. The film is a production with lavish special effects that takes as its subject a group of comic-book superhero characters. Because of this, we assume that the film will be positioned as an example of the fantasy action adventure genre, and expect it to have a requisite number of violent fight sequences building towards a viscerally overwhelming climax. But this is not the case in *X-Men*, which is notable for its relative lack of action scenes in favour of a concentration on character development. Such a focus, which operates against the generic expectations of the film, only begins to make sense when we find out that the film has been planned as the first in a, the producers hope, long series of features. In this context, the role of the first film becomes the laying out of the terms of the series as a whole, the initial delineation of narrative elements – character types, character pasts and histories – which will be expanded out over 10 or 20 hours of story-time, rather than the usual two.

In this respect, film sequels and series become more aligned with television drama series than with the cinematic paradigm. And perhaps this is not coincidental. Increasingly, film producers are looking towards television material for their inspiration, or simply for a straight transfer from television to cinema. What gets transferred along with the subject matter and characters is an assumption that exposition will be carried out across many hours.

In an extension of this point, we are seeing the emergence of what might be called the 'mutated serial': a number of films which integrally involve interaction between television (cable more than terrestrial, with its endless recycling of old product building up nostalgia for the past and familiarity with generic conventions) and cinema. *The X-Files* (1998) is a good example of this, operating as it does both as a stand-alone cinema feature and as an episode of the cult television series. Although it can stand alone, the full implications of its plot can only be fully appreciated if one understands what it is revealing to us about the wider and longer narrative constructed through many episodes of the series on television. In some sense we are seeing certain instances of films which form a particular series, having their basic narrative trajectory outlined and perhaps sketched in, but with the specific details of individual 'episodes' left until the time of individual production.

The need for big-budget films to cater for all tastes leads to cross-genre films:

[The banks] wanted pictures with an 'upside potential' which meant roughly, Robert Redford and Paul Newman together, with Barbra Streisand singing, Steve McQueen punching, Clint Eastwood jumping, music by Marvin Hamlisch, all in stereo, on the wide screen, going out as a hard-ticketed road show where you have to book your seats, based on a no.1 bestseller which was no.1 for sixty weeks and a television show which was no.1 for at least a season.

(Wyatt, 1994; p.78)

Substitute Keanu Reeves and Brad Pitt for Redford and Newman, Madonna for Streisand, George Clooney for McQueen and, a little perversely perhaps, Jim Carrey for Eastwood, mix in a sizeable measure of digital effects, and the same demands appear to still be in place. The pressure on each huge-budget movie to succeed spectacularly at the box office requires that it is packed with 'major talent' (or what is seen at the time as such); talent which comes at a price, thus pushing up the budget ever higher.

As well as causing spiralling costs, the combining of disparate performing talents with the now almost ubiquitous visceral special effects produces film texts which cannot fit neatly into a generic pigeonhole. The instances of cross- or mixed-genre film-making are increasing. Indeed, the quote from Wyatt just cited indicates something of this, in the need to accommodate diverse acting, singing, dancing talents within the same film.

But again, this is not purely a modern phenomenon: films have almost always comprised multiple genres. A Western might have had a musical element (*Destry Rides Again* [1939], for example, in which Marlene Dietrich sings a few songs), a melodramatic dimension (*Johnny Guitar* [1954], directed by Nicholas Ray), or be largely positioned within the comedy genre (*The Paleface* [1948], starring Bob Hope as a cowardly dentist in the Wild West). There has therefore always been a tendency for films to combine diverse generic elements in an attempt to try to offer a broad audience appeal. Has anything substantially changed to make this a more prevalent or obvious phenomenon in modern American film-making?

In general theoretical terms, it is not at all invalid for this cross-pollination to occur. The elements of each individual genre are at least partly interchangeable between genres. For example, most films have heroes and villains, many are founded on a quest or journey, many involve shoot-outs, either between the forces of good and evil, or factions of the evil. In this respect, the work of the Russian formalist Vladimir Propp in analysing the Russian folk tale proves useful. He argues that a group of narratives, seemingly disparate in terms of the stories they tell and the characters they use, can be stripped down to a set of functions, modules of narrative and character formulation. So, for example, we have *dramatis personae* such as 'the hero,' 'the victim', 'the helper', 'the donor', and narrative functions such as the violation of an interdiction – an order for one or more of the characters not to do something – which sets the narrative itself on its journey towards resolution. Although this approach is overly schematic, it is still useful in understanding how aspects of character and narrative can cross over genres and allow two, or even more, genres to intermix within a single film. In one major scene in *The Matrix* (1999), Keanu Reeves and Carrie-Anne Moss stride into the high-security building of the enemy organisation to rescue Laurence Fishburne's character, with guns strapped to their bodies. When they do so, they are explicitly echoing innumerable scenes from genre films of all kinds from cinema's past, from the four over-the-hill Westerners walking down Main Street to rescue Angel from the forces of the evil Mapache in *The Wild Bunch* (1969) through to Rambo rescuing MIAs in *Rambo: First Blood Part II* (1985) or *Rambo III* (1988).

A culture of cross-fertilisation has grown up, of borrowing ideas, influences, and signatures from other works. The most obvious place where this is happening is popular music, with its practice of sampling: capturing and manipulating snatches of other works and incorporating them into new forms. More generally, the idea of freely mixing styles, references, and specific moments from other works is a feature of post-modern art which can be seen, for example, in the novels of Thomas Pynchon or the playful self-referentiality of a television series such as *Moonlighting* in the 1980s.

Noel Carroll identifies the form this takes in films as being that of allusion: films nowadays relentlessly alluding, or referring, to other films in cinema's own history. 'Allusion, specifically allusion to film history, has become a major expressive device, that is, a means that directors use to make comments on the fictional world of their films' (Carroll, 1982; pp.51–2). In Carroll's opinion, the reason for this lies with the generation of film-makers emerging from the film schools since the beginning of the 1970s, all educated in the history of their own cinema to a systematic degree unknown to previous generations of American film-makers. So, to some extent, the ability to reference previous works in new films becomes a marker of a film-maker's quality, their education, their knowledge. Martin Scorsese has acknowledged this phenomenon as a self-conscious element in his own film-making style:

> After Hours *is to some extent a parody of Hitchcock's style. Over the years his films have become more emotionally meaningful for me. By the time I realised he was moving the camera, it was over and I had felt the effect of the movement emotionally and intellectually. So if you take the scene in* After Hours *when Paul is running with the invitation in his hand – there's a shot of a hand with the ground below – basically this refers back to the moment in* Marnie *where she's holding the gun and going to shoot the horse.*
>
> *(Christie and Thompson, 1996; p.101)*

For Carroll, this trend includes imitating film-historical referents; inserting classic film clips; referring to a received pantheon of film-makers; retreading archaic film styles, and mobilising conventional, transparently remodelled characters, stereotypes, moods, and plots. The audience for such works is expected to read such references as self-conscious play rather than plagiarism.

To a large extent television has, for some time now, taken on the role of genre producer. Its ceaseless flow of product, speed of creation and ease of consumption require constant recycling of standard plots and story-lines and character stereotypes. It is also necessary to identify clearly the genre-type of its individual programmes, to fix slots in the schedules where certain types of programme will occur: news at 6.00 p.m., soaps between 7.00 p.m. and 8.00 p.m., adult drama between 8.00 p.m. and 10.00 p.m., and so on. Within this context, cinema is freed from the role of strict genre provider, and can experiment more freely with generic elements.

The time frame of sequel production is an interesting aspect of the subject in general. There is no absolute standard for this, although many sequels, and sequel series, such as the Rocky movies – *Rocky* (1976), *Rocky II* (1979) and *Rocky III* (1982) – seem to be made on three-year cycles (the same, incidentally, as between each of the *Thin Man* sequels of the 1930s and 1940s). This is understandable, as it would take that long both for a film to prove its success at the box office and for the production process to make a follow-up – from decision to proceed through to post-production – to go through its various stages. There is also an interesting tension between the need to capitalise as quickly as possible upon a hit movie, before audience interest wanes, and a desire to raise audience expectation by withholding their pleasure at revisiting a popular success. The producers of *The Matrix* are now in the process of doing this, to ensure that the long-awaited appearance of the second instalment of the *Matrix* saga, like each new *Star Wars* episode, becomes an unmissable event.

Keanu Reeves and Hugo Weaving do battle with the aid of digital wire removal and time-slice cinematography in *The Matrix* (Andy and Larry Wachowski, 1999) THE MATRIX © 1999 WV Films LLC.

There are other factors determining the time frame of sequel production. The now endless circuit of exhibition of films on cable television channels ensures that past popular successes are kept in the public eye. In such circumstances, framed by a television discourse dependent upon episodic development, the public interest in an original film is maintained, and almost inevitably generates a desire to see further developments in that story and its characters.

Another factor influencing the making of sequels is that of a star or director wanting, or perhaps more frequently needing, to make a sequel to a past success of theirs in order to try to rejuvenate a career which might be in some degree of difficulty. We might see this as the reason, for example, why Peter Bogdanovich and Cybill Shepherd made *Texasville* (1990), the sequel to *The Last Picture Show* (1971), one of the seminal films of the early 1970s. They would almost certainly argue that their interest lay solely in a desire to see how the characters created for the original film had fared later in life. One might also look at Francis Ford Coppola's decision to make *The Godfather Part III* (1990) some 16 years after the second instalment was made in 1974 (itself only two years after the original in 1972). Having resisted pressures to make a third instalment of the saga for 15 years, his decision finally to do so was at least partly caused by a string of relative failures in the years prior to 1989. *One From the Heart* (1982), *Peggy Sue Got Married* (1986), *Gardens of Stone* (1987), and *Tucker: The Man and His Dream* (1988) were all unsuccessful at the box office. The film he made after *The Godfather Part III, Bram Stoker's*

Dracula (1992), however, was successful. But in general, Coppola can be seen falling back on the security of a well-known and highly respected subject matter in order to recoup some of the losses occasioned by the failure of these other films.

GENRE AND TECHNOLOGY

The technological state of the film industry has always been one factor involved in determining the types of film that have been made at any point in Hollywood's history, or at least, the prominence of a certain genre over others at that time. So, we see that musicals (*Whoopee!* [1930]; *Broadway to Hollywood* [1933]) became a popular type of film in the late 1920s and early 1930s, once synchronised sound had been added to the range of technical options from which a director might choose in making his film. And, again, the production of biblical and historical epics and Westerns (*Land of the Pharaohs* [1955]; *Ben Hur* [1959]; *The Man From Laramie* [1955]) increased from the early 1950s when widescreen formats such as CinemaScope offered the chance to show expansive landscapes and huge vistas.

The possibilities offered by new technological developments can therefore add a further factor influencing the choice involved in making a film which has a certain narrative structure and is operating within a certain generic framework. The most prevalent and increasingly ubiquitous technological development of the last two decades has been in the area of digital effects. There are very few films now made which do not employ digital effects work of some kind or another, even if it is only localised repair of scratched film frames.

The use of computer-based digital work over the past 20 years is a good example of the way in which a new film technology affects the shifts in the kind of film that might tend to get made as the technology is slowly absorbed and normalised within the industry. Early uses of computer-generated imaging, because of its rather artificial, too-clean, look, were confined almost exclusively to the fantasy and science-fiction genres: *Alien* (1979), *Flash Gordon* (1980), *Tron* (1982). The ultimate, general, failure (*Alien* excepted) of these films at the box office (*Tron* eventually made $33 million) caused the industry temporarily to turn its back on the use of computer-based image generation. Activity in this area was directed instead towards the advertising industry where the intense scrutiny and attention to detail in image creation meant that imaging software programmes were gradually pushed to ever more sophisticated levels. The reintegration of computer imaging into the film industry at the end of the 1980s remained in the generic area of science-fiction and fantasy. James Cameron was the key player in engineering this development, in his desire to create specific kinds of extraordinary, 'out-of-this-world' images in his films *The Abyss* (1989) and *Terminator II: Judgement Day* (1991). It took another few years, and steady improvement of the detailing possible in CGI processes, for the use of digital images to expand into the more 'realistic' genres such as historical romance (*Titanic*, 1997). So we see the emergence of a new technological possibility in the film industry initially being used primarily, if not exclusively, in certain genres, before being slowly accepted by all areas of film-making.

The advent of DVD as a major distribution format for films is one element of a process which is having a significant effect on the types of film being chosen for development, and how they are made. Again, *X-Men* provides a good example of this. Eddy Friedfeld, in the *Empire On-line* article on industry attitudes to DVD, notes that '[t]he DVD format allows for bonus footage, interviews, commentary and other perks so attractive to directors that many now work on a DVD version of the film, even as they shoot the one that will go to theatres'. Director Bryan Singer, interviewed for the same article, has commented that '[y]ou definitely think about the DVD from the moment you start shooting the theatrical film' (Friedfeld, 2000; p.1). The possibilities offered by DVD – its behind-the-scenes documentaries, explanations of how elaborate special effects were created, storyboards and production photographs, trailers and outtakes – open up the film to self-reflexive commentary, a means of determining and foregrounding its generic placement and production specificity.

The kinds of film made by contemporary American film-makers are certainly not controlled by special effects technologies. There are certainly many generic films that do not focus themselves around digitally created images. But it has been the case in recent years that such films have dominated the industry. This bias can be attributed to the need to reap the huge box-office dividends upon which modern Hollywood increasingly depends to balance the books in an age of exponentially rising production costs. There is, however, evidence that the trend might at least partially be changing. Writing in 1999, Peter Bart predicted that:

> *action films, especially sequels, may become an endangered species by next summer [1999] . . . The explanations were more pragmatic than strategic. Aware of the sky-high salaries Warner Bros. had paid on* Lethal Weapon IV, *stars involved in other sequels had pumped up prices as never before. As a result, studios desperate to hammer out sequels to hits like* Men in Black, Jumanji, *and even* Rush Hour *found themselves coming up empty-handed.*

> (Bart, 1999; pp.278–9)

Bart argues that the negative reaction to certain high-profile action block-busters, most notably *Godzilla* (1998), has prompted the industry to shift focus to producing small-scale comedies, using *There's Something About Mary* (1998) as a template, or slasher movies using casts of largely unknown youths. The attacks on the World Trade Centre and the Pentagon in September 2001 threatened to intensify this shift. The release of *Collateral Damage*, starring Arnold Schwarzenegger in a plot which involved terrorists blowing up a Los Angeles skyscraper, was held back several weeks because its subject matter was judged to be too close to the real events in New York. *Spiderman* (2002) in which the superhero was scripted to scale the World Trade Centre, and *Men in Black 2* (2002), which was originally planned to climax there, also had to be revised in the light of events. As John Sutherland noted only days after the attacks, '[n]o one in New York is going to pay $10 to see computer-generated simulations of skyscrapers being blown up. At least, not for a month or two' (Sutherland, 2001; p.10).

Sutherland's closing prediction that the painful memories of 11 September might prematurely fade and allow big-budget action blockbusters with explosive special effects to re-emerge and once again dominate the market has, to a large extent, proved accurate. The latest blockbuster release at time of writing, *Spider-man* (2002), opened to a record weekend box office of almost $115 million and has earned $605.8 million worldwide to date (June 2002). A survey of current releases in summer 2002 might reveal a rising number of small-scale, human-relationship, films gaining respectable box office. *Monster's Ball* (2001), for example, with a budget of only $4 million, built gradually over the months after release to take over $30 million at the American box office alone, at the same time as its star, Halle Berry, won the 2002 Best Actress Oscar. It is still, however, the hundreds of millions of dollars taken annually at the box office by the small number of blockbuster films, and currently primarily those based on comic-book characters, which continue to dominate the thinking of executives at the major studios.

The history of the American film industry has partly been one of cycles of popularity for certain genres; an ebb and flow which have made certain genres popular at times and unpopular at others. A good example is the Western – one of the most enduring genres until the 1980s, but currently out of favour. What goes around comes around, however, and the Western will return at some time in the future as a genre with audience appeal. The important point is that Hollywood has always responded to these shifts in audience taste, demonstrating its resilience and ability to adapt and persevere. The problem with the modern industry is that the old securities of production line pro-cesses and regular audiences have gone. Moreover, the fewer, more expensive, films that are produced take longer to make and have more pressure on them to perform spectacularly at the box office. It is, therefore, no longer so easy to predict and respond to any new shifts in audience proclivities. Modern mainstream American film-making is becoming more of a lottery as time goes by. Each new hit, especially the surprise successes, sends the industry scurrying off in its new direction, making clones of clones, each of which, it is hoped, will capitalise on that new audience configuration. Perhaps in time this frenzied approach will run its course and commercial film-making will return to smaller, cheaper, more personal films – a kind of return to the beginning, at least in terms of the time period covered by this book. Certainly, Bart's comment about *Godzilla* and *There's Something About Mary*, quoted above has more than an echo of the situation at the end of the 1960s. Then, the trend of big-budget, star-laden musicals flopping at the box office ushered in a 'movie brat' generation interested in making smaller, more personal films. The terrorist attacks on the World Trade Centre and Pentagon in September 2001 have undoubtedly intensified this interest, at least in the short-term. The longer-term effect of the attacks on audience interest in the action-blockbuster is less certain. We will have to see over the next few years whether history is poised to repeat itself.

CHAPTER EIGHT

Fixing it in Digital

How digital is Hollywood, really?
It's getting very digital. Nobody's doing it just to be hip – the costs are too high.
People are taking a good look at what they need . . . Nonlinear editing is a wave
that's breaking in a huge way. I see the editors resisting it. I see the studios
embracing it, often not for the right reason: not because it enhances creativity,
but because it reduces post-production time and costs. It's here, and everybody
knows it.

(James Cameron, interviewed by Paula Parisi for Wired *magazine,*
May 1996, p.105)

The history of Hollywood over the past decade or more is of an industry
dominated by the development of a particular kind of technical process:
digital imaging. Whether a film has explicitly and widely used such techniques in its creation or not, no film has escaped being framed within its
boundaries. Use of digital techniques can span a wide range of needs, from
simple removal of a visual glitch, through to the creation of extravagant and
visceral visual imagery depicting impossible worlds, such as are seen in the
wholly digitally created world of *Star Wars Episode II: Attack of the Clones*
(2002).

BRIEF HISTORY OF SPECIAL EFFECTS WORK IN AMERICAN CINEMA

Of course, there have always been special effects in film-making. Such visual
flourishes as dissolves, wipes, fades, multiple exposure, and so forth have
been used from the earliest years of cinema. The post-production optical
effects department of RKO was famed throughout the 1930s and 1940s for

the sophistication of its work in this area: in *Bringing Up Baby* (1938) an optical composite (combining two separate images from two separate strips of film into a single image) allowed a baby leopard to be put into the same space as the actors Katharine Hepburn and Cary Grant. The RKO department also created the many breathtaking optical effects and trick shots which give *Citizen Kane* (1941) its extraordinary visual richness. Matte paintings, in which a portion of the finished film image is painted on glass, which is placed in front of the camera, have been used for decades: in *The Adventures of Robin Hood* (1938) the mediaeval castles situated in lush English countryside are all painted images. The little figures of the human actors on their small section of country pathway appear to be riding through this virtual space, but are the only 'real' elements of the image.

Such techniques became staples at all of the major Hollywood studios throughout the studio period and beyond. Indeed, many of them are still potential tools in the armoury of the special effects experts. It would be a mistake to think that modern digital techniques have totally swept away the old, traditional, manual ways of creating images. However, in many ways the latter have been superseded by the advent and development of digital technologies that have provided effects workers with a whole new toolkit with which to create their 'non-real' imagery.

BRIEF HISTORY OF DIGITAL TECHNOLOGY IN AMERICAN CINEMA

In 1967, the Mathematical Application Group Inc. (MAGI) created the Synthavision system which enabled the operator to build objects up out of basic polygonal shapes (spheres, cubes, triangles) which were then smoothed out to form contoured surfaces. The objects were lit to give a modelled look, and movement from single image to single image was effected to build up animated sequences. These were then outputted to 35mm film via a colour film recorder.

In the mid-1970s, the Scanimate system could be used to control an electron beam through a raster (a grid of minute holes) to build up a range of effects, including the simulation of certain camera movements: pans, tilts, and so forth. It was used to produce some of the effects in *Star Wars* (1977), among other notable films. The next generation of system – Caesar – had a small digital computer controlling the processes, and could be used to create sequences involving animated characters.

In the 1973 film *Westworld*, Yul Brynner's robot vision was created by reducing the pixel information of the images he 'sees' so that they become crude grids of coloured squares. More significantly, in 1976, in the sequel, *Futureworld*, the effects crew drew a grid of lines on Peter Fonda's head, in order to plot a series of co-ordinates of his face. These were then used to create an artificial version of his head. This technique is still used, most notably in *Toy Story* (1995) (see below), and *Terminator 2: Judgement Day* (1991) in which the face and body contours of actor Robert Patrick were scanned and fed into a computer to create the lifelike human features of the T-1000 Terminator.

Throughout the 1960s and 1970s, computer graphics were developed almost solely within academic institutions, such as MIT and Iowa State, and the research and development divisions of large industrial corporations, such as General Motors and Bell Laboratories (Darley, 1990; p.42). These organisations were the only institutions with large enough mainframe computers to handle the massive amount of data required to create the images. One of the most important areas of research and development was in military simulation environments: the creation of credible warfare arenas in which armies fight simulated battles with believable degrees of realism. The success of such exercises is dependent upon the accurate simulation of reality: lives depend upon it. The fruits of such research and development imported into the creation of new images in feature films inherited that high degree of believability.

Alien (1979) was one of the first films to show the results of this research: its wire-frame image of the surface of the planet onto which the main characters land at the start of the film was created at the Royal College of Art in England. By 1980, electronic compositing arrived, and began to replace the physical optical compositing method: two separate film images being electronically scanned and combined via a mixing console.

Tron (1982) represents the first significant breakthrough of digital computer graphic effects work in American film-making. Such images make up approximately 20 per cent of the film. The computer-circuitry landscapes of the film's diegetic world were digitally created, as was the simulated circuitry of the characters. The latter was achieved by green-screening parts of the actors' costumes, which were made in a tone of green that could allow them to be replaced by digitised images of electronic circuitry at a later date.

Tron failed at the box office, however, and set back the cause of digital effects work within American film-making for several years. The exercise was seen as being too uncertain and too expensive to warrant the risk. As noted in Chapter 7, the development of such imagery was taken up instead by the advertising industry. The creation of glossy, high-production-value advertisements, in which every frame of every image is minutely scrutinised and manipulated until it is perfectly without blemish, was a natural environment for the development of high-cost digital processes, which created a kind of imagery never seen before.

It took several years for the film industry to become aware of these developments and, more significantly, to become convinced that they were dependable enough to be used in high-budget film production. The man credited with almost single-handedly bringing about this transition is James Cameron, although he has, perhaps uncharacteristically, downplayed this innovator role in interviews:

> There was something happening that I don't think anyone could push forward or hold back – there was an opportunity to ride that wave at exactly the right time. We took that opportunity on The Abyss, we took it again on Terminator 2, and we took it a third time to found Digital Domain. But before I became involved in computer graphics, there was a good ten- or fifteen-year history of pioneering work, with people writing the code necessary to do 3D imaging and figuring out how to do polygonal modelling . . . It was all being done, but it was being done in rarefied environments, at universities and in the R&D labs of big software companies. It hadn't reached the artists yet, per se. It hadn't cross-pollinated into the film industry, which had both the art and the money to make it a broad cultural phenomenon.

> *(Parisi, 1996; p.76)*

In *The Abyss* (1989), Cameron employed digital animation processes to create the water-alien – the pseudopod – which appears at the climax of the film; although he only did so after having considered traditional models and matte-work (Cameron began in the industry as a miniature-artist on *Battle Beyond the Stars* [1980] and a matte-artist on films such as *Escape From New York* [1981]). In all, even though the process of creating the 20 or so effects shots took millions of dollars and eight months, the cost and effort were justified for the technical advance and product differentiation produced.

Cameron's *Terminator 2: Judgement Day* was a more significant step forward in terms of incorporating digital special effects in a mainstream big-budget film. The pseudopod in *The Abyss* could have been created using conventional methods if the digital version had not worked, because the creature was not central to the plot but entered late on for specific effect. The T-1000 Terminator in the later film, however, was central to the story throughout the film, and was on screen for a substantially larger percentage of the film's length. It therefore had to be believable.

> [T]he success or failure of the film is really predicated on the success or failure of the digital technique. The great leap of faith is that we were ready, or could risk a US$90-plus million negative – which is a pretty high investment – on a group of people at ILM who couldn't guarantee that they could do what I wanted them to but said, 'We think we're ready.'

> *(Parisi, 1996; p.77)*

The success of the film – it was the box-office leader in that year, with worldwide receipts of $516.8 million – was instrumental in convincing the American film industry that such effects work was achievable. More significantly, it showed that the inclusion of such effects would add substantial production values (and, hopefully, box-office revenue) to any film in which it was used. *Terminator 2: Judgement Day* ushered in the fantasy adventure, digital-effects mega-productions which were to dominate the 1990s.

DIGITAL AESTHETICS

Computer-generated digital images have been criticised from many quarters for their overly smooth, weightless quality: 'these fantasy objects laden with the irresistible gravity of the real, and at the same time with the elusive weightlessness of dream' (Romney, 1997; p.205). Certainly, this neatly summarises the qualities of early digital images which practitioners in the field have been striving hard to improve over the past few years. Early manifestations of such visual effects – such as *The Mask* (1994) in which Jim Carrey's famed rubbery physicality was extended into the grotesque and flamboyant slapstick actions and facial reactions of the eponymous central character – succeeded only in so far as they remained firmly in the world of the cartoon.

As software programmes and computer platforms, such as Avid, Paintbox and Harry, developed, allowing subtler and more sophisticated graphic techniques to be achieved, the subject matter of effects-foregrounded feature films could extend into referencing the nominally real, physical world that we all know. But that world remained in many respects an unreal one – filled with gigantic spaceships, aliens and liquid metal robots. These various objects and beings display many points of reference for us – whether the hardness of metal, tough scales of lizard-like skin, or the slippery quality of mercury – which allow us to understand the physical properties of the objects and the world being depicted on screen.

The description that is most commonly used in discussions of digital effects is 'painterly'. For George Lucas, digital imaging is 'the process of a painter or sculptor. You work on it for a bit, then you stand back and look at it and add some more onto it, then stand back and look at it and add some more. You basically end up layering the whole thing' (Kelly and Parisi, 1997; p.74). Thomas Elsaesser argues that the painterly quality of digital film-making

requires a new kind of individual input, indeed manual application of craft and skill, which is to say, it marks the return of the 'artist' as source and origin of the image. In this respect, the digital image should be regarded as an expressive, rather than reproductive medium, with both the software and the 'effects' it produces bearing the imprint and signature of the creator.

(Elsaesser, 1998; pp.205–6)

It is marked by a certain surface gloss, a smoothness which comes from an electronic version of painting – drawing lines to create the shape of objects and then applying colour to areas of that object. Such a process eradicates imperfection – lines and surfaces are perfect, without blemish or wrinkle. It is the objective of the digital paint program to make sure that such imperfections are removed from the process. Unpredictability is removed. Digital clothes do not snag on branches or furniture. Extras in the background of digitally created crowd scenes do not make awkward gestures or movements that spoil a take. Unless, of course, the digital creators *want* the clothes to snag. Then they simply tweak the program and the effect appears.

The painterly aspect of the digital imaging process partly controls the pace and timing of editing for scene construction in effects-heavy films. This is partly because such images are not totally believable. Digitally created images can remain on screen only so long before the visual 'cracks', so to speak, begin to appear. The surfaces of the walls of the Coliseum in *Gladiator* (2000), for example, are too smooth because they lack the countless tiny imperfections which real stone possesses. Although, admittedly, their brevity is also due to the high cost of creating them, as well as their role in generating the fast-moving action of the scenes in which they appear, digital images generally appear on screen in fragments, diverting the eye and then disappearing before their visual quality can be scrutinised too closely. Editing patterns tend, therefore, to be faster, rapid-fire sequences of very short shots, showing fragmented bodies and objects; an often confusing and ambiguous diegetic space and action.

The exception to this general aesthetic process is a version of the 'money shot': the payoff for an audience that has been denied a sustained look at the desired object – whether the massive lizard-monster in *Godzilla* (1998), the gargantuan alien spaceships in *Independence Day* (1996), or the catastrophic effect of a meteorite hitting Earth in *Deep Impact* (1998). At the climax of *Deep Impact*, when the meteorite has crashed into the sea and created a massive tidal wave that is sweeping towards New York, a rapid series of shots shows the population panicking and preparing for impact. Then, the 'camera' cuts back to an extreme long shot of the entire Battery Park seafront area of New York as the wave reaches land. In a shot whose length is manifestly longer than any of those which have preceded it, we watch as the wave, higher even than the World Trade Centre, crashes over the city, effortlessly knocking over some of the tallest buildings in the world. Such an image-sequence (24 frames

Effects specialist Peter Jopling composits an image at Mill Film

per second, each individually and painstakingly drawn, painted and rendered at enormous cost) is designed to awe the audience into submission, to make it finally surrender to the believability of the digital world being created. The ironic thing is that it still does not quite succeed – we notice the insubstantiality of the wave and the buildings; they do not have quite enough mass and substance, they seem to float (forgive the pun) in partial weightlessness. Perhaps the best-known 'money-shot' of recent effects movies is the scene in which the first actual sight is given of the dinosaurs in *Jurassic Park* (1993). This kind of moment has been commented upon by several writers, especially Michele Pierson (1999, p.167) and Geoff King (2000b, p.43):

> *The mode of arts-and-effects direction characteristic of science-fiction cinema in the early 1990s is very much directed towards establishing a spectatorial relation to its computer-generated special effects that is wondering, and even contemplative. In action-driven science-fiction films like* The Abyss, Terminator 2, Lawnmower Man *(Brett Leonard, 1992),* Jurassic Park, Stargate *(Roland Emmerich, 1994), and* Johnny Mnemonic, *the presentation of key computer-generated images produced a distinct break in the action. These temporal and narrative breaks might be thought of as helping to establish the conditions under which spectators' willed immersion in the action – their readiness to be carried along by 'the ride' – is suspended long enough to direct their attention to the display of the digital artefact. Effects sequences featuring*

CGI commonly exhibit a mode of spectatorial address that – with its tableau-style framing, longer takes, and strategic intercutting between shots of characters – solicits a contemplative viewing of the computer-generated image.

(Pierson, 1999; p.169)

The objective of many of the practitioners of digital effects is to move from that partially referenced unreal world to the real. For Fred Raimondi, visual effects supervisor at Digital Domain: 'My goal is to do completely photo-real computer-generated scenes that are completely and totally believable – where the viewer would look at it and not be able to identify the technique, not be able to say, "was that photographed, or was that computer-generated?"' (interview in *Electric Passions*, Channel Four TV, 1996).

But what if photorealism is not the aesthetic goal? Could it be an outmoded aesthetic – rather like the flatness and disproportionate figures in early mediaeval paintings when compared to the Renaissance interest in proportion and perspective?

Still, before we take that route of muscle and blood, perhaps there's room to salvage the immateriality of digitals for more fruitful use. At the risk of invoking some vaporous idealist code of aesthetics, I'd say there's still every possibility for CGI to be used in the service of poetry – by which I mean, simply to create images that are not shackled to the sensationalist hyper-real but have some consciousness of their own constructedness . . . There is also the option – practically unexplored in the mainstream, for obvious reasons – of using computer effects to loosen the hold of realism altogether and explode the economy of the film frame. In Prospero's Books *and* The Pillow Book, *Peter Greenaway fragments the image, critically measuring the signifying power of the screen against other readable surfaces – painting, books, the human body. The latter film, in particular, consciously offered itself as a provocative if overly aesthetic manifesto for a new digital cinema.*

(Romney, 1997; p.224)

Of course, Romney is referring to a particular kind of film-making here – art cinema, even avant-garde cinema. For such 'alternative' film-making styles, digital effects can indeed open up new avenues of non-representational expression, new artistic possibilities. For the mainstream cinema, however, images have to refer to what is real and represented. Digital images have to look like something believable, and look as if they behave according to real-world physical laws (gravity, mass, inertia, etc.), however outlandishly. However, some critics argue that the logic of CGI images inserted into real-world environments (i.e., those which really exist, and have been conventionally photographed) is not to seamlessly integrate both together, but to have the latter foreground the artificiality of the former:

> *The privileging of electronic depiction . . . here depends upon its marked difference from cinematographic space rather than upon its integration with it (however much integration may be 'promoted' by the narrative.)*

> *(Sobchack, 1987; p.261)*

The point, surely, is that a tension exists between computer-generated and photographic imagery, a tension between visual integration and visual distinction, which lends current CGI images their particular and peculiar effect: as simultaneously both believable and impossible:

> *The enjoyment of special effects lies, perhaps, in allowing ourselves to be deceived while knowing that this is not entirely the case . . . We can let ourselves go, surrender to the wonders of convincingly rendered dinosaurs or ships, but at the same time retain an element of distance and control through our awareness that we are allowing ourselves to delight in an illusion; and further, that we are delighting in it precisely because of its quality as illusion. We are able to stand back just far enough to be able to enjoy both halves of the equation.*

> *(King, 2000b; p.56)*

That complex aesthetic has characterised big-budget Hollywood film production throughout the 1990s, and will no doubt continue to do so for years to come.

There is also a tension between the space opened up for the contemplation of the complex, digitally created image, and the lack of contemplation produced by a narrative driven forward in order to hide the limitations of plot and environment. Of course, this is more applicable in the case of a certain kind of film – the action-fantasy or sci-fi genre – rather than for films in general. Other kinds of film try very hard to hide their CGI work: whether the simple removal of wires in stunt-work, such as that which allows Schwarzenegger's stunt-double to perform a dangerous motorbike leap from a bridge in *Terminator 2: Judgement Day*, or the generation of large crowds in films such as *Forrest Gump* (1994) or *Elizabeth* (1998). There is therefore a difference between invisible and visible special effects:

> *As their name suggests, invisible special effects are not meant to be noticed (as special effects) by film spectators. Visible special effects, on the other hand, simulate events that are impossible in the actual world (but which are possible*

in an alternative world), such as the dinosaurs in Jurassic Park *and* The Lost World.

(Buckland, 1999, p.184)

The effect of such digital work is different for every spectator; there is a shifting scale of relationship between the two, depending on the individual. An older member of the audience, perhaps, will be more immersed in the fiction, and more willing to unthinkingly accept the CGI image *within* the narrative context. A young video-game playing technology enthusiast, on the other hand, has come to the film at least partly to identify and then appreciate the effect *outside* of the narrative (King, 2000b; pp.44–5).

ANYTHING IS POSSIBLE

Anything is possible right now if you throw enough money at it, or enough time. We have the right tools, or we can combine tools, to do anything. That doesn't mean that it's easy, that it's straightforward, that it's intuitive, or that it's cost effective. The goals within the next ten years are to make the interface with the film-maker more intuitive and easier to use, to bring costs down and to create a cohesive field out of all these disparate tools.

(James Cameron, in Parisi, 1996; p.77)

The real development and absorption of computer-based digital effects into the fabric of the American film industry was a result of the exponentially decreasing cost of computer memory across the 1990s, as computers became an essential part of so many aspects of human life and work. ' "In my lifetime, the cost of the basic tools of my trade – of making images with a computer – has gone from about $500,000 to about $2,000 dollars," he says. "It's a factor of 200 or 300 to one" ' (Tyler, 2000; p.1). Cameron's comment that opened this section – that anything is possible with enough time and money – is a refrain that has been endlessly repeated by those in the digital effects industry over the past few years. There is a definite perception that the development and learning curves of digital effects have reached their apogee, and the full potential of the arena has been realised in practical terms.

This situation has several implications. Firstly, it is now possible to produce any image a film-maker desires, no matter how fantastic or extravagant. Such a possibility might be seen to confirm the out-of-control, surface-over-content, style of film that many commentators, including Peter Bart (1999) and Jonathan Romney (1997), have criticised the American cinema for producing over the past decade. And, indeed, it is hard not to agree at least partly with this judgement. The perfection of digital imaging effects and techniques does initially seem to point towards their continued use in future overblown, surface-image-with-weak-story, styles of film-making. The poorly sketched and cliché-ridden three-way relationship between father, daughter and her lover in *Armageddon* (1998) was roundly criticised in reviews on the film's release. The love triangle in *Pearl Harbor* (2001) has received a similarly poor response, especially in comparison to the impressive special effects of the air attacks. So, although the director of photography on the film, John Schwartzman, might say that '*Pearl Harbor* is really a love story – it just so happens that the second act is set against the backdrop of the Japanese attack. The bombing only comprises 35 to 40 minutes of the film,' the article in which he makes this point later notes that 'The most talked about aspect of *Pearl Harbor* will undoubtedly be the scenes depicting the Japanese bombardment of the unsuspecting Americans' (Probst, 2001; pp. 39, 43).

On the other hand, the situation whereby 'anything is possible' normalises the presence and potential of digital. If anything is possible, the power of new images – known as 'impact aesthetics', each new image having to top the effect of the previous one – gets progressively weakened, giving the films in which they appear less potential advantage over competitors in the marketplace. Every effects film becomes rather too much like every other one. In such an environment, other factors come into play as the element which will give one film an advantage over its rivals: for instance, a strong and gripping story, or emotionally affecting acting. In a perverse way, the perfecting of digital effects, seen as having been so responsible for the dumbing down of American cinema over the past ten years or so, might be responsible for the return of story and acting skill to future American cinema:

> The real danger, many experts say, is that audiences eventually will no longer be thrilled by the 'wow' factor. 'To a certain extent, we're jading an audience,' Hayes [visual effects supervisor, Tippett Studio] says. 'How much more can you really do?' Some already see signs of special-effects burnout. 'We call it "cinema puritae", a whole generation that rejects special effects. Audiences are craving something real that feels real,' says James B. Meigs, editor of Premiere magazine. He points to last summer's sleeper hits as evidence that audiences are eager for less flash. The Sixth Sense had practically no special effects and grossed nearly $300 million, and The Blair Witch Project, made for $60,000, went on to take in $140 million, the most successful independent film ever.
>
> (Soriano, 2000; p.1)

Digital effects will therefore become absorbed into the very fabric of US film production, not only the high-end, big-budget blockbuster, as one of a range of techniques available to film-makers. Indeed, this has already been the case for several years. Digital effects are now so endemic throughout American (and not just American) film-making that many of them pass completely unnoticed by audiences. Spacecraft attempting to land on flaming asteroids in *Armageddon* (1998) foreground their digital effects as enjoyable in their own right. In contrast, the subtler use of digital effects to create the Norwegian army in the background of a shot in Kenneth Branagh's *Hamlet* (1996) or the feather fluttering to the ground in the opening shot of *Forrest Gump* (1994), is designed to be invisible. Here, they act as an aid to the production process rather than an explicit effect intended as the audience's main source of enjoyment.

The terrorist attacks on the Pentagon and, more particularly, the World Trade Centre, has significantly affected the role and effect of digital special effects in blockbuster films. It was a repeated refrain in the immediate aftermath of the attacks that the explosions caused by the airliners striking the towers and their collapse soon afterwards, was like a scene from a big-budget special effects film. Or rather, that it was even more visually stunning, dwarfing any effect that a CGI artist could ever imagine or create. For the past few years, computer-generated imaging has been getting gradually more sophisticated, able to produce increasingly photo-realistic objects. The destruction of the twin towers of the World Trade Centre had two effects: in the event itself to look like a special effects movie and in the aftermath to make equivalent computer-generated scenes in movies something which were suddenly less impressive, more easily seen-through as illusion. *Armageddon*-style digital special effects now had a real-life benchmark against which they could, and inevitably will be unfavourably compared.

EFFECT ON PRODUCTION

Computer-generated images can help to save on location costs. Scenery for certain scenes of a movie can be simulated digitally, making it unnecessary for full production units, director and stars physically to travel to, and stay in, those locations. This scenery can be fantastic and otherworldly, as in *Star Wars Episode II: Attack of the Clones* or real-world, as in some of the panoramic shots in *Gladiator*, which mix and match buildings, sunsets and hills from various locations. Even if they do go on location, film-makers do not need such critical set-up times to get everything perfect. If light is fading as an important and expensive shot is being filmed, the production does not now have to close down and try again the following day, when it might be delayed again by rain or other unforeseen distraction. Now the light levels can be adjusted by computer, shadows added to simulate strong sunshine. For many cinematographers, such as Russ Carpenter, this is cause for concern because:

> as an individual, I'm asking, how much is this picture going to change in postproduction? What happens if I walk in one day and somebody surprises me – for example, if I can see the actor's eyes. He's been lightened up. That's a real issue . . . For me, you need to form a relationship with the director, with the production designer, with a post/effects facility where the communication is. So I welcome the digital revolution, and yet I have some trepidation.
>
> (Carpenter, 1995; p.26)

Cutting production and post-production time is especially necessary with hugely complex, big-budget effects films. There is a point, however, at which the equation of costs saved versus costs incurred by digital effects work reverses itself. So we find, for example, that although the concept of 'fixing-it-in-digital' allowed the location shooting of *Twister* (1996) to remain on schedule, the extensive 'fixing' work itself was costly.

> it . . . served to double the ILM shot count. 'We ended up with more than three hundred shots,' related Bromley [ILM visual effects producer] . . . To accommodate the considerable increase, ILM rapidly assembled a large crew of about thirty technical directors, thirteen compositors, nine rotoscope artists, nine match-movers, and five modellers, along with texture artists, computer graphics supervisors and co-ordinators.
>
> (Luskin, 1996; p.74)

Ironically, *Titanic* (1997), a film which epitomises such cutting edge processes with its digital realisation of the ship charging through the open seas and digitally created actors ('avatars') walking its decks, is the most striking example of the complex relationship between physical production and digital post-production effects work. While it was always intended that digital effects would play a major part in creating the images of the film, one might ask why the makers of a film whose use of digital imaging was so overhyped would want or need to physically build, almost full-scale, 90 per cent of the ship in a dry dock in Baja, Mexico. Furthermore, many of these digital-heavy films demand extreme physical labour of their actors. For instance, Keanu Reeves and Carrie-Anne Moss trained for months to perfect the gravity-defying wire-leaps of the actors in *The Matrix* (1999), as did the actors in *Crouching Tiger, Hidden Dragon* (2000). Kate Winslet and Leonardo DiCaprio had to endure hours in freezing water in *Titanic*. Russell Crowe and his fellow actors had to train for several months to learn the swordplay which would make the brutal fighting in *Gladiator* look convincing.

The answer comes from Paula Parisi in her account of *Titanic's* production history. The cost of totally creating the film by computer, and the difficulty of matching actors' movements and actions within that virtual space, would have been three times greater than that of physically building the space and allowing the actors to inhabit it (Parisi, 1998; p.182). Digital imaging work can be a cost and labour saver, but only in certain circumstances. At other times, nothing beats doing it for real.

What is actually more usual is that shots will involve a combination of digital effect and real action. Again, examples are numerous. The stunt-people falling off the upturned stern of *Titanic* at the climax of the film are replaced mid-fall by digital versions of themselves. The fireballs hurled from authentically built catapults in *Gladiator* become replaced, mid-flight, by digital fireballs so that actual fire does not rain down on the extras pretending to be the Germanic hordes in the opening battle of the film. It is this slippage between real and digitally simulated objects which really marks modern film-making using digital imaging techniques. The physical confirms the virtual, whether on the large or small scale. In *Titanic*, 90 per cent of the ship was built to back up its computer-generated images. In *Jurassic Park*, a full-sized model of a dinosaur's foot is used to persuade us that the following full-shot of the digitally generated dinosaur exists in the same frame of reality as the foot itself.

A related issue is one of penetration of the digitally created space. Traditional effects work has always been marked by a certain two-dimensionality, of the actors and physical space existing on a flat plane which cannot be entered as a 3-D space. The perfect representation of this has always been the matte painting referred to at the beginning of this chapter. A flat painting, even if it is simulating a 3-D space such as a deep landscape and castle, cannot be penetrated by the camera, which is forever forced to remain on the other side of the plane, looking in, as it were.

Digital effects, on the other hand, have reached such a stage of development that they can simulate not only 3-D bodies (whether objects or humans) but also 3-D movement around those bodies. When the monster appears for the first time in the streets of New York in *Godzilla*, a complex camera movement sweeps through 180 degrees of diegetic space, turning around both the monster's body and a panic-stricken member of the public fleeing before it, as they both run down the street. The camera sweeps around both real and virtual object at the same time, convincing us that the two share the same space. The digital simulation of physical bodies is one stage of the process. A second, and perhaps most important phase, is the digital simulation of camerawork which enters the space inhabited by those objects, and moves around those objects to show them from all angles, because it allows film-makers finally to be able to persuade us that that space is whole and total.

Significantly, the complex 180-degree camera movement comes after a sequence of several static, or at most laterally moving, shots which have kept the monster frontal to the camera plane. The shift to panning camera marks the shift from 2-D to 3-D digital imaging of space. Similarly in *Gladiator*, the sweeping circular camera movement that swirls around the gladiators as they enter the Coliseum acts to confirm that they really exist in a physical space. The labour involved in creating the effect is seen to be worthwhile because it fundamentally increases the believability of the film's diegetic world. As the art director of the film commented on the commentary track of the DVD release: 'Spectacular shot. You couldn't have done this shot 5 years ago, not to that degree of plotting. It took them a long time to do. It was a very expensive one to do. Circular again, like the others.'

This advance is typified by the example of *Twister*. The film-makers shot a lot of the location filming using handheld cameras, moving in and around the real space. They knew that the sophistication of ILM's digital software would enable them to accommodate the complex camera movements with digital elements (such as the tornadoes obviously so vital to the scenes) to form a seamless diegetic space (Wiener, 1996; p.37). The handheld shot, so emblematic of 'reality filming', can now be used to confirm the reality of the virtual images generated by computer.

Much of modern blockbuster film production is now being carried out by digital effects teams working under supervisors in small companies located some miles away from the central production process. In this context, it might be an apposite moment to ask whether the traditional notion of the auteur still holds valid in today's American film industry. Ridley Scott, on the commentary track accompanying the DVD of *Gladiator*, notes at one point that filming a grand sequence such as the arrival of Joachim Phoenix in Rome and his meeting with the senators, is now, as he puts it, 'an act of faith'. Brief segments of action are filmed in which real actors move in small areas of real location space. These then have to be stitched together with the large-scale digital imaging of the magnificent buildings in which the characters are supposed to be located and by which they are supposed to be surrounded. The final realisation of the images which the audience sees on screen is increasingly the responsibility of effects artists and their overseers rather than the film's nominal director. Of course some 'high-tech' directors – such as Scott, Lucas and Cameron – see to it that they are at least aware of the labour and techniques involved in digital imaging, even if they are not actually the ones doing the final image creation. Other directors, to varying degrees, abdicate their responsibilities in this area, such that the final look, texture and *mise-en-scène* of their films are the product of someone else's creativity and labour. As Albert J. La Valley has noted: '[f]or many young people, knowledge of special effects techniques now offers a kind of lure of stardom and power within the industry previously available only to screenwriters, stars, producers and directors' (La Valley, 1985; p.141).

This spreading of auteurist responsibility can extend to the production process itself. On *Twister*, for example, representatives from Industrial Light and Magic were on hand to advise the director Jan De Bont, of the parameters within which certain shots could be filmed. That is to say, their advice in terms of the ease or difficulty of 'fixing it in post' affected the actual filming process itself:

> *Effects specialists from Industrial Light and Magic were on the set to make certain the exposed footage would accommodate the computer graphics De Bont had planned. 'Whenever we set up any shot that was going to include CG,' Green [cinematographer] says, 'we'd get together and talk. It didn't require exposure changes or special filters or anything like that. We'd arrange the composition to allow room for tornado or for trucks tumbling through the sky or for houses blowing apart. We were never doing the show 'alone' – there were always the as-yet unseen digital effects to be taken into account.*

> *(Wiener, 1996; p.37)*

The auteur of many contemporary American films using digital effects – and that now means most of them – must increasingly be seen as a dispersed entity, consisting of several creative personnel, from director and art director through to effects supervisor and effects artist(s):

> *In fact, one of the problems of CGI is that it unsettles the notion of authorship: we are no longer entirely sure where images come from. Should we attribute them to the director of a film (can we honestly talk about Spielberg's dinosaurs or Jan De Bont's twisters?) or are the real authors the effects houses that generated them – ILM, Digital Domain, Pixar? Or perhaps we should attribute them to the technology itself, as if to an invisible god, the ghost in the movie-machine?*

> *(Romney, 1997; p.210)*

In a sense this has been the result of a blurring of the boundary lines between production and post-production. In earlier times, production was where the images and, to a lesser extent, the sounds of the film were created. Post-production was where a certain amount of smoothing out was performed and where seamless transitions were effected between certain shots and sequences. Nowadays, production is where images of the film are partially created, and post-production, now a greatly enlarged period of time, is where the greater proportion of imaging is created and united with the images created during the production period.

The sharing of auteurist responsibility is also a consequence of a shift from stand-alone customised programs which allow only individual, expert, operators to create images to universal programs, which enable such effects work to be subcontracted out to teams of people in several discrete companies, and sections of films to be created simultaneously. On *Batman Forever* (1995), for example, 14 separate effects houses were employed concurrently to create sections of the film's digital imagery, including Blue Sky/VIFX for the batwing underwater sequences, Composite Image Systems, Illusion Arts Inc., and Pacific Data Images. This is what King, amongst others, identifies as a move towards a 'decentralised or "post-Fordist" production system . . . what post-Fordists term "flexible specialisation" in the production process – the general shift to an environment in which film packages are assembled on a one-off basis with different elements of each package supplied by a large number of small providers' (King, 2000b; p.68). The creation of a sub-industry of specialist digital effects houses to service the needs of the film industry has become a feature of the American film landscape over the past decade.

However, as King goes on to note, caution must be exercised in this respect. The development of such new production practices has not been paralleled by similar changes in the financial or distribution sectors of the industry. Furthermore,

> *[t]here have also been moves towards some re-centralisation at the production and post-production level. As far as digital effects is concerned, the majors have begun to take over: 'To date, the studios have chosen either to buy established entities outright (Sony with Imageworks, Disney with Dream Quest); take substantial stakes (Fox with VI Effects, DreamWorks with PDI [Pacific Data Images]); or form their own in-house divisions (Warner Bros.)' As ever, the majors are happy to leave the risks of innovation to outsiders . . . moving in to reap the benefits at a later stage when potential profitability has been demonstrated.*

> *(King, 2000b; p.68)*

What we have been seeing in recent years, and what has been alarming certain practitioners, has been the removal of the indexical, of the reference to the actual and the real, of the assurance that what we are seeing up on the screen is an irrefutable photographic record of what was truly there at the moment of filming. There is a certain integrity to such a belief which, some fear and believe, is being undercut and compromised in digital-effects cinema. So, for example, when we see Liam Neeson and Ewen McGregor flanking, and talking to, the digitally animated alien creature Ja-Ja Binks in *Star Wars Episode 1: The Phantom Menace*, there is an essential unbelievability to the image because the two actors cannot really be sharing the same space as the computer-generated character. But it is more complicated than this: the two men are not sharing the same space either, at least in a literal sense. The performance of each comes from different takes, so that when Neeson talks or gestures to McGregor, the latter's response is not actually to that word or gesture, but to another which happened later or earlier.

The question which must be posed is whether, and, if so, to what degree, this is fundamentally different from the case, noted earlier, of *Bringing Up Baby*, where optical compositing seemed to place Katherine Hepburn in the same space as a baby leopard. The two beings are not existing together in the same moment of time in this sequence either. But the difference is that they both had actually been in that space (a drawing room set) and had been photographed there onto a filmstrip of individual photo-frames, by a movie camera. The fear of many is that the non-physicality of Ja-Ja Binks will eventually become the unreality of the human actors as well.

Already we are seeing this happen in localised instances, usually in desperate circumstances such as the death of an actor mid-production. Both Brandon Lee in *The Crow* (1994) and Oliver Reed in *Gladiator* had their faces digitally overlaid onto stunt-mens' bodies in certain shots of their films in order to preserve the continuity of the scenes and of the narrative in general. In *Jurassic Park*, because of the difficulty and danger of the stunt, a stunt woman dangling from a ceiling grate with a dinosaur snapping at her ankles had her face replaced with that of one of the child actors in the film. These are small moments indicating a future wider-scale possibility of digitally creating artificial human beings who have no actual existence:

> [M]any in the special effects industry question whether silicon actors will ever pose a real threat to the carbon-based variety. Dennis Muren, visual effects supervisor for Industrial Light and Magic and nine time Oscar winner, is sceptical of the creative benefits. 'What's the point,' he wonders. 'If you want to put Marilyn Monroe in a movie, you could get a terrific actress, give her a great make-up artist, six months of studying and voice training, and she could do a better Marilyn Monroe than we could ever do.'

> Jim Blinn questions whether synthespians make economic sense: 'A dinosaur doesn't exist, so it's practical to simulate it. With human beings, however, having a staff of 20 people all working on the lighting, the modelling, and the

motion might not be a great trade-off, because you can replace that whole team with one human actor who can do what the director wants.'

(Tyler, 2000; p.5)

Another significant implication of digital processes in contemporary American film-making lies not in post-production effects but, rather, in the shooting process itself. More and more film-makers are turning to digital video cameras, rather than the traditional 35mm or 70mm film camera, as their means of image-capture during production shooting. And this is as much the case with big-budget blockbuster film-making as with low-budget independent film-making:

> *[T]hough Star Wars creator George Lucas is among the highest-profile users of DV, 'What we [Sony] are bringing to the market is not only meant for Lucas and these big-budget movies. What we're seeing in our pavilion here is a lot of European medium-budget movies, and those film-makers are very enthusiastic about it.'*
>
> *(Horowitz, 2000; p.1)*

Digital video shooting has the fairly obvious advantage that the material shot is already in digital form, and can therefore be directly imported into a digital editing and effects environment during post-production. Such ease of transfer can not only give to film-makers a higher degree of control in getting exactly the right look for their films, but can also be extremely cost-effective for those conscious of the limited funds and resources at their disposal. As Melvin Van Peebles, director of the seminal blaxploitation film *Sweet Sweetback's Baadasssss Song* (1971), has commented:

> *It was very frustrating [with the film]; I had to run back to the lab a thousand times to get exactly the tint, exactly the amount of superimposition that I wanted to use from one step to the other. However, if I use digital, I can see what I've got, and instead of going to the optical house, I can do the optics digitally and control 100 per cent of the outcome . . . The financial aspect also is important. What it saved in ease of use was very important, but nothing like the happiness I was able to achieve when working at my editing table and realising what I saw would be what I got.*
>
> *(Horowitz, 2000; p.2)*

The independent film *The Last Broadcast* (1998) was an all-digital video feature, as is Spike Lee's production, *Bamboozled* (2000). According to Peter Broderick of Next Wave Films, there are three things which indicate the extraordinary future for digital film-making. 'First, new cameras (ranging from $3000 to over $100,000 – for the new HDTV cameras) which continue to improve and become lower in price; secondly, the availability of software for desktop computers to edit movies and do post-production at home; and, thirdly, the success of transfers from video to film' (Wasserman, 1999; p.2).

SYNERGY

The desired end point of converting the film image (and its sound) into digital form is to effect a synergy with product in other media, all of which have also been converted to digital. So, whether that material is still-image photograph or artwork, music from, or designed to form, a soundtrack, or video game environment and characters, it can all be easily exchanged and interlinked. Information taken from one material environment can be used within any other. For example, in order to initially create the toy characters in *Toy Story* a series of actual dolls had to be physically created: 'traditional' dolls which could be held in one's hands. Those figurines were then subjected to a spatial analysis by means of a grid of vertical and horizontal lines being drawn over their three-dimensional forms. The co-ordinates that this process produced were then fed into computers and used to create the computer-generated versions which, when animated, became the characters in the film itself. The same information (co-ordinate references of facial features, length of limb, etc.) could also be fed out to graphic artists wanting to create artwork to support the film's release (images of the characters on posters, T-shirts, burger cartons, and so on). It could also be sent to toy manufacturers to build replicas of the very dolls that had been built in order to generate the mathematical information in the first place. Digitised sound recordings of the actors lending their voices to the characters in the film could be sent to soundtrack compilers, makers of voice-boxes to be put inside the talking-dolls of the characters sold in Disney stores, and so on. The ease of transfer of endlessly repurposed material is the secret of maximising profit on a major feature film produced within a digital environment.

This synergy between various media is a fundamental focus of the modern conglomerate companies; companies who see film – cinema – not as a stand-alone medium, but as one amongst many, all interacting and re-deploying information generated in the others, making that information perform the maximum amount of work, an operation which, in turn, ensures maximisation of profits. The photographed film strip forms only part of the material by which an image in modern digital cinema is created; as Lev Manovich notes: 'Digital cinema is a particular case of animation which uses live action footage as one of its many elements' (Manovich, 1999; p.180).

In an analogous way, film is just one amongst several media forms which, together, form the total media landscape now controlled and orchestrated by the large conglomerates.

DIGITAL CINEMA

A development that could, until very recently, have been placed in Chapter 9 of this book, on the future, has now become a reality: digital cinema. In digital cinema, no film-print is physically carried back and forth between distributors and cinemas. Further, it is no longer projected by being pulled at a rate of 24 frames per second through the gate of a projector in front of a light beam, which shines the image through the projector lens and onto the cinema screen. Instead, one copy of the film, in digital form (cassette; file on a computer server) is held at a central source and sent as a digital transmission out to any number of cinema projection booths, and from there via a video projection unit, onto the screen. Such a procedure is simpler, more direct, and substantially less expensive, than the traditional way of creating the thousands of individual print copies of a film which are now inevitably required in these days of mass, saturated release patterns. '[E]ven just in the domestic marketplace, we spend about half a billion dollars a year, in the film industry collectively, on release prints' (Parisi, 1996; p.79).

Such a move will not in itself fundamentally alter the blockbuster mentality of the American mainstream film industry, because it will still ensure the mass saturation of the market to maximise profits on a film before word of its weaknesses gets out. It may, however, alleviate the financial pressure on production of films by reducing the overhead which must be covered by box-office returns. 'The cost of converting to digital projection systems is . . . formidable – $100,000 per projector multiplied by the more than 34,000 screens in the United States alone – and theatre owners and studios have very different ideas about who should pay the tab' (Lyman, 1999; p.1). But, then, the costs of converting to sound in the late 1920s were also astronomical: some $500,000 million over a few years. Conversion of cinemas following the introduction of CinemaScope in the 1950s, while not as expensive, still involved substantial sums of money: some $25,000 for theatres seating more than 2,000 people. What makes such investments financially viable is the enormous longer-term profit which results from the rejuvenation of the public's interest in wanting to go to the cinema.

DIGITAL SOUND

So far, the majority of the work that has been done on the significance that digital processing technologies promise for the film industry has been focused on visual imaging. But digital systems are also at work transforming the quality and creative options open to sound recordists and editors as well. This expanded possibility comes in part from the higher technical specification of digital processes. Since the information is in binary form – 0s and 1s rather than waveform – digital sound is not prone to the distortions, surface noise and hiss common to its analogue equivalent. Consequently, sound engineers can add layer upon layer of sound (dialogue, effects, music) without any perceptible loss of quality. This ability has transformed the nature and quality of film soundtracks.

The impact of digital sound on the aesthetic formation of the film itself lies in the degree of manipulation that it allows film-makers to exercise in creating the film's spatial world. Bob Fisher, discussing the work of Jeff Wexler, writes that he:

> believes re-recording mixers will be intrigued with the ability [the system] provides for taking a voice, or other sounds, and panning it around the theatre. But, in order for that to be effective, it has to be supported by the script and general concept of the movie . . . 'Dialogue should generally come from the front of the theatre,' Wexler said. 'But you now have the ability to immerse the audience in a very specific sea of ambient sound, for example, in a crowd scene. There are times when you want to envelop the audience in ambient noise so they feel like part of the crowd. I think we can do these things much more effectively now . . . CDS [Cinema Digital Sound] provides the bandwidth which we need to be much more subtle in our use of sound . . . Over the long-term, I believe we will see a better marriage between sound and images. The dynamic range of CDS mirrors the real world. It has moved the threshold. We can recreate total silence for dramatic impact. You can use contrasts in sound the same way that you do it with images. But, you never want the audience to be aware of what you are doing with sound on a conscious level. It has to be natural.'

> (Fisher, 1990; p.75)

Something like this prophecy seems to have transpired, although the outcome is not, perhaps, as positive as the above writer and practitioner were suggesting. Digital sound's enabling, amongst other things, of a 'better marriage between sound and images' has resulted in a overdetermined literalness of sound–image relations. Endless multi-layering, possible because of the cleanness and lack of distortion of digital sound, has created dense, overworked soundtracks. Every object you see on screen is now accompanied by its 'authentic' fully realised sound effect. As the stunt-people/avatars tumble down off the tilted poop deck of the sinking ship in *Titanic*, for example, every thud and crunch is rendered faithfully, as is every swish of metal wire as it snaps and whips across water and every creak and scrape of metal across metal as the ship slowly breaks apart. Soundtracks today can tend to be too doggedly and accurately representational, pinning down every object and action in realistic sonic effect. Audio hyper-reality has come to match its visual counterpart.

Digital sound is also having a serious impact on the exhibition sector of the film industry. Prints using digital sound tend to last far longer than those that do not, because there is less degradation of sound quality across repeated use. But, again, the process has a downside, at least in the short term. Sound quality from digital prints is no doubt qualitatively better. However, the quality of soundtracks now being mixed for optimum performance on those digital prints is not being replicated on ordinary analogue optical prints to be used in smaller, second-run cinemas. As a result, the sound quality in secondary cinemas can often seem unbalanced and muddy.

In an attempt to ensure that the quality of film sound is improved and maintained, George Lucas' Lucasfilm has proposed a set of standards, or performance parameters (as opposed to a technical system) regarding how film sound should be reproduced in a movie theatre and at home. The ultimate aim of these standards is to ensure that people watching a film in the cinema or on their home cinema systems, should hear the same sound the film's sound mixers heard when building the soundtrack.

In the long term, of course, the expectation is that all cinemas will have digital sound capability. However, with several competing systems available (including the aforementioned CDS; SDDS |Sony Dynamic Digital Sound, which premiered with *Last Action Hero* in 1993|; and DTS |Digital Theatre Systems, which also premiered in 1993, with *Jurassic Park*|), the situation is likely to remain confused for some time to come.

CHAPTER NINE

Back to the Future

Reports of [cinema's] death have been greatly exaggerated.

(Adapted from telegram to Associated Press from Mark Twain, 1897)

The future of cinema will be physical, at least partly. Traditionally passive (or immobile, rather than passive, since several theorists have argued that the spectator performs a continuous questioning and hypothesising as they watch a film), the audience is poised to become literally active as it experiences audio-visual texts in various custom-designed forms in the future. A range of both real and virtual environments is being developed, which will reframe cinema within new contexts. 'Film' will no longer be a filmstrip, but a stream of digital information. The spectator will no longer be passive, but will be asked to perform a variety of actions, make a variety of choices and decisions, and move through a series of carefully arranged physical spaces in order to experience fully the new media forms.

Many of these formats – theme parks, interactive computer programs (both stand-alone and via the Internet), virtual reality, and so on – already exist, some in embryonic form, others more fully developed. The purpose of this chapter is to examine how likely it might be that any or all of them will be fully developed as a viable media entertainment.

DVD

Digital Versatile Disc (DVD) is a relatively recent new digital distribution format for feature films. The DVD format was initially praised for its superior sound and image quality, relative to the VHS videocassette. Furthermore, unlike a videocassette, the DVD's worth is judged not simply on the quality of its main feature film, but on the amount and quality of its supplementary material, whether interviews, out-takes and/or deleted scenes. Indeed, the original term represented by the acronym – Digital *Video* Disc – was replaced with Digital *Versatile* Disc to reflect this potential.

The two-disc DVD of *The Abyss* (1989), for example, contains both the original theatrical version and special edition versions of the film; behind-the-scenes footage and a 'making of' documentary; a visual effects reel; multi-angles of the pseudopod sequence; as well as trailers, photo gallery and cast biographies. The DVD of *Men in Black* (1997) even offers a pseudo-editing program that allows the user to edit short scenes together using alternative takes. Taken as a whole, the increasingly large amount of supplementary material surrounding the feature film on DVD places the film itself within a substantially new context, in which it is no longer the sole, or even the main, attraction. The 'text' now consists of a series of separate texts – the feature film itself plus all other materials – which the user puts into individual and unique combination in the process of viewing any or all of them. But the relegation of the status of the feature film to just being one amongst several programmes on a DVD should not blind us to the fact that it remains the *raison d'être* and centre of the endeavour. Without the feature film, there would be no reason to gather together the supplementary materials. They all justify their presence on the disc in relation to it.

DVD allows the user to view the material non-linearly. That is to say that, instead of starting at the beginning of a film and proceeding in real time through to its end, the user can hop around between scenes, accessing and replaying them as desired. While in some ways not a totally new concept, since video has for the past 20 years allowed spectators to interrupt the linear flow of the viewing of a film and to fast-forward or rewind at will, DVD makes this manipulation of the text substantially easier. Moreover, the ease of being able to do so is built into the very logic of the DVD format itself: it is one of its main attractions and selling points. This notion of non-linearity and interactivity is an important one in any discussion of modern media forms and new identities for cinema, as we shall see in forthcoming sections of this chapter.

THEME PARKS

Film-based theme parks are not a new phenomenon; they have existed since the 1950s (at least) with the opening of Disneyland in California in 1955. Douglas Trumbull is seen as having been instrumental in the development of the modern version. By his own account, he saw the potential for theme park rides during work on Stanley Kubrick's *2001: A Space Odyssey* (1968):

It had this huge sequence at the end of the movie which took the audience on a trip into space. It wasn't about plot, or story or character development. It was about what I call now an immersive experience and that made me believe that it was possible in the cinema to create experiences where the audience gets to be the actor in a sense, and gets to be in the movie rather than looking at the movie.

(Billion Dollar Funfairs, *Central Independent Television, 1998*)

While it may seem a little strange to include theme parks in a chapter on future developments in the American film industry, I have done so because their future importance to that industry promises to be considerable. Indeed, they have become a major phenomenon in the last decade, with the construction of several substantial sites in different parts of the world, the latest of which, both opened in 1999, are MCA's Universal Studios Japan (cost: $1–2 billion) and Island of Adventure, in Florida (cost: $2.5 billion).

On the face of it, theme parks seem a clumsy development. Physically located in one place, with people having to travel significant distances to visit them, they consist of a series of brief, intense physical experiences rather than a sustained escapist fantasy. Why have they become so popular, and so central to the contemporary American film industry? The primary reason is because they are spectacularly successful, economically. 'For the parent company, the theme park is a machine for the rapid generation of cash' (Davis, 1996; p.403). Well over 200 million customers a year visit American theme parks, over 55 million visiting the ones in Florida. Two thousand people an hour experience the *Jaws* ride at Universal Studios, Florida; 2,300 people an hour for *Terminator 2:3D*; 2,400 people an hour for the *Twister* attraction, both also at the Universal site. Each of these short shows – lasting five to ten minutes – costs as much as a two hour-plus movie screening:

Today, the motion simulator is undoubtedly the leading-edge of the commercial movie-based LBE [Location-Based Entertainment] industry, not least because of the high volumes of paying customers that can be accommodated in a short period of time. The intensity of excitement that can be condensed into less than five minutes makes the ride feel much longer than it really is and conveys a sense of 'value for money' comparable with much longer entertainment experiences (e.g., conventional feature films). This is particularly so when the ride itself is preceded by an imaginative 'pre-show' that prepares the audience. And, of course, charging as much for a ride as for admission to a movie gives rides a strong appeal to operators.

(Anon, 1995; p.225)

As James Zoltak, West Coast editor of *Amusement Business* magazine, commented in the documentary *Billion Dollar Funfairs*, if, at a conservative estimate, 12 million people a year visit a theme park, each paying $25–30 dollars for a ticket, they generate a great deal of revenue. And this figure does not even account for the additional income from concessions and merchandise, which effectively doubles the figure to somewhere between $700 million and $1 billion dollars. But with theme parks forced to add major new rides every year or so, each costing $100 million to build, that revenue is needed (*Billion Dollar Funfairs*, 1998).

For the conglomerates, park ownership is also about a particular kind of synergy – not only between their film interests and ride development, but also between these and their real estate, restaurants and hotel chain ownership. All of the major conglomerates have theme park operations: 'Significantly, in the 1990s, most of the chains built in the 1960s and 1970s have been integrated into media conglomerates. The "big five" owners are Disney, Anheuser-Busch, Time-Warner, Viacom (Paramount) and MCA' (Davis, 1996; p.401). Although many customers are assumed to come only for the day, even if they have to drive for several hours each way, every theme park has a range of accommodation and eateries to allow people to stay for several days if desired. As Davis comments, 'A theme park and its surrounding real estate create a tourist district, complete with the opportunity to license or operate profitable adjuncts: hotels, campgrounds, restaurants, parking garages, souvenir shops, cruise ships, casinos and golf courses . . .' (Davis, 1996; pp.405–6). This is franchising on a massive leisure scale, within which film is merely the originating source. Though I say merely, it has a very important, not to say vital, role to play. Film sets up the deep emotional and psychological terms which are then followed through in other, more physical media, as I will explore shortly.

In many ways, there is a straightforward affinity between feature films and theme parks:

> . . . the Hollywood theme has multiple uses. Parks need regular, even annual infusions of new attractions, whether these be rides, character shows, parades, performances, or short films. Hollywood, with its seasonal, frequent change – traditionally tied to school years and family vacations – helps solve the 'what's new' problem. It follows roughly the same annual promotional rhythm as the theme park. Although it takes years to design and build a new rollercoaster or ride, performances and merchandise areas can be rethemed quickly: attractions can change in order to support the year's big film releases. In 1994, for example, Universal Studios Hollywood featured sets from 1993's blockbuster Jurassic Park, while the opening of a walk-through Flintstones movie stage was timed to coincide with that film's theatrical debut . . . There is even some

evidence that cartoons and films are being styled at early stages with potential theme park attractions in mind, the relevant question perhaps being 'Will this story be good to ride?'

(Davis, 1996; p.407)

As indicated at the end of the above quote, such is the importance of theme park attractions to the major film studios that new film scripts are vetted as they come into the studios to find suitable sequences and material to make new rides. In *Billion Dollar Funfairs*, Gary Goddard, chairman and CEO of Hollywood's Landmark Entertainment, commented that the minute a new film project is announced, the theme park developers are keen to enter into talks about possible development of rides based on the idea. The implications of this are huge. It means that for new film projects to be green-lighted these days, there is an increasing desire for them to contain high-action, visceral scenes or sequences which could be turned into theme park rides. With this process firmly in place, it is little wonder that the all-action blockbuster remains a cornerstone of American mainstream cinema. Again, this production emphasis may well be compromised, at least in the short-term, by the terrorist attacks on America on 11 September 2001. The public's willingness to put themselves into situations of extreme physical danger, albeit simulated, will understandably be compromised by the memory of thousands of people having done so in reality during the destruction of the twin towers.

There is a degree of unpredictability in the relationship between films and theme rides. For a ride to be developed from a movie, that movie has to be successful at the box office. It has to be, in order to generate enough public interest to make the ride something people want to come and experience. But the development period of a ride is longer (several months) than the period needed to determine whether a movie is a major hit (a few weeks). Therefore, the ride has to begin development before the movie is released. If the film then fails at the box office, a lot of money can be wasted on developing the ride.

The pressure on film-makers to predict the market becomes intense. Each new big-budget film release not only has to return huge profits at its own box office, it also has to support the success of a $100 million theme park ride as well. This double bind increases the pressure on film-makers and studios to play safe, to base film plots and action around stunts, chases and special effects rather than character development.

Such is the importance of theme park shows and rides to the overall marketability and profitability of a major film these days, that the leading directors of those films are becoming closely involved with their development. Steven Spielberg has had an active role in the design of the *Jaws*, *ET* and

Back to the Future attractions and is now the creative consultant for Universal Studios theme parks. Roland Emmerich, director of *Independence Day* and *Godzilla*, sees advantages in the producer/director of the film also being the one who designs the ride, because that will ensure that the spirit and tone of the film are faithfully transferred to the new environment.

Some commentators have expressed concern that the intimate connection of theme park rides to feature films will result – or already has resulted – in a reduction in the importance of narrative and character development and an increase in spectacular events in these movies. Just such a phenomenon has been identified as having been in progress for at least the last ten years, as has been described elsewhere in this work. But such a stark binary opposition is too simple a take on a complex interaction between the two media. Douglas Trumbull has commented that '[w]hen we're trying to find a movie that lends itself to being a ride, we look at action sequences, chase sequences, physical dynamic motion. Things that lend themselves to some kind of very powerful visceral but short simulation experience. A love story doesn't usually lend itself to that' (*Billion Dollar Funfairs*, 1998). But there is evidence that narrative is important to the success of many of these attractions. Indeed, it could be argued that it is essential to keep the narrative in feature films because otherwise the 'movie attraction' (the ride) will have no context. Instead, it will have to build that context *and* deliver its visceral thrills itself, within its intensely short time frame. Most rides, such as Universal Studios Florida's *Dudley Do-Right's Ripsaw Falls* water-splash ride, and *Dr Doom's Fearfall*, in which guests are hauled to the top of a tall column and then released to fall extremely rapidly under carefully controlled conditions, last only a few minutes.

In fact, many of the more elaborate theme park rides and attractions do attempt to set up a narrative context for themselves. This is done through the addition of introductory sessions before the actual ride, which are designed to orientate their spectators for what they are about to experience. A further, more calculating, reason for such sessions is that they are designed to make an event seem longer so that the spectator feels they are getting their money's worth. Take, for example, three of the most ambitious attractions and rides: *Terminator 2:3D*, and *Back to the Future: the Ride*, both of which are housed at Universal Studios theme park, and *Wayne's World*, housed at Paramount's theme parks. The *Terminator 2:3D* attraction preludes the actual main event with an introductory contextualization, given via television monitor, by Linda Hamilton, one of the actors in the original film. This format is repeated in other attractions: in *Back to the Future: the Ride*, Christopher Lloyd, as Doc Brown, similarly appears on video to explain the premise of the ride to the audience as they stand in queue waiting to take it (King, 2000b, pp.175–85). This task is undertaken at the *Wayne's World* attraction by Mike Myers (Wayne), who prepares his guests for the wooden roller coaster appropriately known as 'The Hurler' (Davis, 1996; p.409). Such arrangements and strategies allow the organisers to control the flow of people moving through the attractions, while simultaneously extending the experience in less costly ways than would be the case if they increased the length of the rides themselves.

Theme park rides have been likened to the 'cinema of attractions' of the earliest years of film, in which narrative was minimal and the main intent of the film (and its makers) was to deliver to the audience a show, a magic trick or sensational action (Gunning, 1986). There may well be these connections to be made between the two forms, separated by a century. However, what I am more interested in identifying here is the role to be played by foreknowledge of stories in both cases. When the earliest films began to tell stories to their audiences it was often necessary, and assumed, that those audiences would already know the stories, because they came from well-known news events (such as the Boer War), fairy-tales (*Jack and the Beanstalk*, 1902), or biblical stories (*Passion Play*, 1897). Spectators brought to the film viewing pre-knowledge of the narrative they were about to be told, and that pre-knowledge was used by the film-makers as a kind of shorthand, a means of cutting out parts of the storytelling process and allowing the audience to 'fill in the gaps'.

A similar, but inverse, process is at work in the movement between film and movie attraction at theme parks today. A ride often plays upon the fact that most people who visit it have already seen the film on which it is based. As Phil Hettema, senior vice-president of attraction development at Universal, notes:

> *In a movie you have 90 minutes to tell a story and there's a tremendous amount of background information etc. that you can absorb, and come to this experience with all that background information. So a lot of the storytelling has already been done for us, we only have to give them cues to bring that back into their memory. And once we've done that, they're already half way there, because we only have $4\frac{1}{2}$ minutes to tell them their whole story.*

(Billion Dollar Funfairs, *1998*)

For Murray Smith '[the movie] provides a primary narrative baseline which both endows isolated movie icons with meaning and emotional resonance, and provides a backdrop against which to toy with these associations in other media contexts' (Smith, 1998; p.14), while for Geoff King, 'The meaning and resonances carried by film icons are important commercial considerations, helping to ensure that expensive theme park attractions have a ready-made audience and are able instantly to establish clear and positive associations in the minds of potential visitors' (King, 2000a; p.8).

In a strange, and perhaps perverse, way, therefore, the development of primarily sensation-based media forms, such as theme park rides, which have their source in feature film subjects, might actually mean the *retention* of strong story lines in those films. Having already experienced the feature film, and remembered its story line, spectators feed those memories into their experience of the ride. The emotional effect of the theme park movie attraction is, in fact, dependent upon the narrative input of its users. Without their memory of the larger narrative, to which the ride can only refer in a condensed way, the visceral thrills of the ride itself become contextless.

We can only speculate as to what future form(s) the interrelationship between film and theme park attraction will take. Conrad Schoeffter has commented that '[t]he cinema auditorium of the future will be a modified flight simulator. You will literally fasten your seat belt for the ultimate flight of fancy. That is why you're seeing alliances forming between the motion picture and aircraft industries' (Schoeffter, 1998; p.115). However, others are more cautious. Geoff King, for example, counters Schoeffter's vision by observing that '[t]his might happen, but there are plenty of economic reasons why it might not, at least in the foreseeable future. Hollywood seems unlikely to invest the vast sums required while the major studios are doing very nicely from the current format, a lesson taught by most instances of technological change or continuity' (King, 2000a; p.8).

The American film industry has always been hard-headed about any major technological upheaval in its methods of operating. The coming of sound in the late 1920s, for example, was undertaken only after Warner Bros. took the risk and proved the viability and potential popularity of talking pictures with *The Jazz Singer* (1927). Once convinced, the industry poured hundreds of millions of dollars in only a few years into re-equipping its studios and theatres for sound. Modern Hollywood will have to be convinced that there is similar economic viability in turning all of its cinemas into movie attractions, with special motion-control booths and multiple media equipment to provide the visuals, physical events (explosions, crashes, tornadoes, etc.) and human actors performing live on stage. I doubt that this will happen. It makes more economic sense to keep such experiences in a particular place – the theme park – and leave cinemas to show films (albeit as digital projections). That way, the conglomerate owners of both can double their audience – enticing people to go first to one and then to the other based on the first.

The theme park attraction has the added benefit of prolonging the money-making life of a film which would otherwise have a relatively short theatrical run, followed by sale to video, cable and satellite. Even with these ancillary markets, a film's main financial life is measured in a few years. A theme park ride can be maintained indefinitely, because its attraction is one of pure physical sensation. Moreover, 'the deep vaults of the parent company contain valuable, recyclable assets: Universal has rides based on *Back to the Future* and *ET*, affixed with the "magical bankable" name of Steven Spielberg' (Davis, 1996; p.410). That is to say, films that might have been seen to have passed their sell-by date are now, potentially, being given a new lease of life as a theme park attraction.

THE INTERNET

Nothing has created quite such a cultural and social stir as the Internet and World Wide Web in recent years. For many, their emergence and development has been hailed as a more significant communication medium than either cinema or television. Integral to this perhaps hyperbolic valorisation has been the promise that the Internet will become a major distribution channel for films in the years to come.

The issue of movies on the Internet has become a hotly contested one in the last year or so, largely because the American film industry has both attempted to become involved in it and to control the efforts of individual Internet operators to offer non-licensed films via their services. As with its rejection of, then partnership with, television in the 1950s, or its competition with, and sequestering of, foreign talent at various times, Hollywood can be seen to be playing a cat-and-mouse game with the Internet. It is cautiously establishing contacts and generating initiatives with interested Internet parties while also seeking ways to achieve dominance over the phenomenon as a whole.

Certainly, there is much activity in this area, activity symbolised, in many ways, by the partnership between Time Warner and AOL (America On-line, one of the largest Internet service providers, with over 20 million subscribers), announced in early 2000. The benefits to both companies have been clearly stated:

> . . . this is really a merger that allows each of the companies to get a piece of the Internet future that they could not themselves provide. In Time Warner's case, AOL really helps them move onto the Internet, in a coherent and mass fashion. They were one of the early old media companies to embrace the Internet and have had some successes there, but not all of their attempts to organize the vast content that they have, have been real hits with consumers.

> What we're seeing here essentially is the maturation of the Internet as the platform for what will be the 21ˢᵗ century entertainment media universe. And what we've seen in this deal is not merely the conglomeration of some

technology with some media, but essentially the first shot across the bow of the 21ˢᵗ century media landscape.

(Lehrer, 2000; p.1)

Because of the exponentially increasing speed and diversity of new media technologies, the modern media landscape is being increasingly seen as a bewildering and confusing place in which people are losing their bearings and old certainties. One of the supposed attractions of Internet/media partnerships is to sort out this confusion and form clear plans for their future use.

> *Because beneath all this is this unrelenting fact, which is that the Internet has fragmented and created a very heterogeneous media landscape. And it's very troubling for these big companies because we've shifted from this homogeneous, simple [situation] the three networks and a couple cable stations, to this great wash of stuff. Part of what this merger now has to do is figure out how to aggregate all these people, how do we in a sense capture their attention in this fragmented world? That's why you're going to see more and more of these very big mergers between Internet companies and well-known media companies. It's all about trying to recreate an ability to capture the consumer, capture the public's attention in an increasingly fragmented world.*

(Lehrer, 2000; p.1)

Other commentators are more sceptical, seeing such alliances as limiting choice rather than increasing it under controlled conditions. The World Wide Web is being seen by many as the increasingly 'World Narrow Web', because the major players like AOL-Time Warner – fewer, larger and more powerful – are coming to control access to the Internet and Web, and can therefore determine what content is put onto them, and how access to it is marshalled and orchestrated. Sony is involved with Ifilm.com, while Warner Bros. have invested in Atomfilms.com, which has recently been acquired by shock-wave.com, a subsidiary of Macromedia Inc. (Olavsrud, 2000; p.1). As with many other examples in the past, the Hollywood majors buy into new talent and initiatives which appear to pose a threat to their continued operations. If Internet films fail, the threat has been warded off; if they succeed, Hollywood will find itself at the cutting edge of a new and financially lucrative distribution medium.

A user may, for example, have to fight their way past numerous advertisements for the conglomerate's other products before getting to the material they want. That material, more significantly, may have to be (inevitably will be) subscribed to before being accessed. We have been seeing this happen for years on cable and satellite, where prime feature films are offered on pay-per-view for a period before they become part of the ordinary schedule of films on offer every day. The premiere films become a bargaining chip in efforts to make consumers subscribe to ever more specialised, and ever more expensive, services.

The (supposed) difference in the case of the Internet is that it has always been democratic: a phenomenon that is not under the control of any one institution or company. The more that big mainstream features are made available on the Web, the more cluttered the environment will be and the more likely that the smaller, independent movies will be missed by their potential public, thus replicating the current theatrical and video situation.

Specific content may well not be on offer at all, if the conglomerate decides it no longer wants to provide it. Such an event occurred simultaneously with the AOL Time-Warner merger announcement in January 2000, when Disney's ABC channel was suddenly removed from Time-Warner cable networks. Power resides not with content providers but with the distribution channel providers. This is the reason why media companies and Internet companies are teaming up – to nail down freedom of access to valuable content (current blockbusters, libraries of film and television classics) so that profits from charging people to access it can be maximised.

In fact, several initiatives have already been set in motion in an attempt to capitalise on the potential of the Internet as a new film distribution channel. Film directors Steven Spielberg and Ron Howard, for example, through their companies Dreamworks SKG and Imagine Entertainment, set up Pop.com. Pop.com was intended as an on-line entertainment site devoted to creating and broadcasting original content such as live Web events, animations, video on demand and streamed video segments called 'pops', which last between one and six minutes.

The initial venture failed, partly because loudly announced projects involving major Hollywood stars, such as Eddie Murphy and Steve Martin, failed to materialise, and partly due to a crash in the dot.com market, which sent waves of nervousness throughout the Internet community. However, the two film-makers have now transferred their efforts to another Internet site, countingdown.com, for whom they are currently making short animated films based on dreams and nightmares they have both experienced.

One other significant event in this initiative is that one of the site's users left an Internet bulletin board message for Spielberg asking him to check out a short he had made titled *Award Showdown*, which features a claymation Spielberg fighting with a claymation George Lucas. Spielberg complied, liked the film, and the managers of the site posted it there the following month. In a modest way, we can see this representing the democratic potential of the Internet, in that users can become creators, using the Internet to make contact with those who can help them do something with the material they create.

Not everyone will get the attention of a Spielberg or a Lucas, but other potentially valuable interconnections will be made.

A more ominous connection between Hollywood and Internet providers comes with the case of Scour.com, a file-sharing company that used loopholes in the current copyright legislation to allow its users to access and swap the works of major media artists and companies. Michael Ovitz, who has represented many of the movie industry's top stars and has helped shift the balance of power between actors and studios, was one of the leading investors in Scour. The film industry was open in its condemnation of the site's operation and took legal action. Jack Valenti, president of the MPAA (Motion Picture Association of America), commented that: 'This lawsuit is about stealing . . . Technology may make stealing easier, but it doesn't make it right' (Borland, 2000; p.1).

Again, the first incarnation of Scour fell foul of legal measures and bankruptcy at the end of 2000. By March 2001, however, it was back, although now owned by CentreSpan Communications and offering a considerably modified set of operations, which promised control not only over the further copying of downloaded materials, but also over the use people would be making of its site. As things stand at present, the decision of the film industry to co-operate is still in the balance.

There are also technical problems still to overcome before any of this delivery potential can be realised. Current Internet technology, essentially using narrow-band telephone wires, is wholly inadequate as a medium for carrying the massive amount of data required to play a feature-length film on the Internet. This, together with the sheer volume of usage generated by even a modest viewing public, would make demands on the system which it simply could not deal with:

> *Assume that all national video programming is distributed by direct broadcast satellite, leaving local content to local digital services. Then if every television station in the United States had a local Web page with substantial local video content, and if the audience for such material approached the present-day audience for local TV programming (around 5 to 10 hours per TV household per week of the 50 hours of total viewing), there clearly would be insufficient capacity in local telephone systems to deliver the service. Almost any scenario in which standard quality video is offered interactively (that is, on demand) to millions of ordinary viewers results in the collapse of present distribution systems. The interactive integrated video future requires much more capacity than we have, not only in national backbones, but in local distribution systems that link up with individual households.*

> *(Owen, 1999; p.313)*

This is why such films as are currently available on the Web are short (a few minutes at most), tiny (occupying a small window on the computer screen) and of low resolution (blurred, jerky motion). For example, one of the films Ifilm.com offers is *405* (2000), a film lasting two minutes and fifty-eight seconds, which shows a Jumbo jet landing on a main road, as seen in the rear view mirror of a driver on that road. Made by two men, Jeremy Hunt and Bruce Branit, on their home computers, it has a very simplified *mise-en-scène* – one man in a car, driving slowly down the road; a Jumbo jet slowly approaching him from behind – and a well developed soundtrack of atmospheric noise and effects. The film had more than a million viewings within a few months of appearing on the web.

Internet movies have tended to be the province of the independent artist who sees the Internet as a useful means of distributing their works to an audience without the need of major studio assistance. The Sundance Film Festival launched an Internet section at its gathering in 2001. Again, this potential may well become compromised if the mega-mergers between media and Internet companies develop as argued above.

However, there are indications that new viewing options are opening up to potential 'audiences' (actually, single users), which uniquely suit short films rather than features. New technologies such as WAP mobile phones and hand-held, palmtop devices are new receivers for film material sent over the Web. Because of the nature of the viewing method – on the move and while waiting for transport, service, etc., short films make ideal material.

An interesting recent example of this is a series of advertisements for BMW cars, created by leading film industry talent. Five films have been produced, collectively entitled *The Hire* (2001), commissioned by BMW for their website, bmwfilms.com. Their directors include John Frankenheimer, Ang Lee, David Fincher, and Guy Ritchie. BMW has even developed a new software programme to help the films run smoothly when streamed to the user's viewing appliance. What is most interesting about this project is the way in which it signposts an interaction between several high-affluence elements and the short film form as advertisement. These short films are meant to be seen via technologically sophisticated machines – computers, palmtops, etc. – by people who have specifically sought them out. These spectator/users will want to see the films in specific circumstances (on the move, at any time, on demand) which do not require them to free up two hours of their time, and which will project the image of a certain status. Further, each short film, while retaining high production values and exciting levels of action, can be quickly and easily digested. The significant investment made by BMW in their production (an undisclosed secret) signifies the seriousness with which they are being taken. If they are successful, further short-film cycles by other directors for other companies are likely to follow (Pulver, 2001; p.4). Significantly, the Ifilm.com short film website is heavily advertising the *Hire* series of films, in a reciprocal arrangement designed to heighten awareness and interest in short films on the part of the public.

The directors of *The Hire* cycle of short films are all leading industry practitioners, but the trade works both ways. It is the stated aim of most, if not all, of the new Internet short-film makers to use that platform to attract industry notice. As Ifilm, one of the major sites for these films, announces in its own publicity:

Hollywood is watching. Your film here.
IFILM is changing the rules of film-making by giving film-makers a free worldwide showcase for their work. Many of our film-makers have already been 'discovered' by some of the thousands of entertainment industry professionals who visit us every day. We are proud to share their success stories below:

Gene Laufenberg, 'Sunday's Game', 9:36
After this film premiered on IFILMpro, director Gene Laufenberg signed a two-picture deal with Fox 2000.
....
Jeremy Hunt and Bruce Branit, '405', 2:58
In June 2000, Hunt and Branit – the duo behind IFILM's most-viewed film of all time (with more than 1 million hits . . . and counting) – signed with Creative Artists Agency to negotiate writing and directing deals.

(Ifilm, 2000; p.1)

There is an undoubted creative uniqueness about films made to be shown on the Internet. As it currently stands, however, the Web is little more than a free advertisement, or calling card, for film-makers frustrated by their inability to break into the tightly controlled mainstream movie industry in America.

The other attraction of the Internet in terms of movies is its interactivity. Users do not only sit and watch a film as it plays on the Web, but can also call up supplementary material (interviews with film-makers, biographies, production notes, etc.) at the same time. We can see this happening already on the websites of the major movie companies, who all use the Web to advertise coming releases by streaming trailers together with supporting materials. Although relatively primitive at the moment – again because of technical limitations – this aspect of the Internet's potential as a movie distribution channel will undoubtedly expand in the future.

What will transform the use of the Web as a movie distribution medium will be the shift from narrow- to broadband: cabling large enough to be able to carry the size of data streams involved in feature-length movies. Currently this technology has been commandeered by the cable operating companies, who are jealously guarding it, and the riches it produces. AT&T, for example, has been conducting a $20 million test of its broadband equipment in Boulder Colorado since November 2000. Critics accuse the company of using delaying tactics to prevent open access for competitive services. Dr Mark Cooper, director of research of the Consumer Federation of America, argues that

> All these tests do is establish how long they can hold off before they are forced to open up the network to competition . . . The feasibility of open access has been proven for a couple of years now, up in Canada. The $20 million they're spending on these 'tests' is a good investment when you look at all the customers they have exclusive access to. By the time the networks are opened up, they will have most of the first generation of broadband Internet users in their pocket.
>
> *(in Wagner, 2000; p.1)*

And again, the AOL–Time Warner merger is significant in this respect, as it integrally involved Time Warner's development of their Road Runner broadband service. Road Runner is the exclusive Internet service provider on Time Warner cable until the end of 2001:

> For AOL, I think this is largely a deal about technology; that is to say, America Online has been the dominant leader in what might be termed the sort of first stage of Internet usage, that is people going on-line for e-mail and Web surfing. But they have not had much of a strategy to go to the next level, so-called broadband access, where access to the Internet would be much faster and will allow for much more complicated tasks. For example, one of the things the two companies talked today about is streaming video through your computer, whether that would be you just call up a video that you want to see, or to watch live news through the Internet in a way that one would through television, downloading music, these kinds of applications that right now are very difficult to do at the access speeds that most consumers have to the Internet. Time Warner, with its Road Runner service, potentially has the ability to deliver that, and AOL wants to be the content on what's going into those homes. So it makes sense from a strategic perspective, and of course, it also creates a globally powerful company that combines both old media power and content with new media speed.
>
> *(Lehrer, 2000; p.1)*

INTERACTIVE CINEMA

DVD and the Internet both promote a notion of interactivity: of the spectator/ user actively participating and engaging with the text; in many ways constructing a unique text for themselves in the process of that viewing and engagement. Interactivity is seen as a great potential threat to the classic traditions of cinema whereby a large group of people sit passively in a darkened room, watching larger-than-life figures on a screen in front of them. Interactivity is supposed to empower the spectator, allowing them to take control of the narrative, change events, influence character psychology and decision-making, and so forth. 'Much of cinema's power over us is our lack of power over it . . . It could be argued that the introduction of viewer impact on the representation is a destructive step for the cinema' (Weinbren, 1995; p.17).

There is a similar level of hype, equal to that which has been generated regarding DVD and the Internet, surrounding the possibilities of interactive film, or interactive cinema, although the terminology becomes somewhat strained and oxymoronic. Interactivity promises to fundamentally change the nature of cinema, to such an extent that we may no longer be able to use the term. Consider this announcement by one of the leading practitioners of interactive film, Glorianna Davenport, director of the Interactive Cinema Group at the Media Laboratory at the Massachusetts Institute of Technology:

The next generation of computer media will feature information-rich, dynamically adaptive distributed environments which seamlessly merge the real and virtual worlds . . . As bits themselves become graspable and manipulable, the separation between maker and consumer shrinks dramatically, while the connection between consumer and story becomes more tangible, personalized and intimate.

(*Davenport, 1998; p.1*)

There are two basic forms of interactive film: collective and individual. The collective version takes the form of a group of users, gathering together in a shared space, watching a narrative unfold. Each has their own computerised console, and uses it at specific points along the way to decide in which direction the narrative should proceed and what the characters should do next; the majority vote winning.

For example, in the ICE (Immersive Cinema Experience) installation, a scenario is laid out in which an astronaut aboard an international orbiting space station in the year 2020 is exposed to a deadly foreign organism from the planet Mars. Using an experimental medical procedure involving injections into the astronaut's body, members of the space team desperately try to locate the disease in a race against the clock. Visitors to the installation view the action on three giant screens, find out information, make choices and interact with the movie using touch-screen consoles. They also compete against each other to achieve the highest game score. In this incarnation, interactive cinema clearly has strong ties to the theme park rides and attractions examined a little earlier, with narrative premise used as the springboard for a participatory experience. It is notable how the competitive element of achieving the highest score has been introduced into ICE in order to offset the frustration that must, almost inevitably, be experienced by visitors. At least a percentage of their decisions will be outvoted and they will see the narrative proceed in ways they do not want. In the individual version, that same decision-making process still takes place, but, as the product of only one user, the path the narrative takes and its outcome will be more satisfying.

In both its group and individual forms, interactive film has obviously developed out of video games and the possibilities offered to users of the latter to control the actions of characters, influence the direction and outcome of a narrative context, and attain the highest final scores. Significantly, the premise of most interactive movies has a character suffering from memory loss in a science-fiction setting. For example, in *Privateer 2: The Darkening* (1996), the main character wakes up one day to find himself in hospital on the planet Crius and has no idea who he is and where he is from. Narrative premise is set up via a doctor who tells him that he was frozen over ten years ago because he had a disease that was not curable then. The purpose of the film/game is to find out whether this is true and who he actually is.

Privateer 2: The Darkening stars Clive Owen as the amnesiac, and also features actors of the calibre of Christopher Walken and John Hurt. Bruce Willis has similarly starred in an interactive movie, *Apocalypse* (1998), an action adventure film in much the same mould as several of Willis's high-action blockbuster movies, except that the user of the interactive game can determine the direction of the plot and Willis's character's action at several junctures.

One of the more interesting attempts to weld interactivity and traditional feature films together is *Tender Loving Care* (1997), again featuring John Hurt. The project was both a film, shot on 35mm and shown in cinemas, and a CD-ROM game. The story concerns a husband, his traumatised wife, a nurse and the mystery surrounding the tragic accident involving their only child. As such it sets up an enigma at the start of the narrative which it is the job of the user to explore by asking questions of the characters and making decisions based on their responses. The cinema film only shows one set of options in this multi-strand narrative potential.

Tender Loving Care indicates a key issue surrounding the potential of interactive cinema. Interactive films do not radically differ from conventional linear film narratives except in that they offer multiple strands, at strategic points (possibly only a handful) rather than truly and fully open narrative structures. Those strands are organised on the assumption that they will be experienced linearly: one might choose one of five possibilities at the first branching point, but the second section which is accessed as a result is designed to always follow section one.

Furthermore, a greater amount of time, money and labour goes into writing, planning and executing such interactive films. Each scene of the film has to have several different optional scenarios created for it. Even in these days of the mega-budget blockbuster, Hollywood is still keen to maintain economic self-regulation. The costs involved in interactive films are currently substantial enough to ensure that only occasional experimentation takes place. However, as the costs of the technologies involved, or their more complex successors, decrease over time, the full potential of these new formats and platforms will surely be more thoroughly explored.

SUMMARY

Having looked at a few of the more exciting but problematic possibilit-ies for film in the future, we must come back to earth and consider the full extent of what might happen to cinema in the future. We have looked so far at the growing trend towards a user's interactive engagement with a wealth of material surrounding the central feature film; the mix of the physical and the virtual (whether 2-D image on screen, 3-D movie attraction or computer game). The important point to grasp about these various developments is that the film itself is becoming only one element amongst many in a diversified package. Whether that exists in one format, like DVD, or more, as is the case when people first see the film then visit the movie attraction, there is no doubt that the role of the film within the general entertainment landscape is changing. Now it can often just be regarded as an initiatory source for ideas worked out more fully in other media (the ride) or as a supporting player, a rationale, for the inclusion of other material about it which becomes the main selling point for the DVD.

But it is important also to recognise that the feature film is still needed; it is what gives the other material and other forms their meaning. As Smith and others have argued earlier, the emotional content of the feature film, its ability to engage us with the lives and feelings of its characters in order to make us care about them, provides the bedrock upon which the other representations of the original film material are developed and played out. Without that bedrock, the other formulations of that material become groundless and immaterial. We cannot be asked to care for a character from a standing start within the few minutes' duration of a theme park ride: the emotional learning curve is too steep. When we experience the *Jurassic Park* ride at the Universal Studios theme park, for example, we are taking with us to that experience the 'relationship' we built up with the characters in that film when we originally saw it. The characters might not appear at any point during the ride, but we invest the experience of seeing the dinosaurs, and the short narrative of the ride as it progresses, with the emotions originally generated by, and in relation to, those characters. So, for example, as the dinosaurs appear during the ride, we can remember the scenes where Grant (Sam Neill) and Ellie (Laura Dern) first see the herd of brontosaurus and feed their, and our, wonder at the new experience. For this reason alone, we can hope that, in spite of these new threats, the feature film is guaranteed a continued existence for years to come.

Modern theme parks are founded on storylines and characters which come from mainstream American cinema. The cost of the parks alone – over $2 billion each just to build, more to keep running – would guarantee the continuity of the feature film as the centre of the American film industry. Given the kind of ride that predominates at such parks – short, intense, visceral – it is also virtually certain that the big-budget action blockbuster will continue its dominance of the box office. Although previous chapters have suggested that the blockbuster might have had its day, due to escalating costs and market insecurity, the potential financial return from a major blockbuster success is still the Holy Grail of American mainstream film-making. And if box office possibly falls a little short of expectation, then the chain of ancillary markets – video through cable and satellite, multi-media games and on to theme park ride – virtually guarantee that any film, no matter how expensive to make in itself, will move into substantial profit.

The most telling example of this in recent years is the film *Waterworld* (1995), which was a box-office flop on release ($88 million domestic and $167 million overseas, on a budget alleged to be $200 million) and was widely and soundly pilloried in the critical press. After a few years of careful release into ancillary markets, and the opening of a theme park ride built around its central premise, however, even *Waterworld* can not only boast a movement into the black, but can also, in some ways, offer a kind of vindication from some of the harsher things said about it at the time of its initial release. The mark of a successful movie, in other words, is that it generates a theme park attraction. The hype is all around the initial box-office success of a big movie on its opening weekend, but the final marker of success or failure comes several years later, when returns from all available versions, formats, markets and merchandising opportunities have been totted up. It is this bottom line that most interests the conglomerate owners.

SUMMARY

Siegfried Zielinski (1999), as the title of his book *Audiovisions: Cinema and Television as Entr'actes in History* implies, sees cinema in its traditional form (as filmstrip projected onto a white screen to a paying audience) to be only one audio-visual configuration in a continually transforming audio-visual landscape. Cinema as we have known, and still largely do know it, emerged at the very end of the nineteenth century, and has continued, more or less unchanged, for 100 years. Various other media – radio, television, cable and satellite – have also emerged and threatened to usurp its dominance in the cultural marketplace. They are all still here, having refused to disappear when the next new media upstart came along, and cinema will do so too. It will change, if only in the degree of its dominance in a cultural landscape which is acquiring new computer-based electronic media forms.

Undoubtedly, new digital cameras will allow anyone who cares to, to go out and film anything they want: friends and family, local events, a story of their own creation. And the Internet will allow them to purchase space on an ISP server and to create a Web page and lodge the film they have made there for anyone to find and play should *they* so wish. The results, by and large, will be amateurish and badly made, and will constitute no threat whatsoever to the major film production studios, which will continue to make one or two dozen big feature films per year, which the majority of the public will prefer to go to rather than calling up made-at-home digital video movies on the Web.

Even when technical standards on the Internet allow feature films to be streamed into homes via computer, there will still be a popular need to go and see films in cinemas, even if they are digital beams rather than projected celluloid. It is not so much the material base which is at issue here, but rather the cultural and social phenomenon. Sometimes, people like to watch films in the comfort of their own homes, and will put up with the smaller screen size and interruption by advertisements in order to do so. At other times, they want a special occasion, want to go out into the night-time social world, to join hundreds of other like-minded souls and watch a film and its stars hugely magnified on a cinema screen. That is part of the reason why big-budget, lavishly mounted films such as *Pearl Harbor* (2001), with its love interest plot supposedly aimed at the female audience and gung-ho action sequences for the male audience, are still being produced, and are still proving hugely popular at the box office. And at still other times, the public might want to take family and/or friends to a movie-based theme park to experience state-of-the-art movie attractions and thrill-rides, scaring themselves witless in reality rather than vicariously.

And that is what the film companies want too, because diversity is a good – for which read, profitable – thing. While people are out at the cinema or away at the theme park, their monthly cable is costing them the same rental as if they stayed home and watched it every evening. In the future, cinema will

243

be many things, all at the same time. It will remain, largely, what it has been for the past century, although now digitally projected in order to save print costs. It will be the source of material that will be repurposed into other media forms, all of which will refer back to the original, which will itself continue to anchor the whole process. To repeat Thomas Elsaesser's observation, cinema 'will remain the same *and* it will be utterly different' (Elsaesser, 1998; p.204).

FURTHER READING

Balio, Tino – *Hollywood in the Age of Television* **(Cambridge, Massachusetts & London: Unwin Hyman, 1990).**

A good survey of the relations between Hollywood and American television from the 1940s to the 1990s. Part one contains a useful range of essays on the early history of this relationship which covers developments in media technologies, economic analysis, feature films on television, and industrial developments caused by the interaction between the two media. Part two covers developments in the 1990s such as pay TV, the made-for-TV movie, the rise of the multiplex, and Hollywood and European television. The breadth of coverage is generally very good, making the collection of essays a useful source of information on the growing interdependence of American television and film-making across six decades.

Bart, Peter – *The Gross* **(New York: St Martin's Press, 1999).**

Authoritatively written by *Daily Variety's* editor-in-chief, this work is a detailed study of the production and release of the significant films made in 1998, as a means of investigating the current state of the American film industry. Bart shows the thinking and rationalisation that went into selecting these films for production, their expectations elicited within the industry, and their public reception. In the process, he shows how Hollywood has effectively painted itself into a corner by its increasing dependence on big-budget blockbusters, which have to become massive box-office smashes in order to go into profit. Against these, he compares a number of smaller, more modestly budgeted films which surprised the industry by returning substantial profits. As a study in the mechanics and corporate mentality of the contemporary Hollywood machine, it makes for compulsive reading.

Biskind, Peter – *Easy Riders and Raging Bulls: How the Sex 'n' Drugs 'n' Rock 'n' Roll Generation Saved Hollywood* **(New York: Simon and Schuster, 1998).**

An anecdotal but extremely detailed account of American cinema in the 1970s. Salacious accounts of the excess and egomania of some of the central figures are mixed with useful period detail and astute analysis of the real workings of the American film industry. Although the first can occasionally obscure the latter two qualities, this work is valuable in providing a sense of how Hollywood's old order was dismantled by the new generation of maverick directors emerging at the end of the 1960s and early 1970s, and how the industry recovered itself by the end of the latter decade. Entertaining, fascinating, appalling and informative.

Diawara, Manthia (ed.) – *Black American Cinema* **(New York and London: Routledge, 1993).**

Divided into two sections – Black Aesthetics and Black Spectatorship – this collection of essays provides valuable coverage of an under-represented area of American film-making. Although its historical scope stretches from the beginnings of cinema to the contemporary period, the majority of essays are located in the Black American cinema of the past three or four decades. Furthermore, the arguments presented in the essays are not wholly positive in tone, and are not afraid to criticise Black film-makers if considered necessary. A useful and illuminating collection.

Gierland, John & Sonesh-Kedar, Eva – *Digital Babylon: How the Geeks, the Suits and the Ponytails Fought to Bring Hollywood to the Internet* **(New York: Arcade Publishing, 1999).**

A detailed, blow-by-blow (virtually week-by-week) account of the interaction between the film and new media industries in the latter half of the 1990s. Based on hundreds of interviews with industry insiders, the study is informative with a tendency towards the anecdotal. However, as an account of the still-developing relationship between the two media industries, it displays a sense of the here-and-now, as well as a certain irreverence towards its subject.

Hillier, Jim – *The New Hollywood* **(London: Studio Vista, 1992).**

An authoritative analysis of contemporary American cinema. The work is split into subject areas, including a study of the organisation of the contemporary Hollywood film industry, women directors, and Black cinema and the representation of Blacks in American film. Informative and provocative.

King, Geoff – *Spectacular Narratives: Hollywood in the Age of the Blockbuster* **(London and New York: I.B. Tauris, 2000).**

A well-developed analysis of the formal properties and industrial implications of the special effects laden, action blockbuster movie. The work is organised thematically and generically, offering a theory of spectacle and narrative, and a series of genre studies, including science fiction, action films, war epics and disaster movies. While it occasionally risks repetitiveness, the range of films under discussion and their detailed analysis is continually thought-provoking. This is a useful survey and sheds new light on digital effects theory.

Kolker, Robert – *A Cinema of Loneliness: Penn, Kubrick, Coppola, Scorsese, Altman* **(New York: Oxford University Press, 2000).**

A detailed series of examinations of some of the leading American directors of the last thirty years, arranged thematically rather than chronologically. Theoretically dense, with much subtle and sensitive reading of key films, the book frames each director within his historical and cultural context, and expands outwards to explore his influence on subsequent generations of American film-makers. For example, Scorsese is linked both backwards to Hitchcock among others, and forward to Tarantino. Immensely thought-provoking.

Lev, Peter – *American Films of the 70s: Conflicting Visions* (Austin: University of Texas Press, 2000).

Lev's book offers a series of individual film analyses, organised thematically, in order to chart how they represent the major issues of American society – race, feminism, politics, conspiracy, and Vietnam – of the 1970s. The thematic structure allows Lev to fully explore each area, showing how it imbued a range of films. Each film analysis is handled sensitively and astutely.

Levy, Emanuel – *Cinema of Outsiders* (New York: New York University Press, 1999).

A detailed, authoritative and comprehensive survey of American independent cinema of the past two decades. Levy is an enthusiast for independent cinema, and offers a consistently sensitive reading of the major films and their creators without recourse to sycophancy or bias. The book is loosely organised both chronologically and thematically. This both works and fails, by allowing disparate elements to be juxtaposed in ways which can obscure the sense of historical space. This criticism should not, however, detract from a substantial work that is one of the most important works on American independent cinema to date.

Lewis, Jon – *The New American Cinema* (Durham & London: Duke University Press, 1998).

A useful collection of essays. Divided into three sections: Movies and Money, Cinema and Culture and Independents and Independence. The first section contains studies of auteur cinema and financial and marketing strategies in contemporary American cinema. Section two offers a range of political interventions, with studies on race, gender and Oliver Stone's political sensibilities. Section three offers specific studies of film-makers including John Cassavetes and essays on the status of American independent cinema.

McDonald, Paul – *The Star System: Hollywood's Production of Popular Identities* (London: Wallflower Publishing, 2000).

A short, but informative history of the Star System. Only the second half of the book covers the post-Second World War period, but the survey – precise, economical, and accurate – is still very useful. This is represented in a wealth of detail in both text and tabulated form, combined with astute observations and is compressed into barely 120 pages.

Neale, Steve & Smith, Murray (eds) – *Contemporary Hollywood Cinema* (London: Routledge, 1998).

Contains a good range of essays from an impressive list of contributors. The work is split into four sections. The first – Hollywood Historiography – offers two theoretically weighty essays on the philosophy of Hollywood history and post-classical historiographies. The second – Economics, Industry and Institutions – covers corporate practice and the periodisation of film history, globalisation, the major independents, and a first hand account by producer James Schamus of the economics of independent cinema. The third section   Aesthetics and

Technology – is the largest, and offers both general histories and individual film analyses. Together, these comprehensively explore the interrelation of film technology and film aesthetics. The final section – Audience, Address and Ideology – offers a similar combination of general surveys (of the yuppie horror film, Black independent cinema, the women's picture) and specific film analyses (*Basic Instinct*). Together, the range and detail of the contributions makes this a valuable work on modern Hollywood cinema.

Nowell-Smith, Geoffrey and Ricci, Steven (eds) – *Hollywood and Europe: Economics, Culture, National Identity: 1945–95* (London: BFI Publishing, 1998).

A useful collection of essays on aspects of the often troubled relationship between Hollywood and the major European film industries, which offers detailed examinations of the various phases of industrial shifts and developments. Both general and specific studies are included to build up a full picture of the subject.

Pierson, Jon – *Spike, Mike, Slackers and Dykes: A Guided Tour Across a Decade of Independent American Cinema* (London: Faber and Faber, 1995).

A personal account of the emergence and development of American independent cinema in the 1980s and 1990s by one of its most important players. Pierson gave significant support to the early work of Spike Lee and Steven Soderbergh, among others. His account of the realities of independent film-making and distribution makes absorbing and revealing reading. His authority comes from first hand experience. A nostalgic, but not overly sentimental account of real history.

Pye, Michael and Myles, Linda – *The Movie Brats* (New York: Holt, Rinehart & Winston, 1979).

A seminal study of the new generation of maverick film-makers who emerged at the end of the 1960s – Francis Ford Coppola, George Lucas, Martin Scorsese and Steven Spielberg. It is organised in two sections – 'The Playground' and 'The Children.' The first section offers a good overview of the substantial changes in the structure and operational processes of Hollywood, which followed in the wake of the industry crisis in 1969. The second section offers a series of individual character studies of the most important new directors of the early 1970s and provides sensitive analysis of their films.

Wasko, Janet – *Hollywood in the Information Age* (Cambridge: Polity Press, 1994).

An authoritative work with a mass of useful information and facts and figures. The work covers all of the major technological developments of the past three decades, from video, through cable and satellite to multimedia and the Internet. It offers critical analysis of the effects on the American film industry of each of these technologies. The potential dryness of the technical material is offset by Wasko's amusing section titles, together with her lively commentary.

Wyatt, Justin – *High Concept* (Austin: University of Texas Press, 1994).

A provocative and thoughtful examination of the phenomenon known as the 'high-concept movie', characterised by a plot that can be summarised in a single sentence, expensive production values, and a virtual guarantee of box-office success. Wyatt looks at all aspects of the subject, from original concept, through its various formal and stylistic elements, how it is marketed to its public, and what it means for the future of the American film industry. Exhaustive in its probing within these theoretical, formal and industrial areas, the book offers an authoritative definition and analysis of the type of film which has come to epitomise the style-over-content nature of modern Hollywood film-making.

BIBLIOGRAPHY

Aksoy, Asu and Robins, Kevin (1992) 'Hollywood for the 21st century: Global competition for critical mass in image markets', *Cambridge Journal of Economics*, vol.16, pp.1–22.

America On-line Transcript (1995) 'Transcript of on-line conference with *Little Odessa* writer/director James Gray'. http://www.flf.com/odessa/odtrans.htm

Anon. (1995) 'Location-based entertainment: a global phenomenon', *Screen Digest*, October, pp.225–33.

Anon. (2000a) 'Sam Mendes interview', *6degrees online*, March. http://www.6degrees.co.uk/en/2/200003ftsammendes.html

Anon. (2000b) 'Singer to return for two X-men sequels?', *Empire On-line*, 28 July. http://www.empireonline.co.uk/news/news.asp?2412

Ascher-Walsh, Rebecca; Daly, Steve; Fierman, Daniel; Flynn, Gillian; Gordinier, Jeff; Hochman, David; Jensen, Jeff; Kargar, Dave; Nashawaty, Chris; Rich, Joshua; Shaw, Jessica; Steffens, Daneet; Svetkey, Banjamin (2000) 'Who deserves to be a millionaire?', *Entertainment Weekly*, no.528, 3 March, pp.23–8.

Auster, Albert and Quart, Leonard (1988) *How the War Was Remembered: Hollywood and Vietnam* (New York: Praeger).

Bakara, Amiri (1993) 'Spike Lee at the Movies', in Diawara, M. (ed.) *Black American Cinema* (New York and London: Routledge).

Baker, Houston A. Jr. (1993) 'Spike Lee and the commerce of culture', in Diawara, M. (ed.), *Black American Cinema* (New York and London: Routledge).

Balio, Tino (ed.) (1985) *The American Film Industry* (Madison, Wisconsin and London: University of Wisconsin Press).

Balio, Tino (ed.) (1990) *Hollywood in the Age of Television* (Cambridge, Mass. and London: Unwin Hyman).

Balio, Tino (1998) '"A major presence in all the world's important markets": the globalisation of Hollywood in the 1990s', in Neale, S. and Smith, M., *Contemporary Hollywood Cinema* (London: Routledge).

Bambara, Toni Cade (1993) 'Reading the sign, empowering the eye: *Daughters of the Dust* and the Black independent cinema movement', in Diawara, M. (ed.), *Black American Cinema* (New York and London: Routledge).

Barnouw, Erik (1990) *Tube of Plenty: the Evolution of American Television* (New York and Oxford: Oxford University Press).

Bart, Peter (1999) *The Gross* (New York: St Martin's Press).

Base, Ron (1994) *Starring Roles* (London: Marquee Publishing).

Baxter, John (1996) *Steven Spielberg: The Unauthorised Biography* (London: Harper Collins).

Beaupre, Lee (1968) 'Dickstein's "Star" Strategy', *Variety*, 4 September, p.2.

Billion Dollar Funfairs (1998) documentary on the modern theme park business. Director: Richard Blanshard, Central Independent Television. Tx: Channel Four, 14 July.

Biskind, Peter (1998) *Easy Riders and Raging Bulls: How the Sex 'n' Drugs 'n' Rock 'n' Roll Generation Saved Hollywood* (New York: Simon and Schuster).

Blaine, Nancy (1993) Interview with Ang Lee, *Los Angeles Village View*, 13 August, p.34.

Boddy, William (1993) *Fifties Television: The Industry and Its Critics* (Urbana and Chicago: University of Illinois Press).

Bordwell, David, Staiger, Janet and Thompson, Kristin (1985) *The Classical Hollywood Cinema* (London: Routledge & Kegan Paul).

Borland, John (2000) 'Movie studios target Scour with copyright lawsuit' CNET News.com, July 20.
http://news.cnet.com/news/0-1005-200-2302214.html?tag=rltdnws

Borneman, Ernest (1985) 'United States versus Hollywood: the case study of an antitrust suit', in Balio, T. (ed.) *The American Film Industry* (Madison, Wisconsin and London: University of Wisconsin Press).

Braudy, Leo (2000) 'Afterword: rethinking remakes', in Horton, A. and McDougal, Stuart Y. (eds) *Play It Again, Sam: Retakes on Remakes* (Berkeley, Calif. and London: University of California Press).

Buckland, Warren (1999) 'Between science fact and science fiction: Spielberg's digital dinosaurs, possible worlds, and the new aesthetic realism', *Screen* vol.40 no.2, Summer, pp.177–92.

Carpenter, Russ (1995) 'Wielding the double-edged sword: digital post and effects', panel discussion transcript, *American Cinematographer*, May, pp.26–32.

Carroll, Noel (1982) 'The future of allusion: Hollywood in the seventies (and beyond)', *October* 20, Spring, pp.51–81.

Cercel, Elif (1999) 'Interview with Sam Mendes, director *American Beauty*', online at *DirectorsWorld*, 22 September.
http://www.directorsworld.com/article/mainv/0,7220,118929,00.html

Chandler, Clay (2000) 'For Chinese studios, a foreign challenge: state-owned film industry faces WTO rules', *Washington Post Foreign Service*, December 21.

Christie, Ian (1985) *Arrows of Desire: The Films of Michael Powell and Emeric Pressburger* (London: Waterstone).

Christopherson, Susan and Storper, Michael (1989) 'The effects of flexible specialisation on industrial politics and the labour market: the motion picture industry', *Industrial and Labour Review*, vol.42, no.3, April, pp.331–47.

Cogley, John (1985) 'HUAC: the mass hearings', in Balio, T. (ed.) *The American Film Industry* (Madison, Wisconsin and London: University of Wisconsin Press).

Conant, Michael (1985) 'The Paramount decrees reconsidered', in Balio, T. (ed.) *The American Film Industry* (Madison, Wisconsin and London: University of Wisconsin Press).

Cook, David A. (1998) 'Auteur cinema and the "Film Generation" in 1970s Hollywood', in Lewis, J. (ed.) *The New American Cinema* (Durham and London: Duke University Press).

Crisp, Colin (1997) *The Classic French Cinema 1930–1960* (Bloomington, Ind: Indiana University Press and London: I. B. Tauris).

Darley, Andy (1990) 'From abstraction to simulation: notes on the history of computer imaging', in Hayward, P. (ed.): *Culture, Technology and Creativity in the Late Twentieth Century* (London: John Libbey and Co. Ltd.).

Davenport, Glorianna (1998) 'News from Princeton University Office of Communications', April 2.
http://www.princeton.edu/pr/news/98/q2/0402-daven.html

Davis, Susan G. (1996) 'The theme park: global industry and cultural form', *Media Culture and Society*, vol.18 no.3, July, pp.399–422.

de Grazia, Victoria (1998) 'European cinema and the idea of Europe, 1925–95', in Nowell-Smith, G. and Ricci, S. (eds) *Hollywood and Europe: Economics, Culture, National Identity: 1945–95* (London: BFI Publishing).

Dixon, Wheeler Winston (2000) 'Fighting and violence and everything, that's always cool: Teen films in the 1990s', in Dixon, W.W. (ed.) *Film Genre 2000: New Critical Essays* (Albany: State University of New York Press).

Electric Passions (1996) – director: Paul Madden for Screen First. Tx: Channel Four, November.

Elsaesser, Thomas (1998) 'Digital cinema: delivery, event, time', in Elsaesser, T. and Hoffman, K. (eds) *Cinema Futures: Cain, Abel or Cable?*, (Amsterdam: Amsterdam University Press).

Eyman, Scott (1999) *The Speed of Sound: Hollywood and the Talkie Revolution, 1926–1930* (Baltimore: Johns Hopkins University Press).

Fisher, Bob (1990) 'Cinema digital sound: the next step', *American Cinematographer*, vol.71 no.9; September, pp.73–8.

Friedfeld, Eddy (2000) 'Hollywood's new obsession', *New York Post Online*, 5 November.
http://www.nypost.com/11052000/entertainment/15395.htm

Frook, John Evan (1992) 'Miramax Paradiso', *Variety*, 21 September, p.106.

Gibbons, Fiachra (2001) 'Hey dude, gross-out flicks are a turn-off', *The Guardian*, 21 April, p.5.

Griffin, Nancy and Masters, Kim (1996) *Hit and Run: How Jon Peters and Peter Guber Took Sony For a Ride in Hollywood* (New York: Touchstone).

Guback, Thomas H. (1985) 'Hollywood's international market', in Balio, T. (ed.) *The American Film Industry* (Madison, Wisconsin and London: University of Wisconsin Press).

Gunning, Tom (1986) '"The cinema of attractions": early cinema, its spectator and the avant-garde', *Wide Angle*, vol.8 no.3/4, pp.63–70.

Hack, J. (2001) 'Pure vision', *Dazed and Confused* magazine online, transcript by Jonathan Fussel.
http://worldfilm.about.com/movies/worldfilm/gi/dynamic/offsite.htm?site=http%3A %2F%2Fwww.angelfire.com%2Fab%2Fharmonykorine%2F

Hayward, Philip (ed.) (1990) *Culture, Technology and Creativity in the Late Twentieth Century* (London: John Libbey and Co. Ltd.).

Higson, Andrew (ed.) (1999) *'Film Europe' and 'Film America': Cinema, Commerce and Cultural Exchange 1920–29* (Exeter: University of Exeter Press).

Hillier, Jim (1992) *The New Hollywood* (London: Studio Vista).

Hilmes, Michele (1990) 'Pay television: breaking the broadcast bottleneck', in Balio, T. (ed.) *The American Film Industry* (Madison, Wisconsin and London: University of Wisconsin Press).

Horowitz, Lisa (2000) 'Movie watching on the web', *Directors' World* online, http://www.directorsworld.com/article/mainv/0,7220,117999,00.html

Horton, Andrew and McDougal, Stuart Y. (eds) (2000) *Play It Again, Sam: Retakes on Remakes* (Berkeley, Calif. and London: University of California Press).

Horton, Andrew (1998) 'Cinematic makeovers and cultural border crossings: Kusturica's *Time of the Gypsies* and Coppola's *Godfather* and *Godfather II*', Horton, A. and McDougal, S.Y. (eds) *Play It Again, Sam: Retakes on Remakes* (Berkeley, Calif. and London: University of California Press).

IDATE [institut de l'audiovisual et des télécommunications en europe] (2001) 'The Japanese Market'.

Ifilm (2000) 'Success stories', ifilm.com. http://www.ifilm.com/db/static_text/0,1699,1295,00.html

Informa Media Group (2000) *Global Film: Exhibition and Distribution*.

Jarvie, Ian (1998) 'Free trade as cultural threat: American films and TV exports in the post-war period', in Nowell-Smith, G. and Ricci, S. (eds) *Hollywood and Europe: Economics, Culture, National Identity: 1945 95* (London: BFI Publishing).

Jeancolas, Jean-Pierre (1998) 'From the Blum-Byrnes agreement to the GATT affair', in Nowell-Smith, G. and Ricci, S. (eds) *Hollywood and Europe: Economics, Culture, National Identity: 1945 95* (London: BFI Publishing).

Junnarkar, Sanjeep and Hu, Jim (2000) 'AOL-Time Warner Merger', CNETNews.com, 10 January. http://news.com/2100-1023-235400.html?legacy=cnet

Kelly, Kevin and Parisi, Paula (1997) 'Beyond *Star Wars*', *Wired*, February, pp.72–7, 102–6.

King, Allan [President, Director's Guild of Canada] (1999) 'The "Runaway" production: a Canadian response'. http://www.whites.com/articles/1.html

King, Geoff (2000a) 'Ride-films and films as rides', *Cineaction* 51, pp.3–9.

King, Geoff (2000b) *Spectacular Narratives: Hollywood in the Age of the Blockbuster* (London and New York: I.B. Tauris).

Kolker, Robert (2000) *A Cinema of Loneliness: Penn, Kubrick, Coppola, Scorsese, Altman* (New York: Oxford University Press).

La Valley, Albert J. (1985) 'Traditions of trickery: the role of special effects in the science fiction film', in Slusser, G.S. and Rabkin, E.S. (eds), *Shadows of the Magic Lamp: Fantasy and Science Fiction in Film* (Carbondale and Edwardsville, Il.: Southern Illinois University Press).

Lehrer, Jim [transcript] (2000) 'AOL-Time Warner merger', *PBS Online Newshour*, 10 January. http://www.pbs.org/newshour/bb/business/jan-june00/aol_01–10.html

Lev, Peter (1993) *The Euro-American Cinema* (Austin: University of Texas Press).

Levy, Emanuel (1999) *Cinema of Outsiders: the Rise of American Independent Film* (New York: New York University Press).

Lewis, Jon (1995) *Whom God Wishes to Destroy . . .* (Durham and London: Duke University Press).

Lewis, Jon (1998a) *The New American Cinema* (Durham and London: Duke University Press).

Lewis, Jon (1998b) 'Money matters: Hollywood in the corporate era' in Lewis, J., *The New American Cinema* (Durham and London: Duke University Press).

Luskin, Jonathan (1996) 'Riders on the storm', *Cinefex* 66, June, pp.70–85.

Lyman, Rick (1999) 'New digital cameras poised to jolt world of filmmaking', *The New York Times on the Web*, 19 November. http://randlemanland.com/dv2.html

McDonald, Paul (2000) *The Star System: Hollywood's Production of Popular Identities* (London: Wallflower Publishing Ltd.).

Madigan, Nick (1999) 'Runaways inspire taxing questions', *Variety*, 22–29 August, pp.7, 9.

Manovich, Lev (1999) 'What is digital cinema?', in Lunenfeld, P. (ed.), *The Digital Dialectic: New Essays on New Media* (Cambridge, Mass. and London: The MIT Press).

Margulies, Ivone (1998) 'John Cassavetes: Amateur Director' in Lewis (1998a).

Merritt, Greg (2000) *Celluloid Mavericks: A History of American Independent Film* (New York: Thunder's Mouth Press).

Meyer, Kenneth (1995) 'Dramatic narrative in virtual reality', in Biocca, F. and Levy, M.R. (eds), *Communication in the Age of Virtual Reality* (New Jersey: Laurence Erlbaum Associates).

Natale, Richard (2001) 'Take home pay', online article on Eonline.com, 29 May. http://asia.eonline.com/Features/Features/Salaries/index2.html

Neale, Steve (2000) *Genre and Hollywood* (London: Routledge).

Neale, Steve and Smith, Murray (1998) *Contemporary Hollywood Cinema* (London: Routledge).

Noglows, Paul (1992) 'Studios stuck in screen jam', *Variety*, 9 March, pp.1, 69 and 73.

Nowell-Smith, Geoffrey (1998) 'Introduction', in Nowell-Smith, G. and Ricci, S. (eds) *Hollywood and Europe: Economics, Culture, National Identity: 1945–95* (London: BFI Publishing).

Olavsrud, Thor (2000) 'Macromedia's shockwave to acquire AtomFilms', internet.com, December 15. http://www.internetnews.com/streaming-news/article/0,,8161_537181,00.html

Owen, Bruce M. (1999) *The Internet Challenge to Television* (Cambridge, Mass. and London: Harvard University Press).

Parisi, Paula (1996) 'Lights, Cameron, action', *Wired*, May, pp.74–9, 103–6.

Parisi, Paula (1998), *Titanic and the Making of James Cameron* (London: Orion Media).

Petrie, Graham (1985) *Hollywood Destinies: European Directors in America, 1922–1931* (London: Routledge & Kegan Paul).

Pierson, John (1995) *Spike, Mike, Slackers and Dykes: A Guided Tour Across a Decade of Independent American Cinema* (London: Faber and Faber).

Pierson, Michele (1999) 'CGI effects in Hollywood science-fiction cinema 1989–95: the wonder years', *Screen*, vol.40 no.2, Summer, pp.158–76.

Probst, Christopher (2001) 'One nation, under siege', *American Cinematographer*, vol.82, no.5, May, pp.36–49.

Pulver, Andrew (2001) 'Easy Riders', *Guardian Saturday Review*, 12 May, p.6.

Puttnam, David with Watson, Neil (2000) *Movies and Money* (New York: Vintage Books).

Pye, Michael and Myles, Linda (1979) *The Movie Brats: How the Film Generation Took Over Hollywood* (New York: Holt, Rinehart and Winston).

Romney, Jonathan (1997) 'Million-dollar graffiti: notes from the digital domain', in *Short Orders* (London: Serpents Tail).

Rosenbaum, Jonathan (1980) 'Elia Kazan', in Roud, R. (ed.) *Cinema: A Critical Dictionary* (London: Secker & Warburg).

Sanjek, David (2000) 'Same as it ever was: innovation and exhaustion in the horror and science fiction films of the 1990s', in Dixon, W.W. (ed.) *Film Genre 2000: New Critical Essays* (Albany: State University of New York Press).

Schatz, Thomas (1989) *The Genius of the System* (London: Simon and Schuster).

Schoeffter, Conrad (1998) 'Scanning the horizon: a film is a film is a film', in Elsaesser, T. and Hoffman, K. (eds) *Cinema Futures: Cain, Abel or Cable?* (Amsterdam: Amsterdam University Press).

Schulze, Laurie (1990) 'The made-for-TV movie: industrial practice, cultural form, popular reception', in Balio, T. (ed.) *Hollywood in the Age of Television* (Cambridge, Mass. and London: Unwin Hyman).

Seale, Paul (1991) 'A host of others: toward a nonlinear history of poverty row and the coming of sound', *Wide Angle*, vol.13, no.1, January, pp.72–103.

Simonet, Thomas (1987) 'Conglomerates and content: remakes, sequels and series in the New Hollywood', Bruce A. Austin (ed.), *Current Research in Film 3* (Norwood, NJ: Ablex), pp.154–62.

Smith, Murray (1998) 'Theses on the philosophy of Hollywood history', in Neale, S. and Smith, M., *Contemporary Hollywood Cinema* (London: Routledge).

Sobchack, Vivian (1987) 'Postfuturism', in her *Screening Space: the American Science Fiction Film* (New York: Ungar).

Soderbergh, Steven (1999) *Getting Away With It, Or: The Further Adventures of the Luckiest Bastard You Ever Saw* (London: Faber and Faber).

Soriano, Cesar G. (2000) 'Hollywood's altered state', *USA Today online*. http://www.usatoday.com/life/enter/movies/movie657.htm

Sterritt, David (1999) *The Films of Jean-Luc Godard: Seeing the Invisible* (Cambridge: Cambridge University Press).

Storper, Michael (1989) 'The transition to flexible specialisation in the US film industry: external economies, the division of labour, and the crossing of industrial divides', *Cambridge Journal of Economics*, vol.13, no.2, June, pp.273–305.

Sutherland, John (2001) 'Reality Bites', *The Guardian*, Friday 14 September, p.10.

Taylor, Thom (1999) *The Big Deal* (New York: William Morrow).

Think Tank (2000) 'Does Hollywood serve us right?' http://www.pbs.org/thinktank/transcript818.html

Thompson, David and Christie, Ian (1996) *Scorsese on Scorsese* (London: Faber and Faber).

Thomson, David (1985) 'Chinese Takeout', *Film Comment*, September/October, pp.23–8.

Thomson, David (1996) *Rosebud: The Story of Orson Welles* (London: Abacus).

Timberg, Scott (1999) 'Fresh blood', *New Times Los Angeles*, 8–14 July, p.42.

Toeplitz, Jerzy (1975) *Hollywood and After: The Changing Face of Movies in America* (Chicago, Ill.: Henry Regnery Company).

Tyler, Kelly (2000) 'Virtual humans', *Nova Online*, November. http:/www.pbs.org/wgbh/nova/specialfx2/humans.html

Wagner, Jim (2000) 'AT&T broadband's $20 million smokescreen', 1 November. http://www.internetnews.com/isp-news/article/0,,8_501081,00.html

Walker, Alexander (1974) *Hollywood, England: The British Film Industry in the Sixties* (London: Michael Joseph Ltd.).

Walt Disney Pictures (2000) '102 Dalmatians' production information, 31 October. http://movieweb.com/movie/102dalmatians/102dalm.htm

Warner Communications Annual Report 1982, in Balio, T. (ed.) (1985) *The American Film Industry* (Madison, Wisconsin and London: University of Wisconsin Press).

Wasko, Janet (1994) *Hollywood in the Information Age* (Cambridge: Polity Press).

Wasserman, Rey (1999) 'Digital filmmaking is the tsunami of the future'. http://focusin.net/archives/june/digital.htm

Weinbren, Grahame (1995) 'In the ocean of streams of story', *Millennium Film Journal* 28, pp.14–30.

Weintraub, Bernard (1999) 'Disney and Miramax Collide Over *Dogma*', *New York Times*, 5 April, p.C4.

Wiener, David (1996) 'Chasing the Wind', *American Cinematographer*, vol.77, no.5, May, pp.36–44.

Williams, Martyn (2001) 'Murdoch set for $40bn TV deal', *Standard Online*, 16 January. http://www.thestandard.com/article/0,1902,21497,00.html

Wyatt, Justin (1994) *High Concept* (Austin: University of Texas Press).

Wyatt, Justin (1998) 'From roadshowing to saturation release: majors, independents and marketing/distribution innovations', in Lewis, J., *The New American Cinema* (Durham and London: Duke University Press).

Zielinski, Siegfried (1999) *Audiovisions: Cinema and Television as Entr'actes in History* (Amsterdam: Amsterdam University Press).

INDEX